MW00615024

"This book features ⋯ ⋯n professional that is ⋯ ⋯n Kingdom-building ⋯ ⋯n-al anecdotes and bl ⋯ ⋯ge drive the power of Guthrie's book as he eloquently and humbly captures what it means to dream big dreams. This is an inspirational read that provides Christian colleges and universities a wealth of knowledge and the potential to learn and grow in the pursuit of faithfulness to the Lord through their calling to faith-based education."

Shirley V. Hoogstra, J.D., President, Council for Christian Colleges & Universities

"Dave Guthrie has always dreamed big, and his dreams are not *luftgespinste* (pipe-smoke fantasies). Each essay bound here envisions the implications of the kingdom of God for the pursuit of learning, particularly for the institutions that he has served. His zeal is contagious and his ideals are compelling."

Don Opitz, Ph.D., Chaplain at Grove City College and life-long friend of the author

"Anyone working in Christian Higher Education should give themselves the gift of reading and reflecting on Dave Guthrie's book *Dreaming Dreams for Christian Higher Education*. This insightful and challenging examination of our work together as educators both in and beyond the classroom is both challenging and inspiring. Guthrie holds us accountable to create institutions of strong ideals and cohesive models that engage the holistic growth and learning of students as Christian educators should be uniquely positioned to do. Guthrie's presentation of thoughts over time allows us to reflect on the past to create vision for the future. I look forward to reading this with others and dreaming dreams for my students, my institution and my profession."

Julie DeGraw, Ph.D., Vice President for Student Affairs, Valparaiso University

"Over the course of my journey in Christian higher education I've been richly blessed to work alongside David Guthrie and what is abundantly clear is that he loves the Lord and loves higher education. Christian higher education is indeed at a crossroads and this timely and timeless text is filled with insights, challenges, and even laments, that remind us—a people of hope—to remain faithful until the end. Guthrie's clarion call to reconfigure higher education is a call to reimagine. May we in the Christian academy have ears to hear, eyes to see, and the courage to do the work that leads to transformation for our campuses but ultimately for the kingdom."

Todd Allen, Ph.D., Professor of Communications, Messiah University

"If you're a colleague in Christian higher education—whether that be a faculty member, a student affairs professional, or part of the dreaded administration—you understand how tasks can become dry, tired, and wearisome; it's easy to be drained and discouraged. Instead of mere management in higher education, this thoughtful collection of essays feels like the warmth of the sun after a long, dark winter. Equal parts refreshing and convicting, Dave Guthrie distills his educational wisdom and invites the reader to envision a Christian higher education still worth pursuing."

Alex Sosler, Ed.D., Assistant Professor of Bible and Ministry, Montreat College

"Guthrie's *chef-d'œuvre* offers readers a glimpse into an educator's heart. These series of essays chronicle an unfolding dream for Christian higher education providing insight and foresight to a culture at a critical crossroad. The time could not be more critical for such a conversation catalyzing collection of essays to rewaken the vision for Christian higher education in a post-COVID world."

Eric J. McIntosh, Ph.D., Research Associate, The Thriving Project, Azusa Pacific University

"All of us dream dreams, I'm sure we do. But few—even those who loudly proclaim the name of Jesus—dream in a way that is really consistent with the deepest truths of the universe: that in this good, fallen, but being-restored world, Christ's Lordship requires us to rethink everything. For some, it may seem too difficult, but for others, it opens up vistas of adventure and new possibilities, summoning us to become agents of critique, change, and reform. Dr. David Guthrie has always seemed to me a dreamer of this second and best kind: critical, hopeful, imaginative, playful, Biblically-inspired, serious, but whimsical; demanding but kind. After reading through this incredible collection of talks, essays, presentations, and reports from the field of higher education, I am sure he is the kind of dreamer that makes God smile. *Dreaming Dreams for Christian Higher Education* is simply a must read for anyone who wants to 'think Christianly' about this particular arena, but I think it should be read by anyone who wants to see how it's done—how to integrate one's deepest convictions with one's vocation, how to resist compartmentalization and live a hope-filled, seamless life. It is my own great pleasure to recommend this amazing collection of fascinating pieces and dream with Guthrie that this volume could make a real difference."

Byron Borger, Owner, Hearts and Minds Books

"Thank you David Guthrie for this timely and potent reminder to those of us in Christian Higher Education that we are in the wisdom development business. *Dreaming Dreams for Christian Higher Education* points us to the important task of connecting belief and practice, 'knowing and doing, thinking, and living' into a learning environment that prepares graduates to offer wisdom based discernment to a world lacking in this commodity. This book is both a call to return to the *raison d' etre* of higher education while at the same time basing our practice solidly in our current cultural and professional realities".

Skip Trudeau, Ed.D., Vice President for Student Development, Associate Professor of Higher Education, Taylor University

"With precision, candor, and lament, Guthrie rouses Christian higher education to gaze upon its drowsy satisfaction with lesser visions by lovingly awakening its imagination to a more faithful and embodied rendering of gospel realities within contemporary educational contexts. Anchored in the earnest conviction that all institutions of higher learning are inherently and unavoidably formational, this collection of thoughtful reflections persuasively heralds the need for a more deliberate pursuit of wisdom, discernment, vocation, and coherence as organizing principles for the robust and enlivened Christian higher education of the future. Guthrie masterfully holds practical realism and aspirational possibility in a hopeful tension, inviting the reader into the kind of courageous and creative action that catalyzes all worthy endeavors."

Michelle Louis, Ph.D., Associate Professor, Doctoral Higher Education, Azusa Pacific University

"There are rare moments when individuals so fully invested in a field open the vault of their wisdom and let in the curious wanderer. With this text, David Guthrie affords students, scholars, and practitioners the privilege of deep and thoughtful engagement with his career-spanning dream of the Christ-animated college. The dream Dr. Guthrie invites the reader into is not fantasy, utopia, or unbridled optimism. Rather, the dream is incarnational; rooted in a time, place, and among people that produce a difficult but beautiful struggle to be about God's work in the calling that is Christian higher education."

Nathan F. Alleman, Ph.D., Associate Professor, Baylor University; Higher Education Studies Research Fellow, Texas Hunger Initiative

"Christian higher education must continually renew and reimagine what it means to faithfully advance our distinctive calling. *Dreaming Dreams for Christian Higher Education* is a treasure trove of practical wisdom exploring what it means to pursue and embody our deepest purposes. David Guthrie invites readers to invest graciously and intentionally in Christian higher education. Infused with genuine conviction and hope, this volume promises to inspire Christian higher education leaders to dream faithfully and to sustain trustworthy dreams even amid the real challenges we encounter."

Cynthia A. Wells, Ph.D., Associate Professor, Messiah University

"As a professor of education at Pennsylvania State University, who has experience as a parachurch campus minister, a professor at Calvin College and Geneva College, and an academic dean at Geneva, Guthrie has a panoramic perspective on the forces that have shaped and reshaped American higher education over the past generation. These essays explore a wide range of timely topics, including curriculum revisions, church-relatedness, postmodernism, and student development. Eschewing Pollyanna hyperbole about the glories of Christian higher education as well as jaded cynicism about the challenges facing it, Guthrie offers a realistic and ultimately hopeful analysis of contemporary Christian higher education. Parents, educators, and administrators will find these constructive and engaging essays well worthwhile."

P.C. Kemeny, Ph.D., Dean, Calderwood School of Arts & Letters, Grove City College

DREAMING DREAMS FOR
CHRISTIAN HIGHER EDUCATION

Dreaming Dreams for Christian Higher Education

By David S. Guthrie, Ph.D.

Foreword by Bradshaw Frey, Ph.D.
Afterword by Eric Miller, Ph.D.

Falls City Press

DREAMING DREAMS FOR CHRISTIAN HIGHER EDUCATION

2108 Seventh Avenue
Beaver Falls, PA 15010
www.fallscitypress.com

Cover Design by Rafetto Creative
www.rafettocreative.com

Library of Congress Cataloging-in-Publication Data

Guthrie, David S. 1956—

     p. cm.
  Includes bibliographical references.

Identifiers:
  ISBN: (paper) 978-0-9864051-8-1

  LCCN: 2020943954

Subjects: Christian universities and colleges | Education, higher | Postsecondary education   I. Title.
  BV1464.G56 2020 (print)

Printed in the USA

CONTENTS

For my dear ones, my family—Cindy;
Sam, Hannah, and Banner; Andy and Claire; and Molly.

Foreword

The drive from Pittsburgh to Chicago is long and relentless. Flat, flat, flat along the Great Lakes plains, the journey seems like it'll never end. For nearly ten years I'd take the drive annually with a couple of professor-mentors from the University of Pittsburgh and, sometimes, a colleague from Geneva College. We were on our way to an academic conference typically housed at the downtown campus of Loyola University. Inevitably the trip-filling conversation would revert to the rich memories of our two mentors' careers in higher education, even though many of the stories had been told often over the years.

The ones that I enjoyed the most were stories of projects. Not specific academic projects but intellectual projects. Moments in the university when the ideas of the academy intersected the pressing needs of the society and professors rallied to their role as public intellectuals. They loved to tell the story of a visionary department chair who knew how powerful a well-constructed department could be if there were some surgical subtractions and strategic additions. The epic then developed into years of maneuvering to make such a plan the reality. It was particularly powerful to the company in the car because the "strategic additions" had included them!

The most compelling part of the epic was their conviction that the intellectual project held promise beyond the effective training of students. It offered a place to stand amongst similar departments in other universities. A way to clarify issues and advocate urgent policies that would affect the education of their students, the direction of the university and quite possible the society at large. Hyperbole? Yes, possibly. Visionary? Inspiring? Yes, absolutely. It made the stakes of higher education tangible and important. And it stood in vivid contrast to the drab, bureaucratically driven university committed to a neutered technical expertise or a mediocre representation of widely divergent theoretical perspectives.

These fellas had an agenda. They were aiming at transformed students and meaningful faculty roles in the running of their school and in speaking to the issues of the day. Their learning wasn't primarily for career building or personal back-patting but for the civic good. The last of these trips was nearly twenty years ago and yet in the current embattled higher education climate it seems almost like a lifetime.

Their stories resonated with me because I was immersed in just such a project. Certainly, the stakes were modest though the dreams expansive. A group of folks converged in a small church-related, liberal arts school and launched a master's program in the study of higher education. That group shared a cohesion seldom found in higher education these days, a unitary perspective. What my mentors from the University of Pittsburgh had watched develop with political precision and adroit institutional maneuvering was present from the program's launch. Drs. Terry Thomas and Don Opitz, ably assisted by Deborah Michalik, crafted a program at the intersection of a college and a campus ministry organization. It was Thomas's vision and he and Michalik spirited it through a halting faculty. Opitz, a foundational advisor, who was the director of training for the Coalition for Christian Outreach at the time, secured the campus ministry's support. It enjoyed enthusiastic support from the college's president and provost.

However, there was a huge missing piece. The project needed a leader, one with extensive background in the discipline of American higher education, someone with administrative experience to routinize a fledgling program and a visionary. Just such a person was the Dean of Students at Calvin College (now University), David Guthrie. The invitation went out and was accepted.

Guthrie, Thomas, Optiz, and I were all western Pennsylvania natives, had done our undergraduate degrees in small church-related colleges in the same area and then had worked together in campus ministry. We each had a seminary degree. We grew up in an area dominated by Scots Presbyterians and at a time of significant spiritual awakening on the heels of the upheavals of the 1960s. That awakening in the region revolved around the youth ministry Young Life, The Pittsburgh Experiment, The Ligonier Valley Study Center, The Pittsburgh Leadership Foundation—and especially for us—The Coalition for Christian Outreach (CCO). Our work and the work of the CCO was driven by a transformative vision that Christian faith was powerful enough to change institutions as well as individuals.

The project landed at one of the small, church-related, liberal arts colleges in the region, Geneva College. The proposal for a Master of Arts in Higher Education (MAHE) passed a faculty vote by the narrowest of margins, but it didn't matter. We were off and running. But a project, if it's to be more than a trendy new program or simply a pragmatic addition that covers a newly discovered niche in the market, must be more than shared experience or common interests. If it's to have significance and staying power, it has to be rooted in a tradition. And it has to be a deep tradition (as Alasdair MacIntyre describes in his *After Virtue* and *Three Rival Versions of Moral Enquiry*). For this group the tradition was the reformed tradition. Students and colleagues would say to us, "You four are so lucky, you get to work with friends each and every day." They were right—it was fantastic. But what made it work was the deep tradition we all subscribed to. It was our hope that we could add a voice to other Christian voices trying to speak into what had become the unwieldy world of American higher education.

What you will read in these pages is the work of Dave Guthrie, but it embodies so much more. It is the spirit of a tradition infused into a project by four folks (and many others) giddy to be working, learning, and teaching together. Like an emergent faculty member trying to find her voice, we had colleagues who knew us well enough to tell us that our twentieth new idea of the week was just as stupid and pointless as our first. We could argue texts, papers, and curricula. But the final voice was always Dave's. He had a voluminous knowledge of higher education both historically as well as in the contemporary world. He knew the key players and the foundational texts and would patiently wait for all of us to have our say. None of us had Dave's expertise; he also had a way of connecting to colleagues in the field and to students who made him the perfect program director.

So, what does it mean to inhabit a tradition? Is it a matter of reading the right books, checking off the appropriate "boxes" on some orthodoxy chart, or being chummy with leading figures? Not really. It means that you're so deeply formed by the substance of the tradition that it simply becomes the way you think and operate. Dave's collegiality, his non-judgmental demeanor, and his gregarious persona made him a comfortable fit in diverse contexts. And because he lived and breathed a tradition, it never seemed as if he was trying to say what some wanted to hear. He spoke as he saw things. When Guthrie and Opitz procured the largest single grant in the institution's history (a grant that eventually brought the college over two and a half million dollars from the Lilly Endowment) and Guthrie became the academic dean, the stakes of the project got much higher.

To me, this book has much power. It is academic catechesis. How do you stand in a tradition and speak from it? How do you try and "prod the slumbering giant" of Christian higher education? How do you challenge, encourage, contest, and object from within a tradition into the daily concrete workings of an institution? Simply put, this book is a roadmap for just that. Whether it was tackling the theory question of misunderstood verbiage of a tradition, shaping a curricular and pedagogical practice from within the tradition, or even responding to other colleges or prominent gurus in the field, this book displays how it could be done.

In these pages you'll hear Guthrie speaking as a program director, a grant recipient, a dean, and a professor. He's worn all those hats and worn them well. I should tell you reader, I lived through and participated in most of the events that gave rise to these essays. Dave is a powerful public speaker and a dynamic presence. But to review this collection was deeply moving because it touched the deepest level of the project I've been invested in and the tradition I hold.

In the western Pennsylvania that Guthrie, Thomas, Opitz, and I grew up in, we were deeply formed by a Scottish Presbyterian pietism (arguably at some points fundamentalist). We had a parochial view of what our tradition looked like. We each were introduced to a parallel expression of the tradition in the neo-Kuyperian perspective carried to North America by Dutch immigrants. We imagined ourselves as beneficiaries of both branches of our tradition. In fact, we thought we could hold them together because both had been so deeply formative. At one point we even imagined ourselves as being part of a conversation to see a confluence of the two strands. However, the fundamentalist/pietist version of the tradition was never able to embrace the more expansive neo-Kuyperian approach that flowed in Dave's veins. And the deep fragmentation of specialization wedded to its modernist moorings had restructured the college's—and its faculty's—curricular approach more deeply than could be replaced.

As I end this foreword, I wish I could point to a college transformed by an alternative vision for Christian rootedness and scholarly excellence that were hallmarks of Dave's project, the project (and tradition) unfolded in these chapters. But that part of the story is still to be written. It came so close.

How close? The new curricular plan had been discussed and debated at length but had not been approved by the Faculty Senate. Time was running out in the semester, so a special Senate meeting had to be called one evening. The proposal was debated long into the evening. When it came time for the vote the sixty percent vote needed for a major proposal was produced. However, the debate had lasted so long into the evening various faculty members had to return home and the quorum was lost.

Even if the members had stayed the vote was strong enough that the sixty percent was had. It was suggested because of that the proposal passed. Parliamentarians present said it needed to wait until the next Senate meeting. In the meantime, a key supporter had second thoughts fearing the college would not fund the initiative. He substituted a motion that we not move forward with the curriculum renovation until the administration publicly affirmed its willingness to fund the transition. The administration was unwilling to make such an affirmation. The proposal was never revived.

That was also the beauty of the moment. Trying to take on the secularist drift and the myopic tradition squeezing parochialism in one small institution at one decisive moment and almost did it. Not Camelot, but the slow work of institutional transformation that goes on across a broader landscape.

The Presbyterians loved education and were committed to an educated clergy and colleges that could educate them. However, like most American institutions founded in the mid-nineteenth century, they drew too heavily from the epistemology of the Enlightenment. As George Marsden narrates in *The Soul of the University*, the substructure of Scots common-sense realism pulled institutions so significantly into a compromised way of knowing (obviously central for the educational task) that secularization followed for most all of them. Geneva had been pulled out of such a death spiral by a group appointed by their denomination to turn the college back. And so, they did.

Unfortunately, the attempt to harmonize the Scots common sense realism and the neo-Kuyperian perspectives could not co-exist in a small college and the fundamentalist/pietist perspective prevailed. The twin sides of modernism, secularization ,and fundamentalism, are a formidable opponent. The experiment/project with so much hope eventually withered. There was a return to a world characterized by academics like most other colleges and universities, but with a dose of Bible classes, chapel, and rules. But don't let that dissuade you. There was so much that was cutting edge, so much that anticipated health, so much that was fun. Read and imagine what is possible. We used to joke that Dave changed the curriculum of the MAHE program weekly because he always could imagine a better way to deliver the program. Read these chapters and see higher education through the eyes of a visionary. One rooted in tradition, a tradition for health and flourishing.

Bradshaw Frey, Ph.D.
Professor of Sociology and Higher Education
Geneva College

ACKNOWLEDGMENTS

In recounting the faithful that had gone before in the history of redemption prior to Jesus, the writer to the Hebrews in the New Testament is overcome by the sheer volume of those who had been steadfast to the Lord and exclaims, "I could go on and on, but I've run out of time! There are so many more to mention!" As I consider the creation of this book, these words resonate deeply with me. My interest in and passion for Christian higher education represent the gracious investments that so many persons over so many years made in me. My gratitude abounds and overflows:

To my parents, brothers, and extended family and friends who nurtured me to believe and to work hard;

To many of my college professors who helped me to begin to understand biblical theology and the scope of God's redeeming love;

To my Young Life colleagues—both co-workers and high school students at the time—and to my Neshan-nock Presbyterian Church family who made faith real and powerful;

To my contemporaries with the Coalition for Christian Outreach for nurturing me in a compelling vision of the kingdom of God that continues to inspire and challenge;

To colleagues at Calvin (University) that provided tangible means of thinking about institutions as contexts for faithfulness;

To my "Westminny" comrades whose lives remind me to "see why the tide keeps rollin' in and buildin' up the sand tree";

To George, Tom, and Bur. Your love for me for more than 40 years is priceless;

To Geneva and Penn State students who have taught me more about higher education than vice versa;

To my Geneva family who provided me with the glorious opportunity to teach and to lead alongside them, though perhaps, more often than not, through a glass darkly;

To Jerryn, Deb, Allison, Don, Brad, Keith, Terry, and Rick for the privilege of a lifetime to work together so intentionally and so gleefully on something that we believed in so deeply. As I mention later in the book, we were "a small world of the lucky few," and I will never forget.It was and is a gift;

To Keith, for making it possible for my dreaming over the years to have a chance to inspire others to dream anew for the sake of the kingdom, and for "flourishing together"; and,

To my family. Words simply cannot express how profoundly grateful I am for you. I pray that you will always live into the essence of the Christian story—that when you love, you give.

Soli Deo gloria.

I Dreamed a Dream in Times Gone By...

"Livin' the dream" is a common idiom in contemporary American culture. "How's the job goin'?" "Ah, you know, just livin' the dream." Of course, this phrase is perhaps used most often in a sarcastic or ironic way to indicate that things like work are monotonous, uninspiring, or even miserable. In contrast, for a large part of my adult life, I am comfortable saying that I have been livin' the dream—and, most of the time, I mean it. I have not avoided disappointments, loss, disillusionments, and heartache along the way. But, over the course of my life, put simply, I have been richly blessed: to be loved by Jesus, my family, and my friends; by opportunity after opportunity that has shaped me to know myself, my gifts, and my callings; and, by having important, challenging, and inspiring work with truly remarkable colleagues.

I also am one who has been motivated by dreams, by a willingness to imagine and to tackle what-ifs. "We have never done anything like this before at our church, but we would like to give it a try." I am all in! "We want to start this new program. Are you

interested in directing it?" Of course, I am! "Our dream is to
partner with others such that Pittsburgh may come to be known
as much for God as it has been for steel." Sign me up! For reasons
that were not altogether clear to me, and in full recognition that
people like me in this regard can occasionally be thought of as
troublemakers,[1] I have long been inspired to imagine, to entertain ideas, to dream of a way, to take on a project or a challenge.
At least some of the time and in some small ways, I hope that
these efforts have been sourced by a deep desire to honor and
serve the Lord by imagining and pursuing what the Lord may
have in mind for human life in this world. I hope that I have
heeded, at least in part, Allan Boesak's admonition "to resist…
the propaganda that…dreaming a better world is childish, un-
sophisticated, maladjusted, and not [to] be taken seriously by
mature adults, people aware of the 'realities' of life."[2]

The object of my dreaming over the last many years is Christian higher education. Said another way, Christian higher education was my project; it was the thing that I felt called by God to
imagine, to understand, to study. It inspired questions, such as:

If I was to start a Christian college, what would it be like?

What continuities and discontinuities would it have
with existing Christian institutions?

Where would it be located and why?

How large would it be and why?

What would be included in its curriculum and why?

Who would be admitted and why?

Would its faculty be organized by departments?

What would its relationship be to its community?

Would it include graduate programs and why?

How would it be governed?

Would it have residence halls, athletic teams, and counseling centers?

What in the world would a Christian college, on earth as it is in heaven, look like?

I knew that my providence-commissioned project on Christian colleges could not be something just to "think about" in some disembodied, sage-on-the-stage way. Rather, it called me to invest wholly in institutional life, to experience the project in real-time over years, to consider and enact implications of beliefs for actions. I also knew that the point of this project was not about "getting it right." That is unattainable this side of glory. The point instead was to dream and to pursue and to approximate with gusto and based on what I took to be God-inspired dreams. I also knew that the Lord intends vocation and convocation to go together. To that end, my dreams for Christian colleges and universities and the practical pursuits of these dreams were always richer to the extent that it all went forward in league with others.

Looking back on it now, this dream was spawned in my college years as I was challenged to consider the relevance of Christian faith, including in social life and its institutions.[3] It was nurtured in campus ministry with the Coalition for Christian Outreach. Graduate studies in religion and higher education only fanned its flames further. The subsequent 25 years provided me remarkable, multifaceted institutional opportunities—first at Calvin University and then at Geneva College—to attempt to live out of and into the dreams. These opportunities unfolded concurrently with what was a most extraordinary moment for Christian higher education in the United States that included supportive organizational scaffolding (e.g., Council for Christian Colleges and Universities, Association for Christians in Student Development), burgeoning enrollments, the proliferation of thoughtful print material, significant philanthropic support, and the spread of its mission, import, and impact via technology. All of these realities provided important contexts for the dreams as well as significant sources of inspiration and tutelage.

I mention these things for two reasons. First, my sense is that dreams and contexts are related. That is, my dreams regarding Christian higher education encompassed in this book took shape within particular contexts in time. For example, my vision of a way to reconsider teaching and learning at Geneva (Chapters 2, 3, and 6) or my hopes for the efforts of Christian student affairs professionals (Chapters 8 and 9) unfolded in the context of my (and others') perceptions of the moment in time. I will return to this idea a bit more in the Epilogue. For now, however, suffice it to say that it may be that the passage of time provides greater clarity on the relationship between one's pursuit of dreams in the context of particular moments in real time.

This leads to a second consideration. As I write this introduction, the coronavirus (COVID-19) has infected over 5 million Americans and has claimed close to 175,000 American lives. In addition, more than 40 million American citizens are currently unemployed, and many businesses, schools, parks, and sports venues were shuttered for nearly three months. Some are shuttering now. Colleges and universities completed the last two plus months of the 2020 spring semester and beyond with remote learning; commencement exercises were cancelled, postponed, or attempted virtually. In short, normal is up for grabs. What might "dreaming dreams for Christian higher education" look like given new realities that are unfolding because of the coronavirus? How will Christian colleges and universities respond with courage and creativity—and tangibly based on their Christian views of life—to this moment in time?

What follows are snapshots of me living into the dream of Christian higher education given my moments in time and place during the last 20 years. Some chapters are more academic, and others are more practical.

Some of the chapters are more personal or reflective as well, even autobiographical. And, at least one chapter is not explicitly about Christian higher education as such. At the same time, I suggest that the contents of this chapter have considerable affinity with what may be called a Christian view of leading the academy. Perhaps in the future, someone could utilize its contents in some form to craft a more [Christian] confessional treatment of this important topic.[4] Finally, I want to encourage readers not to overlook the endnotes of the chapters, as they potentially offer a trove of resources, though certainly woefully inadequate given all that has been written more recently or that may have been cited no matter when it was written.

I originally prepared and delivered Chapter 1, "The Idea of a Christian College: A Reexamination," for the "Christian Scholarship...For What?" conference at Calvin University on September 27–29, 2001. It was predicated upon several wonderfully provocative conversations and correspondences with a few extraordinary colleagues at Geneva College at the time: Brad Frey, Howard Mattsson-Bozé, Eric Miller, and Don Opitz. I remain indebted to these and to other comrades for their indispensable role in shaping my heart and my voice for Christian higher education.

Chapter 2, "The Project of Christian Higher Education," is an essay that I read to faculty colleagues at Geneva College near the end of my first year (May 1, 2006) as its academic dean. Chapter 3, "The Saga of a Christian College," preceded Chapter 2 chronologically in terms of when I wrote it, but I believe it simply flows better to place them in the book as I have. As readers will notice, they are clearly related in that both ultimately represent an effort to operationalize ideas within institutional and programmatic practices. As noted earlier, I cannot understate the importance of such efforts, as contested and as time-consuming as it may be to do so. Although Chapters 2 and 3 are situated in specific moments in time for a particular institution and its constituents, I am confident that their contents will resonate considerably with the hopes and lived experiences of persons at other Christian colleges and universities. Chapter 2 is a slightly edited version of the original, but Chapter 3 is more substantially redacted to minimize repetition.

Regarding Chapter 3—in January 2006, I read it to approximately 15-20 faculty colleagues at the Wooden Angel restaurant in Beaver, Pennsylvania, after enjoying some delicious pecan balls and coffee together! As readers will readily notice, though overlap with the previous chapter exists (e.g., characteristics of the Christian college "project"), Chapter 3 is framed quite differently, around Burton Clark's notion of institutional saga.[5] In addition, this chapter contains my preliminary envisioning of a revised core curriculum (for the purpose of demonstrating the relationship between principles and practices), which eventually became the pretense for the creation of an ad hoc core curriculum committee, as also mentioned in Chapter 2. One of my great delights in including this essay is to hear once again the voices of so many thoughtful Geneva College colleagues that were earnestly attempting to understand, enact, and further the Christian higher education project.

I wrote Chapter 4, "Educating for [Godly] Wisdom in the Shadow of Empires," for the annual Symposium on Faith and Culture at Baylor University, in October 2011. The specific theme of the conference was "Educating for Wisdom in the 21st Century." Almost 15 years prior, in a chapter that I wrote for a book that I also edited called *Student Affairs Reconsidered*,[6] I suggested wisdom development as the fundamental purpose of student learning. Moreover, I argued that wisdom development pursued with Christian faith in mind was the *raison d'etre* of Christian colleges and universities. I continue to believe this as true.

Chapter 5, "Christian Higher Education and the Challenges of Postmodern Individualism," is an essay that I originally developed for a gathering of faculty, staff, and administration at Grove City College in November 2001, as one feature of both its 125th anniversary and its Vision 2025 proceedings. As an alumnus of

Grove City and as one who also worked there for several years during the mid-1980s, I was deeply honored to be invited to participate in these events. In no small way, what I learned as an undergraduate student—as well as the faculty, staff, and friends from whom I learned during those years—set a course for my faith, my life, and for my career, and I am grateful indeed.

"The R-Word and Its Alleged Relevance to the Academic Enterprise" (Chapter 6) is a short essay that I developed for a faculty luncheon at Geneva College on October 12, 2000. Faculty luncheons were a staple in the faculty development efforts of Geneva College. They provided an informal context not only for exploring numerous topics, but also for hearing one another's perspectives and commitments.

A substantially different and significantly shorter version of Chapter 7, "Leading Academe," was published by the same title in a 2015 book called *Ernest L. Boyer: Hope for Today's University.*[7] Chapter 7, however, is the substantially longer and different, original version that I wrote only to find out that it did not comport with the editors' intended design. That explains why this chapter ends without a robust "summing up," conclusion, or implications. At the same time, in this essay, readers have an opportunity to use Boyer's writings and my analysis of them as a springboard for dialog about effective leadership in the academy for the 21st century.

Chapter 8, "Profiling and Prompting Our Professional Persona and Practice," is an essay that I developed and presented at the Association for Christians in Student Development (ACSD) annual conference at Calvin University on June 1, 1998. I remember that day fondly since early that same morning, my wife gave birth to our third child, a daughter that we named Molly Anna. Since my mother was already with our two sons, and because she knew that she would be well taken care of in the hospital, my wife Cindy suggested that I fly from Pittsburgh to Grand Rapids to give this talk at Calvin—as long as I could be back the next day. So, I did! I also dedicated this presentation to my long-time friend, Steve Everett, who had died quite suddenly and far too young during the time that he was serving at Malone University.

Chapter 9 represents another ACSD opening plenary presentation that I was honored to give. It occurred more than ten years later than the previous one (Chapter 8) and occurred at Messiah University on June 8, 2010. As readers will see under the title, "What Matters in Student Development?" I dedicated this presentation to Bob Reed, my friend and colleague at Calvin University in the mid-1990s. In Chapter 8, I poked fun a bit at Bob. But, by the time of this plenary address in 2010, Bob had died unexpectedly while on a mission trip in Africa. It was my great pleasure then and now to have this presentation—and now chapter—be in his memory.

I wrote Chapter 10, "Student Conduct: Balancing Expectation and Motivation," for the annual meeting of the John Henry Newman Society, held in Washington D.C. in November 2002. Though I knew next to nothing of this organization at the time, I had long been a fan of Newman's vision for higher education. I thoroughly enjoyed my time with these new colleagues and continue to appreciate the thoughtfulness with which they attempt to be faithful in their respective institutions.

"Magnanimity, Higher Education, and Me: Notes to Myself About What I Still Want to Believe and Be" (Chapter 11) is a paper that I presented at the annual Baylor Symposium on Faith and Culture at Baylor University in October 2016; its theme was higher education. I wrote an earlier draft of this essay for master's students in a course that I taught at Penn State in spring 2015, as a commencement address of sorts for them, since they were preparing to graduate later that academic year.

I titled Chapter 12 "Autobiographical Reflections on My Life and Calling(s)." It contains responses that I made to a questionnaire that I was given to complete for a position for which I had applied. This essay reflects so much of what has motivated and sustained me throughout my career and provides partial glimpses of the ways in which I continue to attempt to imagine the Christian higher education project.

Chapter 13, "Vibrant Christian Faith in the 21st Century," is an essay that I prepared for the Lilly Endowment's Christian Faith and Life Consultation, in May 2016. Like the previous chapter, I include it because it conveys a sense of personal commitments that other chapters in the book may not. Also, similarly to the previous chapter, it follows a line of questions that were posed for the conference, and to which I was asked to respond. I did so in the form of what musicians may call "fragments" that, in some way, hopefully reveal a coherent melody.

The epilogue of the book is an "additional word" that invites readers to contribute their own ideas not only to conversations about Christian higher education, but to its practices as well. It offers two specific examples to that end. In league with the preceding chapters, I hope that it will encourage Christian educators and Christian educational organizations to dream new dreams for Christian colleges and universities.

In the epilogue of another recent book, Nick Wolterstorff writes: "The upbringing, the talents, the interests, the loves, the opportunities—they were not of my making. They were given to me. I received them. So, what I feel is gratitude, deep gratitude, for the course of my life."[8] I share Wolterstorff's sentiments quite profoundly in reference to my own life. I simply add that my dreams for Christian colleges and universities have also been heavenly gifts, acknowledging that any error, incompleteness, or flagging effort regarding them is not because of the Gift-Giver, but because of me. I hope that the pages that follow may provide at least some access to my dreams such as they are, and that they may offer at least some inspiration for continued—and more faithful—dreaming about Christian higher education for Jesus' sake.

Notes

[1]One time, for example, I was referred to as a "troubler of Israel." From my perspective, that puts me in really good company, and I will wear that gladly as a badge of honor.

[2]A. Boesak, *Dare We Speak of Hope? Searching for a Language of Life in Faith and Politics* (Grand Rapids, MI: Wm. B. Eerdmans Publishing Company, 2014), 26.

[3]I suspect that commitments in these regards are directly connected to my embrace of Christian faith with a reformational accent. Two other texts came to mind, as well, as I wrote this sentence of the Introduction. They are H. Heclo, *On Thinking Institutionally* (New York, NY: Oxford University Press, 2011) and D. Cunningham, "Colleges Have Calling, Too: Vocational Reflection at the Institutional Level," in D. Cunningham (ed.), *Vocation Across the Academy: A New Vocabulary for Higher Education* (New York, NY: Oxford University Press, 2017), 249-271.

[4]Others, of course, have done precisely this, and I commend their work to readers. Two that come readily to mind are B. Jensen and K. Martel, *Storied Leadership: Living and Leading from the Christian Narrative* (Beaver Falls, PA: Falls City Press, 2015) and K. Longman (ed.), *Thriving in Leadership: Strategies for Making a Difference in Christian Higher Education* (Abilene, TX: Abilene Christian University Press, 2012).

[5]B. Clark, *The Distinctive College* (Chicago, IL: Aldine Publishing Company, 1970).

[6]D. Guthrie (ed.), *Student Affairs Reconsidered: A Christian View of the Profession and its Contexts* (Lanham, MD: University Press of America, 1997).

[7]T. Ream and J. Braxton (eds.), *Ernest L. Boyer: Hope for Today's University* (Albany, NY: SUNY Press), 67-98.

[8]N. Wolterstorff, *In the World of Wonders: Memoir of a Life in Learning* (Grand Rapids, MI: Wm. B. Eerdmans Publishing Company, 2019), 318.

CHAPTER 1

The Idea of a Christian College: A Reexamination

This essay was presented at the "Christian Scholarship...For what?" Conference at Calvin University on September 27-29, 2001.

Introduction

Just over three years ago, on the occasion of the 1998 National Forum on Christian Higher Education sponsored by the Council for Christian Colleges and Universities (CCCU), long-time Wheaton College philosophy professor, Arthur F. Holmes, received the Mark O. Hatfield Leadership Award. The award was created "to honor individuals whose lives reflect the integration of Christ-like character with scholarship and service in the fields of worthy endeavor and who have been champions of Christian higher education." The program rightly attested to Holmes as a "senior statesman" of the Christian higher education movement. A most worthy recipient indeed.

Although Holmes has authored more than ten books and countless articles, the book that redefined and bolstered Christian higher education for more than a generation hence was his *The Idea of a Christian College*, published originally in 1975. At the time, Holmes considered the book simply as one "born out of the hopes and frustrations of an idealistic teacher who had to 'get it off his chest.'"[1] As he told us in a personal conversation this past summer, many of the chapters had been delivered as conference presentations, but all of them represented his deep passion to see Wheaton move toward a more perspectival approach to knowledge and learning. He explained that, in his view, Wheaton's approach at the time (i.e., the 1970s) was "disjunction moving toward conjunction." Disjunction reflected a virtual separation of faith and learning; that is, knowledge was simply knowledge and was delivered in the classroom, whereas the domain of faith was confined to the church and personal behavior. Conjunction offered the possibility of connecting faith and knowledge, but only at those points where it was clear that Christian faith may have had some influence, such as in ethics or moral behavior. Excerpts from the first chapter of his book say it best:

> [The distinctive of a Christian college] should be an education that cultivates the creative and active integration of faith and learning, of faith and culture...it must under no circumstance become a disjunction between piety and scholarship, faith and reason, religion and science...Integration also transcends awkward conjunctions of faith and learning in some unholy alliance rather than a fruitful union. What we need is not Christians who are also scholars but Christian scholars, not Christianity alongside education but Christian education. It shuns tacked-on moralizing and applications... It requires a thorough analysis of methods and materials and concepts and theoretical structures, a lively and rigorous interpenetration of liberal learning with the content and commitment of Christian faith.[2]

Though others before him had championed similar views, Holmes' book captured a moment. His book sprung a movement—Christian higher education—the moniker of which was the integration of faith and learning. Holmes and his book fueled the fledgling Council for Christian Colleges and Universities. Since 1975, by most accounts, Christian higher education and Christian scholarship have achieved considerable sophistication[3] and frequent notice.[4] Opitz and Guthrie summarize:

> A yet-to-be-written history of Christian colleges and scholarship during the last two decades will be quite complimentary: Enrollments at Christian institutions have burgeoned; the language of integration and faith and learning is widespread; literary and electronic media "for Christians" and/or "on Christian subjects" are readily available; evangelical scholarship in many fields abounds; Christian professional associations and inter-institutional alliances have emerged; funded research projects of all kinds have become common; and graduate programs at Christian colleges have emerged. Christian higher education and scholarship is not only "doing well," but may even enjoy a certain popularity.[5]

Although we cannot and should not overlook, much less disparage, the contributions of Christian higher education and scholarship prior to 1975, we simply wish to draw attention to the fact that, in our lifetime, the Lord has richly blessed us as Christian scholars, irrespective of where we work within the larger academy. In addition to the books and articles in our fields that have been written with Christian faith in mind, we have been privy to a common lexicon that helps us to remember who we are, from whence we have come, and what we are doing. In addition to Holmes' body of work, others such as *Making Higher Education Christian, The Scandal of the Evangelical Mind, Faith and Knowledge, Exiles From Eden, The Soul of the American University, Models for Christian Higher Education, The Dying of the Light,* and *The Outrageous Idea of Christian Scholarship* are just some

of the entries in this lexicon.[6] We have also significantly bene-
fited from professional investments, such as faculty workshops,
funded scholarship initiatives, Christian professional associations, and thematic conferences.

Blessings abound, to be sure. Yet despite the rich resources
produced over the last generation to assist us in pursuing faithful Christian scholarship, we feel less than satisfied with Christian higher education and our efforts within it. We wonder, like
Holmes did 25 years ago, if "by and large we have not dreamed
large enough dreams."[7] More specifically, our testimony on more
days than we would like to admit resonates with Holmes and
others[8] that the integration of faith and learning has become cliché. We uneasily experience Sloan's[9] contention that distinctive
implications of faith for knowledge and vice versa elude Christian scholars. And, we often share Richard Slimbach's lament
that "The vast majority of [Christian college graduates] will
reach commencement as Protestants with nothing to protest,
having failed to break through the pale security offered by a cultural Christianity identified with 'the American way of life.'"[10]

Are our testimonies the only such testimonies among faculty of Christian colleges and universities today? We think not.
That is why we wrote this paper. We hope that it will stimulate
conversation within Christian institutions and among Christian
faculty. Perhaps we also have something to "get off our chests."
In any case, what follows are three aspects of Christian higher
education that disenchant us, as well as three new directions that
Christian educators may do well to consider in the years ahead.
We purposely touch on several of the themes that Holmes included in his book, such as the integration of faith and learning
as well as the liberal arts, but we also omit comment on other
topics that he originally addressed. We will also explore additional contexts and issues that simply seemed less apposite 25
years ago. Stated another way, much has happened since 1975,
such that it may be wrongheaded to expect Christian higher education to exist for the same purposes or function in the same
ways it did when Gerald R. Ford was President and an entire

four-year, private college education could cost less than $10K, and the Steelers were winning Super Bowls. To the extent that our efforts can contribute to re-envisioned and revitalized expressions of Christian scholarship at our own (and perhaps other Christian) institutions, *Soli Deo gloria.*

The Disenchanting World of Christian Higher Education

Many colleges and universities—Christian and otherwise—advertise that they wish to shape students in such a way that a noticeable, positive impact will accrue in society through their efforts. Although the mission of American higher education has always purveyed a capacity to change society for the better, one of the clearest expressions of such a goal was offered in a book written just several years after Holmes' *The Idea of a Christian College.* That book was called *Investment in Learning* and was written by economist Howard Bowen.[11] Bowen contends that college is well worth the cost and that our culture has a moral imperative to make it possible for many more students to attend, arguing that those who receive a college education are not only personally bettered in substantial, multifaceted ways, but that American society is subsequently positively affected.

The promise of personal and structural transformation has not eluded Christian higher education by any means. The mission statements of most, if not all, Christian institutions include implicit or explicit reference to what might be called a "transforming vision." Many of them seem to follow Bowen's formula, namely that college will produce personal transformation that, in turn, will lead to societal transformation. The mission of our own institution offers a good example. If you come to Geneva College, our curriculum and co-curriculum will putatively make students servant-leaders such that when they graduate, they will be equipped to transform society for the Kingdom of Christ.

Thus, our first frustration: We are frustrated with the transformational promises of Christian higher education. To be clear, we are not opposed to having and promoting such visions of transformation. We acknowledge that there is something appropriately leavening and hope-giving—both personally and socially—about the college experience. In fact, we resonate with the image offered in the book *Common Fire*[12] that higher education, properly understood, is about cultivating "stewards of the transformation." So, it is not that we are not titillated by talk of transformation. Rather, what frustrates us is the nagging sense that many Christian educators (including ourselves) are not all that interested in transformation, whether it be personally, culturally, intellectually, or institutionally. We fear that we may comfortably fit Alexis de Tocqueville's description of Americans as those who are forever contentedly playing at the margins, carefully avoiding what is fundamental because, after all, what is fundamental may change us and "things." [13] To the point, we wonder if it has integrity to tout transformational promises if our druthers are that the future should look pretty similar to the present.[14] Several examples may illustrate our frustration with transformational language.

With respect to institutional structure, Christian institutions are significantly similar to many other colleges and universities. They emphasize professional preparation, require some number of general education courses, offer courses the same way for the same length of time, advertise many of the same majors, and so on. Given the banner of transformation, we would expect a greater reluctance to mimic mainline institutional structures. Why are we loathe to think about alternative institutional structures—provided that they are accompanied by a compelling Christian rationale—that are given over to a Deep Springs College model of organization, or a St. John's College model, or a 19th century Clark University model, or a Berea College model, or an Evergreen State University model, or a tribal college model, or a Canadian model, or some other yet-to-be known institutional model?

Perhaps a partial explanation is that, as faculty members, we have drunk very deeply from the wells of our academic profession in general and our academic disciplines in particular. We have come to believe that the curricular canon in our field was handed down simultaneously with the Ten Command-ments, complete with the sequence in which the courses were to be delivered. Of course, the pedagogy that we will employ is *a fait accompli*—it is the pedagogy that we received in our own educational experiences. And, we must be careful not to be too passionate in class, too aware of what else is happening on campus, too connected to students outside of class, or too willing to be on committees because academics must not be too anything. In short, we are what historian Paige Smith refers to as academic fundamentalists—we eschew any "truth" that does not conform to our pre-established academic, professo-rial dogma.[15] We cannot overlook the deep irony that we who view ourselves as curious and open-minded—and in service of the Truth beyond us—can also eschew the new, the different, or the future. Is it any wonder that the transformation that our institutions peddle can become diminished, short-circuited, or perhaps unfulfilled altogether?

A related example is that Christian higher education seems enamored by growth. Although we understand the logic that "if you have something good, why not give it to as many as possi-ble," we wonder if such an approach may be counterproductive to transformational outcomes. The prospect of increasing en-rollments is seductive indeed—particularly if it lands one's insti-tution on the front page of the most prominent higher education rag—because we have come to believe deeply that bigger is, in fact, better. And, ballooning enrollments is a clear way to stake a claim within the larger landscape of postsecondary educa-tion. It gives us a voice that we desperately want the head of the snake-like procession[16] to acknowledge and applaud. Thus, if a Christian college's enrollment is increasing, it is ostensibly doing something godly; if it is skyrocketing, God really must have a wonderful plan for the institution's existence. We are frustrated that Christian higher education too easily associates transfor-mation with growth. We suggest that transformation may have as much (or more) to do with quality rather than quantity. If so, we would like to see some Christian institutions that are willing to say, "We're going to keep our enrollment at 400 because, given what we want to do here, we think that 400 is an optimal number of students with whom to do it well."

If an institution has already decided that transformation amounts to preparing Christian students to do well in established systems, then attracting as many students as possible is a potentially lucrative fiscal move. If, however, transformation refers to equipping Christian students to question established systems, to discern nuance and shades in all of life, and to consider alternative approaches, then an "as many as we can get" approach seems like an overload to an educational vision that must be intensive, comprehensive, collaborative, coherent, and personal.

Not too many years back, Calvin College marketed a slogan that was something like "unfitting students for the world." At first blush, such a slogan seemed too countercultural to be Calvin. However, the slogan was intended to emphasize a transformational perspective. Christian education that strived to be authentically transformational would develop students to see differently and live differently such that they would not merely fill existing job openings, do their jobs well, conduct themselves ethically in them, and go to church on Sunday. Rather, they would have caught an "in the world but not of it" vision that propelled them to be critical of institutional structures (including where they work), to be wary of and attempt to fend off the "isms" that exist in God's good earth, to live life boldly and with a sense of wonder, and not to tire from considering new ways to meet humanity's educational, social, spiritual, economic, and political needs.

Perhaps the best way to summarize our frustration with the transformation promises of Christian higher education is to say that we seem overly captivated by what simply is current. Stated in the way that one of this paper's co-conspirators says it, we tacitly endorse what might be called a Constantinian empire. In a Constantinian world, society is mostly good. Though diversity of style and opinion exist, society is still anchored by common agreements about ideals, goals, and values. Clearly, not only does "a center" still exist in the Constantinian world, it "still holds." The role of education is to transmit and reinforce the liberal cultural hegemony to the next generation, preparing citizens to nourish, serve, and augment what already is. Transformation is redefined as the dutiful perpetuation of the inherently benevolent status quo; that is, if the word transformation is used at all.[17]

To go further, life in a Constantinian empire is little concerned with normativity. Foundational questions are largely unasked. How things "should" be is mostly a non-issue. Creational principles are passé. The way things "are" is mostly good, particularly if those who benefit most from the way things are like those things the way they are. From our perspective, this has profound consequences for faithfulness in the educational task. In a classroom context, this may result in relatively tame or altogether absent critiques of American educational, political, and economical systems or of cultural, technological, scientific, or aesthetic understandings and practices. Similarly, a commitment to seeking God's intentions for these same things and helping students do likewise—acknowledging that we and our students will not and cannot understand them clearly or fully— is rendered considerably irrelevant. At an institutional level, the *modus operandi* is largely imitative with respect to disciplinary content, academic structures and policies, pedagogy, student outcomes, and organizational principles. After all, if the vast majority of other colleges and universities utilize these institutional processes and they seem to "work pretty well," how could it be "bad" for Christian institutions simply to co-opt them as their own? In short, a Constantinian outlook persuades us of the unattractiveness of change or innovation since what is normal is also normative.

We are cognizant that our frustrations with the transformation language used by many Christian colleges may hinge on how we understand what is often called "the antithesis" as well as how we view the doctrine of creation and common grace. In fact, we realize that some may think that we are giving the antithesis

too much "play" in our critique. To be clear, we do believe that
the doctrine of creation and common grace gets too much mileage. We use it to bless just about any endeavor imaginable. But,
more importantly, in the comings and goings of institutional life
at our institutions, we also contend that common grace gets too
much mileage even among those who have never heard of it.
Stated another way, our central interest is to wonder aloud about
our frustration that Christian higher education, in many ways,
is simply not all that distinctive. In airing it publicly, we hope
to create conversations that may help to prevent us from doing
what we have always done educationally, if for no better reason
than we have always done it that way. In our view, such an approach lacks Christian integrity.

The second disenchantment concerns what we consider the
primary shibboleth of Christian higher education, namely the
integration of faith and learning. Recalling the biblical context
(Judges 12), the covenantal soldiers of Gilead had a tough time
identifying the Ephraimites by their physical appearance. But,
when the escaping Ephraimites marred the password at the fords
of the Jordan—saying "sibboleth" rather than "shibboleth"—
their masquerade was exposed.

We do not doubt that the integration of faith and learning
remains the password for Christian higher education. It still gets
you "in the door" of Christian colleges. What is disenchanting,
though, is the nagging sense that the phrase currently is considerably vapid or, worse, can be used to mean whatever a person
or institution wants it to mean. To use Berger and Luckmann's
terminology, perhaps the integration of faith and learning is a
"finite province of meaning" for many Christian faculty members. That is, the integration of faith and learning can be, and
is, "experienced" from time to time by Christian faculty members—even powerfully—but it remains behind at the end of the
experience itself. In turn, if the experience is remembered at all,
it is mediated by or "'translate[d]'…into the paramount reality
of everyday life." The net effect is that although faculty members
may encounter the integration of faith and learning, the power

of the encounter remains marginalized in favor of what might be called the taken-for-granted behavior of academic life.[18] We simply wonder about the extent to which the integration of faith and learning ignites the imagination and frames the work of many Christian-teacher-scholars, or launches the visions and innovations of most Christian academic leaders.

In addition, we acknowledge that different Christian traditions should, have, and do add particular nuance to the ways in which they operationalize the integration of faith and learning: Catholic institutions may emphasize wonder in pursuit of the unity of knowledge; Lutheran institutions may highlight developing discernment in the ambiguity of life circumstances; and Anabaptist colleges may endorse an exilic, prophetic voice and servant lifestyle. And yet the church-related institutions that Adrian and Hughes[19] describe seem much more alike than different, not with respect to their respective institutional histories but regarding their current expressions of Christian learning. Further, some books and articles are written as if faith traditions have little to do with particular expressions of the integration of faith and learning, rather the integration of faith and learning is made to sound universal. Both of these observations provide some testimony to our sense that the integration of faith and learning has become cliché. We advertise the phrase, we refer to the phrase, we "just do it," presumably, and yet we do so without plumbing the depths of what it may mean for our work, our institutions, or even ourselves.

If true, perhaps we should be satisfied with cliché. After all, harsher words have been spoken of Christian higher education in the past. For example, Hofstadter[20] criticized the anti-intellectual character of 19th-century American life in general, while Tewksbury[21] described the geographic expansion of Christian higher education in the mid-19th century as the "Great Retrogression." More recently, Noll[22] lamented the scandal of the evangelical mind (i.e., that there isn't one), Sloan[23] leveled the charge that Christian scholars are more Christian than scholar, and Marsden[24] decried the outrageousness of the Christian

mind, largely due to its absence as a thoughtful voice in the
academy. Even Alan Wolfe's article[25] within the last year suggests
that the recent opening of the Christian mind only makes sense
from the standpoint of its up-until-now hibernation. Of course,
a letter to the editor following Wolfe's lead article was much less
kind, although its author was a faculty member at a religiously
affiliated institution:

> [Wolfe] should have sampled the scores of other evan-
> gelical colleges, which…substitute charismatic dogma
> for reflection…As a university professor, I feel it is my
> job to force (politely) my students to question assump-
> tions and to reason rigorously and logically, and then
> to encourage them to follow the logic of the argument
> where it leads. If the first of these essential pedagogical
> activities doesn't happen at Fuller and the second one
> can't, I can only wonder in what sense the school can be
> said to have achieved academic excellence.[26]

Indeed, cliché may represent a step forward from anti-intellectual,
retrogressive, scandalous, me-and-Jesus empty-headedness.

We in no way dispute the anti-intellectual strains within
American evangelicalism or the impact these persuasions have
had on the Christian academic enterprise in general and the integration of faith and learning in particular. We wonder, however, if weak heartedness is as much to blame in the last 20 years
as weak-mindedness was in the previous 100 years. Stated simply, the integration of faith and learning is ostensibly cliché because many simply no longer believe in integration. Our point
is not to argue inexorably for maintaining the word "integration" in the Christian college vocabulary. Rather, our interest is
to call attention to the idea that, by faith, we honor the Lord
as Creator, Redeemer, Sustainer and confess that in Him all
things hold together (cf., Colossians 1). The problem is that we
do not experience a few things—much less all things—holding
together. What seems near to us is a fractured world, not God's
redemption in Jesus Christ. Entropy seems a far better descriptor of our personal and professional experiences. On what seems
like a weekly basis, we sense that we are in the midst of various

wrestling matches in which we are trying to resolve an appropriate balance between the liberal arts and professional programs; to navigate proper relationships between technology and pedagogy, student behavior, and/or educational goals; to discern how little theological sophistication is too little in hiring new faculty; to respond graciously to the relative preparedness of entering and continuing students; and to detect "when tolerance is no longer a virtue"[27] in developing diversity-enriched curricula.

All of this, and yet we cannot even seem to manage a parking space near our offices (although we pray fervently for one)! We also eagerly imbibe the view during graduate school that knowledge is specialized and atomized, we experience tensions in our local, state, national, and international communities on manifold fronts, and struggle to give our families the love they need and deserve. Fortunately, Sunday worship helps us to remember that all things hold together in Him—at least for an hour or so... maybe. In a postmodern world, perhaps integration simply does not work in the college setting or anywhere else. Then again, if integration is by faith, perhaps we need to pray more fervently and regularly, "Lord, help our unbelief."

The weak faith that precipitates the cliché-ishness of the integration of faith and learning is sustained to the extent that we avoid the various resources that would most likely strengthen our faith and our intellectual discourse. Unfortunately, many Christian faculty do not have a functional background in biblical or systematic theology, have not thought very deeply or very long about what the integration of faith and learning would look like in their respective field or pedagogy, and have seldom, if ever, availed themselves of the rich lexicon of written works that we mentioned at the outset. At best, they will say that they are interested in these things but don't have the time. At worst, they may say that it simply isn't their job.

Our concern is if the phrase that represents the heart of the Christian college education is vapid, then what really serves as its animating principle? Or, stated another way, if there is little consensus on or specificity about the integration of faith and learning, then what operates *de facto* as the center of Christian college education? As we stated earlier, we fear that it may be well-intentioned aspirations wrapped in the traditionalist academic ideology of a Constantinian empire.

Third, and finally, we are disenchanted with the liberal arts. At the expense of being uncharacteristically defensive, all of us who participated in the conversations that led to this paper has at least two degrees in traditional liberal arts fields. Although we may not take in as much fine art as we should, we all are deeply committed to philosophy and history, consider ourselves freethinkers, and have learned our grammar and syntax *real good*. That we feel as though we have to couch our disenchantment at all may indicate something about the status that "the liberal arts" is afforded in our institutions, notwithstanding that the majority of Christian college graduates do not graduate in liberal arts majors, a fact that liberal arts faculty will quickly—and pointedly— interject, to be sure. Thus, the first aspect of our disenchantment: We are disenchanted with the seemingly ubiquitous tension between the liberal arts and professional arts on many Christian campuses. On the one hand, we want to provide students with solid foundations, knowledge that lasts, and an appreciation for the past. But, on the other hand, we want to send them on their way with adequate vocational preparation, interpersonal and technical skills, and social adaptability.[28] Students and faculty alike, relative to their "side" in the struggle, pejoratively dismiss the liberal arts as outdated, impractical, and heady and dismiss the professional arts as trendy, non-theoretical, and easy. Liberal arts faculty and student majors are thinkers and professional arts faculty and student majors are doers. We have even heard the comment that the liberal arts provide the Christian content to the curriculum.

At an institutional level, curricular structure is often more a product of the ramifications of the most recent accreditation standards than it is of intentional design. Consider the following pronouncement: "Because we firmly believe in the power of liberal arts education, all students must complete 36 hours in the humanities core—unless a student is an engineering, business, nursing, social work, or education major."[29] As liberal arts faculty will too eagerly attest, so much for firm beliefs. In addition, administrators must contend with the embitterment that accrues as liberal arts faculty and professional arts faculty grouse about inequities in faculty workload issues, salaries, departmental expenditures per student, faculty development funds, equipment and supply costs, and research support. Clearly, the "two-culture phenomenon"[30] is alive and well on Christian college campuses.

All of this is disenchanting to us. Because we believe that these tensions point to a bifurcation of God's world that we think inappropriate—we sincerely yearn for another way to organize and deliver higher education. Although we will suggest a possible first step later in the paper, we offer now that we do not think that a liberal arts *uber alles* is the "right" approach either. Stated another way, we are disenchanted by those who argue that the liberal arts will save us if we just revise our curricula into a "full-force" liberal arts curricula. To reiterate, we are fond of literature, philosophy, history, and we have even been to some museums and symphonies. And, we are not arguing for the elimination of literature, philosophy, history, religion/theology, art, and music from Christian college classrooms.

What we are concerned about is the extent to which these disciplines have been and are currently conceived, delivered, and defended from what John Wilson refers to as a paradigm of "methodological naturalism," rather than from a point of view that attends more closely to a Christian epistemology. According to Wilson, methodological naturalism was *the* "critical innovation" in the American university between 1870 and 1920. It signaled a hegemonic shift from natural theology and Christian moral philosophy to specialized science and sciences, differentially organized institutionally over time in physically and methodologically distinct departments and disciplines, and in service of a new, emerging, good-and-getting-better, fast world. In turn, the humanities (which we often use interchangeably with "the liberal arts") concomitantly emerged in the late 19th century not to bridle or scold the new science but simply as an extension of the new science. That is, consistent with the new science approach, it borrowed its foundational epistemological framework—philological historicism—from the German university, supplanting the Scottish Common Sense approach to knowledge that had fueled it for the previous two centuries in American higher education. Wilson lucidly writes:

> The humanities—understood as subject matter as well as approach—came to substitute for the older claims that knowledge was unified because it rested on Christian claims to universal truth. And within the new model of university learning and the derived curriculum, the humanities displaced—indeed, replaced—the moral philosophical center of collegiate studies in the earlier era…And humanities studies so understood were entirely compatible with—indeed, complementary to—specialized scientific endeavors. So the *arts and sciences university* could be an integral construct, having wholly replaced the religious and theological commitments of an earlier period with specialized pursuit of knowledge and the promise of a progressively unfolding new era. As different as the humanities were, they melded with, and reinforced, the new world of sciences.[31]

Thus, the deep irony and the source of our disenchantment: Liberal arts types doth protest too much. They champion a curriculum (and pedagogy) that historically was not the means of rescuing a college that was little-knowingly falling in love with another suitor, but itself became the eventual replacement for the regnant Christian epistemology of the previous two centuries. Compounding the disenchantment (and the irony) is the apologetic that champions the liberal arts as what makes and keeps our Christian institutions Christian. We are simply not so sure.

Over 25 years ago, Dr. Holmes wrote that a "liberal education is an opportunity to become whole and to see life whole rather than provincially fragmented in one way or another."[32] The historical development of the modern liberal arts in American higher education [ironically] belies such integrality.

Moreover, we wonder if the students at our institutions get the "whole" feeling when they enroll in our humanities courses. We fear that, more often than not, they move on from our classes having crossed out another fragmented piece on their curriculum completion schedule: Renaissance Europe, check; Art History, check; Contemporary American Philosophy, check; Music Theory, check; English Playwrights, check. Maybe the "Christian" liberal arts are the contemporary version of turn-of-the-century Latin and Greek studies.

Liberal arts devotees will quickly counter with pithy rejoinders such as: "The problem is the students;" or, "Sometimes the right thing is the hardest to grasp." True and true. But we wonder if another truth is that the liberal arts are so tethered to their turn-of-the-century history that their product one hundred years hence is the fragmented specialization that was simply inherent in the new epistemological seeds that were sown at that time. And, the harvest is now ripe. Thus, while our everyday knowledge that Berger and Luckmann posit—that which emanates from our disciplinary, Christian, and other allegiances—predisposes us to believe that our liberal arts curriculum has the power to make people and knowledge whole and prepare them to transform society for the sake of the Kingdom, we simultaneously may be blithely unaware that the nature and structure of the very same curriculum is counterproductive to wholeness. If true, perhaps Marsden's thesis in *The Soul of the University* has as much relevance for today's Christian academy as it did for the Christian academies of the late 19th century.

Again, to be clear—and defensive—we deeply believe that Christian education, by its very nature, is holistic education. Moreover, we wholeheartedly affirm that philosophical, historical, literary, cultural, social, economic, aesthetic, and psychological analyses have and do make valuable, rich contributions to a coherent education. Further, we fully agree with Dr. Holmes' interest in his most recent book[33] as well as in our summer conversations to eschew epistemological neutrality and strive ardently for distinctly Christian points of view in our academic efforts. We wonder, however, if the curricular and pedagogical practices that are firmly entrenched in our institutions are delivering the integrality, the perspective, and the transformational vision that we promise. To what extent have we unwittingly and innocently co-opted the curricular and pedagogical structures and practices of mainstream American higher education as our own, without realizing that the epistemological vision to which they are attached provides meanings to integrality, perspective, and transformational vision that may not square with a Christian view of life.

In short, our disenchantment has led us to consider new pathways for Christian higher education, perhaps much in the same way that Dr. Holmes mused 25 years ago. In the next section, we offer three ideas in a humble effort to stimulate conversations that could be useful in reshaping Christian higher education in the years ahead.

New Directions for Christian Higher Education?

Our conversations during the last year were always critical and always passionate. And yet, they were also frequently animated by our heartfelt yearnings for Christian higher education to be different, to be *more* faithful—at least from a vantage point of looking through dark glass. Three particular ideas for institutional *metanoia* rose to the surface with considerable regularity: interdisciplinary learning, wisdom development as an organizing metaphor, and parallel curricula. In closing, we briefly examine each of these yearnings.

First, interdisciplinary learning. It was clear in Holmes' mind that an interdisciplinary approach to learning was critical because it simply was the natural pedagogical byproduct of a Christian institution's commitment to what he called "reflective learning." According to Holmes, reflective learning helps students "see things in relationship, to organize ideas into an ordered whole, to be systematic, to work toward a unified understanding."[34] Unfortunately, the only other thing that Holmes said about an interdisciplinary approach was that it was difficult to consider because Christian college faculty have fallen ill to an epistemological "syndrome" characterized by "gaps between our disciplines." 25 years ago, Holmes proposed an elixir: "Time must first be found for interdisciplinary dialog among faculty."[35]

We heartily endorse Holmes' interest in an interdisciplinary approach. And, we are mildly surprised but enthused that approximately 39% of contemporary Council for Christian Colleges and Universities (CCCU) faculty members say that they have taught an interdisciplinary course.[36] Beyond here-and-there individual courses, however, we wonder if an interdisciplinary approach should be descriptive of the entire educational experience in Christian colleges and universities. Is Christian higher education interdisciplinary higher education? We think that such an idea has considerable merit. Slimbach says it well:

> In addressing the issue of globalization, no single discipline will enable students to see the relationships between deforestation and shopping malls, free trade and urban migration, new technologies and street crime, international aid and increased hunger. They are too readily handled as random, disconnected facts and not as threads of a single cloth. Educating students to *think interdisciplinary* means that merely acquainting students with a variety of disciplinary offerings (as is done in the typical general education program) is insufficient. Our central concern should be to help students *unify* their fragments of knowledge into a cohesive, meaningful, and missional vision for life. But this assumes that we, as educators, see that vision clearly ourselves.[37]

Indeed, perhaps Christian scholars have too easily imbibed of the fragmentation of knowledge that accompanies modernism. After all, our taken-for-granted academic posture simply is that knowledge exists in disconnected parts.[38] Or, perhaps postmodern Christian students really "can't handle the [unifying] truth," even if we delivered it more holistically.[39] Or, perhaps this is simply an arena in which our atomized educational, curricular, and pedagogical works are out of sync with our integrative Christian worldviews. Whatever the case, in our discussions during the last year, we yearned for a unity and integrality to the curriculum that does not have to rely on a capstone course, but could be woven evenly into the fabric of the entire learning experience.[40] From our perspective, there is *still* time to generate interdisciplinary dialog among Christian faculty and other educational leaders to the end that students might embrace a more coherent understanding of—and vision for—life in God's world.[41]

A second yearning arose from the dissatisfaction that we mentioned earlier, namely that the extant tensions between the liberal arts and the professional arts obscure the unity and integrality of God's world and the learning process. Thus, we propose a discontinuation of the automatic association of liberal arts with Christian higher education and a cease fire in the battles between "the heady and the trendy" in favor of another organizing principle: wisdom development.[42] Again, Holmes is instructive in considering this new approach. In his most recent book, *Building the Christian Academy*, he proposes that the "heart and soul" of the Christian academy resides in the biblical concept of wisdom: "[Wisdom]…is not just a body of knowledge or even a depth of understanding, for it requires good judgment that embodies fundamental values inherent in the overall meaning and purpose of life."[43] As Holmes attests, the value of wisdom is that it seamlessly links together knowing and doing, thinking and living. We can imagine no better way to conceive of Christian higher education. We are particularly captivated in this regard by Brueggemann's use of the Old Testament canon as a blueprint for Christian higher education. According to Brueggemann, education for wisdom—which is characterized by its "holy interconnectedness"—is "nurturing people into the practice of discernment." Brueggemann elaborates further:

> The educational task…is to discern and to teach to discern, to attend to the gifts given in experience, to attend to the world around us. It is to read ourselves and that world in its playfulness, to know that what immediately meets the eye is not all there is. It is to know that as

we touch the dailyness of our lives, we are in touch also
with something precious beyond us that draws close to
the holiness of God. In this way we learn that in our
knowing we have not been permitted to know fully, but
only in a mirror darkly (I Cor. 13:12).[44]

We will quickly acknowledge that there is a "rub" with both interdisciplinary learning and enshrining wisdom development
as the organizing principle for what we do. The rub is simply
this: They both will move us beyond our comfort zones of dis-
cipline-determined, departmentally arranged, course-by-course
ordered, slightly-tweak-last-year's-notes, in-a-classroom learning. Stated another way, if we reconstituted what we do and how
we do it around wisdom development and interdisciplinary
learning, our curricula would have to change, and so would we.
Needless to say, changing curricula is more difficult than moving a cemetery, and changing ourselves is even harder than that!
The problem with yearnings though—particularly ones that we
believe have some connection to God's call on our lives—is that
they are difficult to dismiss with a casual "never mind." Thus, we
come to our third potential new direction.

This third new direction begins with two premises. First,
that we cannot consider beginning a new Christian institution
because we do not have sufficient cash among us. If monies were
available, this would be a very attractive option since, as Long
contends, new institutions "may start with innovative programs
and collegiums that define the relationships between different
aspects of learning in unprecedented ways," "force a rethink-
ing of the many issues that are present with respect to the disciplinary structuring of knowledge," and "produce imaginative
repatternings."[45] Alas, we will never be able to afford such new
wineskins. Likewise, old wineskins seem not very interested in
new vintages of this sort.

Thus, our second premise: Christian colleges and universities currently are not interested in large-scale curricular
reform. It is not as if Christian colleges are unusual in this respect. It is simply the case that all organizations have a certain

predisposition toward inertia, particularly if there is any merit to the Constantinian empire idea discussed earlier in the paper. Since most Christian colleges are interested in preservationism of some kind (i.e., of the gospel in general, of a particular faith tradition, of a timeless approach to learning), it may be the case that inertia is more prominent in Christian colleges than in other institutions.

Whatever the case, where do these premises leave us? They leave us with what we are calling a parallel curriculum. The idea has historical precedent. Prior to the Civil War, the classical curriculum persisted as *the* college curriculum. To go to college was to encounter the classical curriculum. However, several new curricular rumblings had already begun at places like Union College, West Point Academy, the University of Virginia, and Rensselaer Polytechnic Institute. By the mid-19th century, both Harvard and Yale established what were called "scientific schools"[46] at which students could pursue "new" studies in engineering, chemistry, applied sciences, modern languages, and a few other areas. These schools offered parallel curricula in addition to the established—and primary—classical curricula of these institutions. At least initially, the scientific schools frequently had separate buildings, equipment, and professorships. In effect, they represented the interest of these institutions to probe cautiously other areas of inquiry and attract additional segments of America's population. Charles Eliot, the president of Harvard in the early years of Harvard's Lawrence Scientific School, commented that the emergence of the scientific schools could be described as "the story of the ugly duckling."[47] It was also the case, however, that Harvard was willing to explore new horizons and interested in innovation. After all, it did not want to jeopardize its status as the nation's first and best.

The rest is history. By the end of Eliot's tenure as president at the dawn of the 20th century, the university model—which was in seed form in the scientific schools both epistemologically and structurally—had supplanted the classical curricular model of the old-time college.

Following the historical academic leadership of Harvard, Yale, and many other institutions, we hope that several Christian institutions may be courageous enough and humble enough to begin experimenting with parallel curricula. More specifically, we hope that several Christian institutions may be willing to consider a parallel program that takes wisdom development as a departure point and then constructs an innovative, interdisciplinary, parallel curriculum based upon it. There simply is little, if anything, to lose.

Conclusion

Over a decade ago, former Yale president A. Bartlett Giamatti suggested that a college was in trouble if it believed that its "value is so self-evident that it no longer needs explication, its mission so manifest that it no longer requires definition and articulation."[48] Our sincere desire is that Christian colleges and universities never travel toward, much less arrive at, such a place. Rather, in the years ahead, we hope that Christian institutions will be willing to be appropriately self-critical and to, as Holmes suggests, dream bigger dreams.

Notes

[1]As recorded in the "The Idea of a Christian College Revisited" that was
written by Dr. Holmes (and included in the Awards Banquet Program) to
commemorate his receipt of the Mark O. Hatfield Leadership Award, during
the Council for Christian Colleges & Universities National Form on Christian
Higher Education, 1998.

[2]A. Holmes, *The Idea of a Christian College, Revised Edition* (Grand Rapids,
MI: Wm. B. Eerdmans, 1989), 6-7.

[3]D.G. Hart notes, for example, that "By the 1990s…the recovery of Christian scholarship among evangelical academics was not simply a desire but
a definite possibility bordering on reality. Gauges for measuring the health
of evangelical scholarship are never scientific, but such signs as the quality
of evangelical colleges, the number of journals devoted to scholarship, and
the contributions of evangelical scholars in specific fields such as philosophy
and history all indicate a vast improvement of conservative Protestantism's
academic fortunes…" ("Christian Scholars, Secular Universities, and the
Problem with the Antithesis," *Christian Scholar's Review*, XXX:4 (Summer
2001, 383-402), 383-384.

[4]A. Wolfe chronicles the "opening of the evangelical mind" during the last
generation in a prominent magazine. *The Chronicle of Higher Education*
covers the disproportional increase in enrollments at Christian institutions
on a front page story. J. Milbank's "radical orthodoxy" receives substantial
coverage in *The Chronicle of Higher Education.*

[5]D. Opitz and D. Guthrie, "Dr. Foster Goes to Gloucester: Improving Christian Higher Education and Scholarship in the Future," *Christian Scholar's
Review*, XXX:4 (Summer 2001, 451-470), 451.

[6]A. Holmes, *The Idea of a Christian College, Revised Edition* (Grand Rapids,
MI: Wm. B. Eerdmans, 1989); A. Holmes, *Contours of a Worldview* (Grand
Rapids, MI: Wm. B. Eerdmans, 1983) ; J. Carpenter and K. Shipps, *Making
Higher Education Christian* (Grand Rapids, MI: Wm. B. Eerdmans, 1987); M.
Noll, *The Scandal of the Evangelical Mind* (Grand Rapids, MI: Wm. B. Eerd-
mans, 1994); D. Sloan, *Faith and Knowledge* (Louisville, KY: John Knox Press,
1994); M. Schwehn, *Exiles From Eden* (New York, NY: Oxford University
Press, 1993); G. Marsden, *The Soul of the University* (New York, NY: Oxford
University Press, 1994); R. Hughes and W. Adrian, *Models for Christian*

Higher Education (Grand Rapids, MI: Wm. B. Eerdmans, 1997); J. Burtchaell, *The Dying of the Light* (Grand Rapids, MI: Wm. B. Eerdmans, 1998); G. Marsden, *The Outrageous Idea of Christian Scholarship* (Oxford: Oxford University Press, 1997). Certainly, others could, should, and will be added, but these works seem to have some fundamental import for Christian scholarship that, if critically utilized, offers significant direction and substance to the Christian academic endeavor. Later in the paper we conjecture that many Christian faculty members' familiarity with these texts may be largely mythical, if they have read any of these works closely at all!

[7]Holmes, *The Idea of a Christian College*, 11.

[8]In a short article produced by the Council for Christian Colleges & Universities entitled "Reintegrating Faith and Learning," Holmes observes that "Integration of faith and learning has become a cliché in Christian higher education. 'Reintegration' would perhaps be a better term for our endeavors" And, J. Mannoia's *Christian Liberal Arts* (Lanham, MD: Rowman & Littlefield, 2000) fully concurs, stating that "the word 'integration' has become a cliché at many liberal arts colleges. This is especially true at Christian liberal arts colleges," 106.

[9]D. Sloan, *Faith and Knowledge*.

[10]R. Slimbach, "Reimagining a Distinctive Christian Liberal Arts Education," in D. Glyer and D. Weeks (eds.), *The Liberal Arts in Higher Education*, (Lanham, MD: University Press of America, 1998), 94. Slimbach's article is quite provocative in that it attempts to redefine Christian liberal arts education in a way that is detached from the common rhetoric and structure of "the liberal arts" but, at the same time, builds on the positive features often associated with liberal learning. We lament the fact that it has not received more exposure and honest discussion in Christian colleges.

[11]H. Bowen, *Investment in Learning* (San Francisco, CA: Jossey-Bass, 1978).

[12]L. Parks Daloz, C. Keen, J. Keen, and S. Daloz Parks, *Common Fire* (Boston, MA: Beacon Press, 1996). The particular reference to "stewarding the transformation" is found on page 223.

[13]A. deTocqueville, *Democracy in America* (Scotland: Mentor, 1956). The section entitled "Why Great Revolutions Will Become More Rare" is particularly relevant in this regard.

[14]We are indebted to Michael Baxter for this general siren call. In discussing an alternative to more traditional models of Christian scholarship he notes: "This alternative, I would concede, may well seem utopian, but in making this concession I also want to make a point that was made ten years ago by Alasdair MacIntyre in the conclusion to *Three Rival Versions of Moral Enquiry*. MacIntyre notes that `the charge of utopianism is sometimes best understood more as a symptom of the condition of those who level it than an indictment of the projects against which is it directed,' because often those who level the charge lack the imagination—or hope—to believe that the future could be very different from the present." See M. J. Baxter, "Not Outrageous Enough," *First Things*, 113 (May 2001), 14-16.

[15]P. Smith, *Killing the Spirit* (New York, NY: Penguin, 1990).

[16]This metaphor is used purposely to connect with the work of C. Jencks and D. Riesman, *The Academic Revolution* (New York, NY: Doubleday, 1968) in which they describe the ascendancy of "the university college" and its eventual primacy in American higher education.

[17]Stanley Hauerwas is often cited for having a similar critique in this regard. In a recent book, Hauerwas humorously quotes one of his critics (Gerald Schlabach) who, according to Hauerwas, understands his position better than Hauerwas himself. Thus, Hauerwas quotes Schlabach who is writing about Hauerwas: "[Hauerwas] rejects Constantinianism because 'the world' cannot be [a community and way of life shaped fully by Christian convictions] and we only distract ourselves from building a truly Christian society by trying to make our own nation into that society, rather than be content with living as a community-in-exile." See S. Hauerwas, *A Better Hope: Resources for a Church Confronting Capitalism, Democracy, and Postmodernity* (Grand Rapids, MI: Brazos Press, 2000), 44.

[18]P. Berger and T. Luckmann, *The Social Construction of Reality: A Treatise in the Sociology of Knowledge* (Doubleday, 1966). Berger and Luckmann's explanation of the dynamic between "the reality of everyday life" and "finite provinces of meaning" may be instructive in understanding the integration of faith and learning as cliché. In the same section that the ideas noted above were taken (24-25), they write: "The theater provides an excellent illustration…The transition between realities is marked by the rising and falling of the curtain. As the curtain rises, the spectator is 'transported to another world,' with its own meanings and an order than may or may not have much to do with order of everyday life. As the curtain falls, the spectator 'returns to

reality,' that is, to the paramount reality of everyday life by comparison with which the reality presented on the stage now appears tenuous and ephemeral, however vivid the presentation may have been a few moments previously. Aesthetic and religious experience is rich in producing transitions of this kind, inasmuch as art and religion are endemic producers of finite provinces of meaning."

[19]W. Adrian and R. Hughes, *Models for Christian Higher Education.*

[20]R. Hofstadter, *Anti-Intellectualism in American Life* (New York, NY: Random House, 1966).

[21]D. Tewksbury, *The Founding of American Colleges and Universities* (New York, NY: Columbia University Press, 1932).

[22]Noll, *The Scandal of the Evangelical Mind.*

[23]Sloan, *Faith and Knowledge.*

[24]Marsden, *The Outrageous Idea of Christian Scholarship.*

[25]A. Wolfe, "The Opening of the Evangelical Mind," *Atlantic Monthly* (October 2000). Retrieved from: https://www.theatlantic.com/magazine/archive/2000/10/the-opening-of-the-evangelical-mind/378388/.

[26]R. Parker, "Evangelical Minds" (Letter), *Atlantic Monthly* (January 2001), 8.

[27]S. Gaede, *When Tolerance Is No Virtue* (Downers Grove, IL: InterVarsity Press, 1993). Though Gaede endorses the biblical goodness of diversity, he also elaborates the error of the postmodern worldview that may lie behind much of the discussion about tolerance and multiculturalism.

[28]Part of the difficulty that surrounds this tension at the institutional level is that our conversations, if they occur "in the open" at all, rarely delve more deeply than the artifact level, or what is readily "seen" or "experienced." Edgar Schein notes that meaning-making and action-taking are improved to the extent that institutional participants go beyond the visible level of artifacts to explore the values and the assumptions the lie behind them. Perhaps Christian colleges should be more intentional about creating the time and space to examine the issue of the liberal arts beyond mere grumblings—from any "side"—at the artifact level. See E. Schein, *Organizational Culture and Leadership* (San Francisco, CA: Jossey-Bass, 1985).

[29]25 years ago, Holmes wrote: "None of us wants the kind of dehumanized brave new world that manufactures men and women to fill jobs" (*The Idea*

of a Christian College, 25). Although we may want to convince ourselves that it is really and only the students who may desire this today, it is difficult to overlook the pressure that Christian institutions must experience to address students' notions of what college is for, particularly given the extent to which many Christian colleges are beholden to tuition dollars. And, yet, this is a central question. What is [Christian] college for? The nature of our disenchantment in this regard stems from our sense that when Christian higher education simply says it is for BOTH liberal learning and professional preparation, it concedes the possibility of a foundational, distinctively Christian organizing principle in favor of simple pragmatism, economic or otherwise. In fact, as long as there remains no principial metaphor to shape and guide Christian higher education in the future, the tensions between those associated with the liberal arts and those connected with pre-professional programs will persist and perhaps worsen. And, no one will be better for it.

[30] P. Lewis and R. Liegler, "Integrating Liberal Arts and Professional Education," in D. Glyer and D. Weeks, *The Liberal Arts in Higher Education* (Lanham, MD: University Press of America, 1998), 47-60.

[31] J. Wilson, "Introduction," in J. Roberts and J. Turner, *The Sacred & the Secular University* (Princeton, NJ: Princeton University Press, 2000, pp. 3-16), 13-14. Later in the book (Chapter 4), James Turner notes that the term humanities was used to separate "secular studies (principally of Greek and Latin texts: the *literae humaniores*) from theological ones, that is, *humanity* as opposed to *divinity*" (76), perhaps further indicating the epistemological shift that occurred between 1870 and 1920. Interestingly, as Turner later states, it is the "new" humanities that fills the gap left by the demise of the "old" classical education (replete with strong doses of Latin and Greek) by the early 20th century, initially as attractive elective courses (compared to Latin and Greek!): "So one reason for the popularity of the humanities was simple and practical: they provided "modern" substitutes for old studies fallen into disfavor" (80).

[32] Holmes, *The Idea of a Christian College*, 36.

[33] A. Holmes, *Building a Christian Academy* (Grand Rapids, MI: Wm. B. Eerdmans, 2001).

[34] Holmes, *The Idea*, 30.

[35] Ibid., 56.

[36] CCCU Faculty Survey: A Report, 1998.

[37]R. Slimbach, "Re-Imagining a Distinctively Christian Liberal Arts Education," 73.

[38]One of the difficulties in broaching the issue of academic structures is that, according to Jeffrey Alexander, they are "virtually invisible," and "...entirely outside the ideological disputes of contemporary university life." Alexander continues: "...from a sociological point of view, the disciplinary basis of undergraduate education is not rational. It emerged for historical reasons that had nothing to do with pedagogy, and functions today primarily to support the creation, evaluation, and maintenance of new knowledge by scholars... Packaging learning into disciplines has nothing to do with how students learning in the early years of college; it has everything to do with the centrality of disciplines in faculty members' professional lives...It would be hard to find a better recipe for mutual alienation and conflict." See J. Alexander, "The Irrational Disciplinarity of Undergraduate Education," *The Chronicle of Higher Education* (December 1, 1993), B3.

[39]We found D. Sheridan's "Modern and Postmodern Challenges to Liberal Education" a useful overview of some of the issues—historical and otherwise—with which Christian educators must wrestle. See *The Liberal Arts in Higher Education* by D. Glyer and D. Weeks (Lanham, MD: University Press of America, 1998), 25-45.

[40]We concur with M. Schwehn in his estimation that "An informing principle like 'unity'really [would] make the Christian university countercultural in the modern world." See M. Schwehn, "A Christian University: Defining the Difference," *First Things* 93 (May 1999), 25-31.

[41]J. Mannoia's discussion on pp. 106-117 in *Christian Liberal Arts* (New York, NY: Rowman & Littlefield, 2000) is instructive here in delineating some of the ways in which such an integrative approach could proceed.

[42]See D. Guthrie's discussion of the development of wisdom as the fundamental purpose of student learning in *Student Affairs Reconsidered* (Lanham, MD: University Press of America, 1997), 39-63. Guthrie utilizes Brueggemann's approach, mentioned later in this paragraph, as a lens through which to shape the purposes and practices of Christian higher education.

[43]Holmes, *Building the Christian Academy*, 5-6.

[44]W. Brueggemann, *The Creative Word* (Minneapolis, MN: Fortress Press, 1982). Citations in this paragraph were taken from the chapter entitled "The

Discernment of Order" (Chapter 4), which focuses on the relationship of wisdom and education and utilizes the Old Testament "writings" as its departure point. However, it also should be noted that the entirety of the book takes as its overarching theme the appropriateness of wisdom as the *telos* of learning.

[45]E. Long, Jr., *Higher Education as A Moral Enterprise* (Washington, DC:- Georgetown University Press, 1992), 95. In our view, Long's book is one of the most underutilized resources for understanding ideas and approaches that seem to resonate with Christian presuppositions and viewpoints.

[46]Dartmouth and Columbia also established scientific schools about this time, although Yale and Harvard are typically considered the pacesetters of this innovation.

[47]"Eliot on the Scientific Schools," *American Higher Education: A Documentary History* by R. Hofstadter and W. Smith (Chicago, IL: University of Chicago Press, 1961), 627.

[48]A. Bartlett Giamatti, *A Free and Ordered Space* (New York, NY: W. W. Norton, 1988), 25.

CHAPTER 2

The Project of Christian Higher Education

*This essay was presented to faculty colleagues at
Geneva College on May 1, 2006, at the end of my first year
as the academic dean.*

As a fitting prelude to his comments on the legacy of the Dutch
aesthete Hans Rookmaaker, Westminster Seminary professor
Bill Edgar described Francis Schaeffer's teaching at L'Abri as
"wide-ranging, imprecise, passionately delivered, and always related to a unifying worldview."[1] The whirlwind of my first year
in general, and of the last month in particular, have led to a less-
than-polished document regarding Geneva's educational future.
At the same time, I take considerable solace that my comments
today might eventually be likened—at least a little—with how
Edgar described Schaeffer's teaching—the adjectives wide-ranging and imprecise probably work the best.

As you know, today is the last day of classes for the spring
semester and for the 2005–6 academic year. Lord willing, within
another two weeks or so, I will be able to testify that I survived
my first year in academic administration. I have many people to
thank for that here and elsewhere, including all of you.

Those who know me best know that I desire to do far more than simply to survive. Likewise, those who know me best know that I desire that Christian colleges, including this one, do far more than simply to survive as well. Perhaps it works well to say that when I am at my best and when Geneva is at its best, I and Geneva have a "passion for God's reign," to use the title of a little book of Jurgen Moltmann essays.[2] In a chapter from that book entitled "Theology in the Project of the Modern World," Moltmann says that he is a theologian both because "in the face of this world, he misses God" and also because he longs for "God's love for life."[3] Taken together, according to Moltmann, they lead to a passion for God's reign. I will return to this theme in just a moment.

I have been at Geneva for just about nine full years now. If understanding and responding wisely to our current moment in time has at least something to do with understanding and responding wisely to the past, I would offer a partial list of internal and external "realities" over the last nine years at Geneva:

1. Faculty do not "look" the same as when I came in 1997. Comparatively, we have more faculty, more women faculty, and more, newer faculty. This is not without consequence. For example, Keith Starcher tells me that faculty opinions about various cultural diversity issues differ based on how long a faculty member has been at Geneva.
2. Financial challenges and conservative, board-mandated fiscal policies have led to what might be described as real and felt cinched belts, and to less-than-stellar faculty morale.
3. Large and continuing deferred maintenance seem to make us look noticeably different than other institutions with which we compete.
4. A four-year Geneva education has officially become a six-figure proposition. This is a difficult reality to swallow, for us as well as for students and their families.

5. Given soaring college costs, the press of vocational pay-off has increased significantly. That is, if families are investing increasingly larger sums of money in higher education, their concern that such an education will "pay off" in terms of good jobs with good salaries has become heightened to say the least.

6. Our competition has increased—some would argue in dramatic proportions—in all "markets"—traditional undergraduate, graduate, and non-traditional adult. Whether one notes the significant renaissance at Robert Morris University, the proliferation of non-traditional adult programs regionally and nationally, or the improved technology-induced distance education programs, it is safe to say that we are "not in Kansas anymore," if we ever were.

7. Leadership changes have abounded. With one exception, there is no affinity between our current administrative leadership and the leadership that was present when I was first hired.

I am certainly cognizant of the fact that those of you who are relatively new to Geneva do not know about these and other things that have contributed to our current moment. And, clearly those of you have been here longer than nine years have plenty more to offer regarding the historical realities of the past that contextualize our present. Nonetheless, I would like to offer one more organizational reality that seems to have had considerable play at Geneva during much, if not all, of my nine years, including our current moment. I am not sure what to name it, but I will call it "unclear identity."

Those of you who have been at Geneva for at least five years will remember the general tone of a faculty retreat that was held in May 2001 at Camp Lutherlyn. This retreat was based on faculty essays on topics such as "What's Troubling Geneva," "Pursuing Excellence at Geneva," "Reformed Identity," and "Enhancing Learning and Scholarship." You will likewise remember essays written by faculty on the topic "Reforming Geneva," or in response to a mini-conference on Geneva's *Foundational Concepts*, or even subsequent essays submitted to *Pro Christo*[4] or presented at regular faculty luncheons. In those essays you will hear colleague Don Opitz say: "The grammar of Geneva College is absent a very important verbal construct—the future tense. Parsing the *Foundational Concepts* will remain little more than an exercise (past perfect, present incomplete, subjunctive-hypothetical) until we learn how to say what these statements mean for how we *will* teach, what we *will* pursue, what we *will* expect from our students, and what values we *will* prize." Or, you will hear colleague Bob Copeland say: "It may sound melodramatic to say that 'there is a struggle going on for the soul of Geneva College,' but it is not far from the truth." Or, finally, if you have been here for more than five years, you will remember Shirley Kilpatrick's brief but clear plea at a recent faculty meeting: "Geneva needs a new metaphor."

In addition, if you have been here for a while, I think that you might agree that we have been less than whole-hearted about things such as the core curriculum, academic strategic planning, fine arts programs and buildings, diversity, master plans, faculty load and salary inequities, and promotional slogans. And, whether you have been here for a while or not, most recently you may have heard Ed Vencio, our new vice president of marketing, suggest that Geneva must make some choices about who and what it wishes to be and become—and that was at his on-campus interview!

So, to summarize: If my partial and quick read of our current moment in time based on the last nine years has any substance, we are an institution that has experienced considerable faculty and administrative personnel changes, an institution that is pressed by significant social, cultural, and economic forces, and an institution that is losing ground with respect to campus facilities at the same time that total student costs now top $100,000 for four years, at least before the discount. Most importantly in my view, however, is that our current moment in time suggests that we are less than clear about what we most want to be and to do.

It is now time to return to the phrase that I mentioned at the outset, namely, a passion for God's reign. Several weeks back I traveled with several Geneva colleagues to Grapevine, Texas to the International Forum on Christian Higher Education, sponsored by the Council of Christian Colleges and Universities (CCCU) every five years. I must confess that I was not terribly excited about going. Other trips to this same conference in the past were far less than invigorating. Apparently, the Lord had other plans. In a pre-conference setting, Dr. Chris Coble, who is our principal contact for the Lilly grant, told a gathering of which I was part that we were in the "seed-sowing business" and that, if we looked carefully, we would see that good first fruits— and even more—were certainly appearing among the students on our campuses. Not only have I always enjoyed the parable of the Sower to which Dr. Coble was referring, but his state-ment was altogether more effective in garnering my attention because I had just finished composing a note of appreciation for an administrative assistant with whom I had worked as a grad-uate student at Penn State. Her name is Trudi and she was being honored for 25 years of dedicated service. When my family and I were preparing to leave Happy Valley for Calvin College in the summer of 1992, she had presented me with Jean Giono's, *The Man Who Planted Trees*,[5] a classic tale of shepherd Elzéard Bouffier. As the story goes, Elzéard planted one hundred acorns a day over a span of 30 years. Over time, these efforts produced quite an environmental transformation and, more symbolically, brought hope and joy to many. A seed-sowing business indeed!

The next morning of the conference, I attended a devotional by Dr. Keith Anderson, the chaplain at Northwestern College in Orange City, Iowa. He began by reading from *The Message* in the book of Ephesians: "In Christ we find out who we are and what we are living for" (1:16). He proceeded to challenge us to prepare a new generation of students to engage and serve the world for the sake of Christ and his kingdom. He then made a few comments on 2 Corinthians 4 using N.T. Wright's book, *Reflecting the Glory*,[6] and concluded with a prayer from Walter Brueggemann's book, *Awed to Heaven, Rooted in Earth*,[7] which is a collection of prayers that Brueggemann has used to begin class over the last 35-plus years of his teaching ministry. One of those poems called "And Then You"[8] struck a chord with me:

> *We arrange our lives as best we can,*
> *To keep your holiness at bay*
> *With our pieties*
> *Our doctrines*
> *Our liturgies*
> *Our moralities*
> *Our secret ideologies.*
> *Safe, virtuous, settled.*
> *And then you—*
> *You and your dreams*
> *You and your visions*
> *You and your purposes*
> *You and your commands*
> *You and our neighbors.*
> *We find your holiness not at bay*
> *But probing, pervading,*
> *Insisting, demanding*
> *And we yield, sometimes gladly*
> *Sometimes resentfully*
> *Sometimes late…or soon.*
> *We yield because you, beyond us, are our God.*
> *We are your creatures met by your holiness*
> *By your holiness made our true selves*
> *And we yield.*

Later that night, at the opening event, fellow participants and I witnessed a video presentation about a partnership between Abilene Christian University and the country of Madagascar in which over 20 students from Madagascar go to Abilene Christian to receive a Christian college education, with the pretense that they will return to their homeland, take jobs in various sectors of society, and contribute to the renewal of their country over the next two generations. As the lights in the ballroom came up, these same students from Madagascar appeared on stage to sing songs of praise to the Lord in their native language.

Then we saw another video about a LeTourneau University program called LEGS in which upper-level engineering students travel to Africa, Asia, and South American during the semester to design, manufacture, and fit artificial limbs for children and adults who had lost arms and legs due to disease, birth defect, or terrorism. We also heard two students from two different Christian institutions talk passionately—and Christianly—about their efforts in the Acting on Aids program. One of these students talked about his vision to raise $100,000 during his college career in the interest of ministering mercy and compassion to children and their families who have been ravaged by this horrific disease.

Later at the conference we heard from noted Christian intellectual, Alistair McGrath, who—along with Elaine Storkey—leads the efforts of Wycliffe Hall at Oxford University, England. Wycliffe Hall is a unique, Christian educational endeavor that exists to speak into social, economic, and political realities of British life—both with words and with actions. Dr. McGrath's two presentations had the distinct feel of fellow countryman Winston Churchill's powerful admonition to his comrades during the turmoil of WWII: "Never, never, never give up!" That is, Dr. McGrath's fundamental message was that Christian colleges and universities had an immensely necessary, significant, and urgent task to embrace and to pursue. The nature of this task, in a phrase, was that Christian colleges must reassure, challenge, and connect students to Christ and His kingdom.

The net effect of the conference on me was no less than to bolster my resolve for the mission of Christian higher education and, more precisely, for our work at Geneva College at this moment in time. It reminded me that we are not simply a

college; that we do not simply teach; that we do not simply offer
courses; that we do not simply have departments and committees and meetings and outcomes and graduates; and, that we
are not simply a coterie of Christians. The conference reminded
me that we are up to something much more than simply "doing
what colleges do." Instead, it reminded me that we have a mission, a project. And this mission, this project is so significant
and so urgent that if we do not embrace it with both seriousness and with joy, and if we do not strive after it both individually and corporately, then something quite precious might be
compromised or even lost. Yes, fellow Hobbits, we must get the
ring to Mordor, for there is much at stake! I think this is why I
resonate so closely with ethicist William May's discussion of the
word *campus*. He notes that the Latin root of the word "campus" literally means "an open field, a flat place," and it connotes
"the traditional site for rival armies to encamp and do battle."[9]
May notes: "...the campus permits us to marshal arguments...
in order that our common life in truth be cherished"[10] and, in
turn, civic life enhanced.

I do not mean to suggest that our project is altogether new.
In fact, one can easily sense the project and its importance in the
language of some of our historic documents. For example, our
Foundational Concepts state that "Christian education endeavors
to develop each student's capacity for the enjoyment of the world
as God's creation, in all its cultural richness, realizing that all of
life as a coherent whole is related to God and to His redemptive
activity." More recently, the document produced by the Panel of
General Education is replete with various features of the project.
For example, one phrase offers: "We want graduates to leave Geneva with a vision for cultural redirection. Our world needs to
hear the voices of articulate, modern-day prophets that measure
what is against what should be. We must also equip our students
for daily faithfulness and for a vision of renewal closer to home,
within reach of their everyday relationships and activities."

Even though our project is not new, however, it strikes me
that crucial projects like ours are always in danger of being
obscured, or minimized, or domesticated, or perhaps even

profaned—"Come now, did God really say not to eat that fruit?" Other competing and compelling projects subtly and not-so-subtly contend regularly for our attention and for our allegiance. Thus, on this day, and for this moment in Geneva's history, I want to offer a few, key components of our mission, of our project, of our institutional calling, and of its seriousness. After doing so, I will also mention several initiatives that I am about to commence, in the interest of clarifying and furthering our project at Geneva College.

First, a few central components of our project:

Our Project is About Helping Students to See More and to See More, More Clearly

Perspectives, stories, projects, worldviews, legitimating ideas, narratives, points of view—in most ways I am not concerned with exactly what word we choose to convey that the Geneva project concerns perspectivalism. What I am most concerned about is that we help students to understand that thinking and living have everything to do with the unavoidability, the centrality, and the richness of perspectives. For example, regarding the history of American higher education in the late 19th and early 20th centuries, Laurence Veysey sees "the story" as "the emergence of the American university,"[11] George Marsden sees "the story" as "the establishment of non-belief,"[12] and Julie Reuben sees "the story" as "the marginalization of morality."[13] The point is simply that: what history reveals, that where one should work, that how technology is employed, that what a human is, that how to raise a child, that what constitutes a good life, that the creation or the interpretation of a sculpture, that what college is for—that all of these things and a world full of other things—depends on one's point of view, on one's perspective. As one thinks in her heart, so shall she be; as one sees, so shall he live.

One implication of this theme is that our educational project must appropriately exhibit both continuity and discontinuity with other colleges and universities. We have continuity with other institutions because we have many of the same subjects, we support many of the same departments, we use many of

the same books, we discuss many of the same "facts," we prepare students for many of the same careers, we have residence
halls and sponsor programs through them, we profess in things
called classrooms, we field athletic teams, we have faculty development opportunities, and so on. And yet, affirming that a
Geneva education is fundamentally a perspectival education
necessitates a discontinuity with other institutions in these regards as well. That is, a perspectival emphasis suggests that we
do all that we do *particularly*—that what we do must be animated by and shaped by the Christian point of view that we say
is true and good and right. So, as I intimated earlier—the subjects, the departments, the books, the facts, the students' career
aspirations, and the like proceed from and toward a fundamental commitment to honor the Lord. You might say that we teach
both perspectives and perspective.

Our Project is About Helping Students to Discern the Times...and to Know What to Do

By their very nature, perspectives are discriminating—they limit, they make distinctions, and they precipitate appropriate judgments and actions. Perhaps another way to think of this is to say
that perspectives provide a foundation for discerning what to
make of things and ultimately how to live. Discernment might
be described as the process by which we attempt to understand
or to "read" the times, past and present. Discernment seems to
have substantial affinity with what the Bible calls wisdom. It necessarily involves coming to terms with what we can affirm and
what we must critique, and subsequently what all of this means
for daily decisions and behaviors.

As regards college education, then, our project is one of
nurturing students for the realities of our age, of raising sons
and daughters of Issachar[14]—doing all that we can to help students "understand the times," and then, to know what to do. At
the same time, we affirm that both the "understanding" and the
"knowing what to do" find their source and enduring strength
in a particular belief—or perspective—that might be summed
up well as "the fear of the Lord." Notice that such a Christian

educational project is simultaneously and intentionally committed *both* to exposing students to the world via coursework and other educational experiences, *and* to helping them craft judgments regarding the extent to which anything and everything in the world to which we expose them is of the world, of the Lord, or a little of both. Thus, Geneva's educational project must hold both in tension, both fearlessly and fearfully—fearlessly, because the earth and all that is therein is the very context of God's redeeming love, and fearfully, because our discerning efforts are never to be autonomous or self-aggrandizing, but always rooted within and drawn toward heavenly honor.

Our Project is About Helping Students to Understand Calling and Vocation

Perhaps one of the most relevant means of assisting students to understand how to signpost Christian faith in daily affairs is to emphasize the arenas to which God calls us by His grace to serve Him faithfully. Accordingly, the Christian educational project at Geneva pays significant attention to calling/vocation; ours is a vocational education. In being and doing so, however, we eschew any suggestion that vocation equates solely and/or inappropriately to job or career. Instead, based on Christian theological, anthropological, and creational concerns, we highlight a multiplicity of vocations that God calls us to consider, through which He calls us to serve, and within which He calls us to signpost His kingdom. In this regard, the Christian educational project at Geneva must strive to be, dare I say, "practical," in that we reach to teach and to model for students—in and out of classrooms, with regard to ideas and with regard to behaviors, in our personal relationships and in our structural processes—how they might enflesh Christian perspective and Christian discernments of the times and, in so doing, serve as what Al Wolters calls "billboards" for God's kingdom to others.[15]

These interdependent and mutually reinforcing ideas represent at least a partial look at the nature of the Christian educational project for Geneva College. As such, they serve as starting points and anticipated goals both to develop and to measure all facets of our educational effort—in the classroom and out of the classroom.

Now, allow me to turn my attention to several plans that I intend to initiate very soon. In offering these plans, I am well aware that you will be at different stages of comfort with what I am about to say. For some of you, the thought of change for any reason is far from your radar; others of you may already be thinking at least some about needed modifications and improvements; and, still others may be thinking to yourselves, "Why has this taken you so long!" In any case, I offer the following four initiatives:

1. I think it is time to review the number of hours in majors at Geneva College—let me try to explain why. While I continue to believe that things called majors are important components of our Christian educational project, my view is that majors are most valuable to the extent that they are in dependent relationship with other parts of the project. In contrast, my read of the contemporary academy is that majors have become fundamental; parts have become the whole; the center not only no longer holds, there is arguably no longer a center or a whole, simply departments and majors. I suspect that Christian colleges, including this one, have not been immune to these developments. Thus, my intent is to work with department chairs and likely with an ad hoc committee, beginning as soon as possible, to examine appropriate relationships between majors and all else based on the nature of our project, and then to consider ways that these relationships might become reified, including the particular number of hours that may comprise our respective majors.

2. In consultation with another ad hoc committee, I plan to explore a new curricular delivery model for Geneva College. To be clear, I am doing so for pedagogical and

curricular renewal reasons. However, I would like to point out that such a new model may help to distinguish us quite well from many other institutions. In my view, to believe that good learning is determined largely or exclusively by how many weeks and hours that one spends in a classroom is to yield to a sort of academic fundamentalism. I fully affirm that curricula and their delivery are sacred activities—Christian educators, of any, should be most mindful of this. However, curricular and their delivery also are not sacred cows, that is, idols—Christian educators, of any, should be most mindful of this, too. That said, the good news is that the model that I have in mind is the Hiram College model that, if pursued, may actually yield more seat hours, not fewer. In this model, each 15-week semester is broken into a 12-week and a three-week session. Such a model ostensibly allows for more focused attention in both the 12- and three-week sections of each semester. Moreover, the three-week session each semester commends itself to an institution such as ours that is beginning to think more about the promise of off-campus study opportunities for our students.

3. I plan to inaugurate a new department at Geneva College, hopefully in the Fall of 2007. I am tentatively naming this entity the Department of Foundational Studies. It will serve as the department that houses, overseas, and supports Geneva's entire core curriculum. It will have a chair, it will have a budget, and it will have considerable standing in the institution because, to paraphrase historian Frederick Rudolph,[16] I believe that an institution's core curriculum is the place that an institution tells itself who it is. The new Foundational Studies curriculum will not simply become the amalgam of all of our current core courses. Rather, beginning this summer, I will convene a working group to develop a new core curriculum. After I offer some framing considerations for the

committee, we will set out to craft a coherent core curriculum, driven by specific hopes for what a core curriculum should accomplish, including its relationships to all else at the college. We will also examine the extent to which current core courses may or may not comport with our nascent proceedings. You will be kept abreast of our deliberations and be consulted for advice and support along the way.

4. The Summer Academy for Christian Scholarship is going forward this summer, but it will take a slightly different shape. In the past, we offered two to four reading groups on various topics that met for roughly four mornings or afternoons during a particular week. This year we will have two reading groups, both of which will focus on the same topic—The Christian Higher Education Project. Each will examine and discuss various essays and/or a book on this theme. In addition, but equally important, the Summer Academy for Christian Scholarship and some part of the August faculty retreat will include several workshops on curricular elements such as "the integration of faith and learning," "diversity," "writing across the curriculum," "off-campus study," "information literacy," "pedagogy," "integrated studies," and "service-learning." You will be invited to participate by attending one of these workshops with an existing course in hand, or with a "possible course" in your head to receive coaching regarding how this course may go forward with a particular element in mind. For example, perhaps you would like some ideas regarding how your "Cinema" course might include a significant writing emphasis; or, perhaps you would like some input regarding how your "American Cultural Studies" course might include a diversity component; or, perhaps you would like some guidance on how your "Market Research" course might include an off-campus element. More information on both the reading groups and the

> workshops will be forthcoming. Suffice it to say for now,
> however, that faculty will receive a modest stipend for
> participating and will be asked to complete some read-
> ing (and hopefully even some reflective writing).

I assure you that other things are also in my and our field of
view, and appropriately so, from faculty load issues to reviewing
department chair responsibilities, from faculty compensation issues to revisiting our international partnerships, from a revised
honors program to a new colloquia series, from the development
of a new master's program in Christian studies to re-envisioning
adult learning programs, and the list goes on. I may have to de-
vise an RFH—a Request for Help—just to begin to get done all
of the things that we need to get done and done well. At the same
time, I believe that these four initiatives strike at the very heart
of the educational project to which we have been called.

As I close, and I hear the words on these typed pages echo
in my own ears, I am reminded of the words of the bumbling
Carl in *The Adventures of Jimmy Neutron*: "I want to fight crime,
but I have to be home by 5:30." Translation: I tremble. At the
same time, I am also reminded of Old Testament theologian
Walter Brueggemann's book, *The Creative Word*.[17] He suggests
that there was something about the very structure of the Old
Testament canon that, in addition to the actual content of the
testament, was intended to have a catechetical impact on the
Israelites in their efforts to know God, understand the times,
and do all as to the Lord. More specifically, he believed that the
content, structure, and integral connections among the Books
of the Law, the Prophets, and the Wisdom Books had the power
by God's grace to convince and to cultivate people into faithful priests, prophets, and kings in God's world. My passion for
God's reign in the part of his kingdom called Geneva College
leads me to hope that, as we yield to that same living Word to
which Brueggemann alludes, the Lord of the ages will enliven
and animate our educational efforts at Geneva in this day. To
that end, I am humbly asking that you will join me in sharing

the hope that ours might be an institution that will never tire of understanding more keenly what must be done to cultivate well sons and daughters of Issachar to the glory of the one who even now sits upon the throne.

Notes

[1] B. Edgar, "Why all this? Rediscovering the witness of Hans Rookmaker," *Books & Culture*, (Jan/Feb 2006), 2.

[2] J. Moltmann, *A Passion for God's Reign* (Grand Rapids, MI: Wm. B. Eerdmans Publishing Company, 1998).

[3] Ibid., 12.

[4] *Pro Christo* was a short-lived, in-house journal that featured essays, poems, and art from Geneva faculty and students.

[5] J. Giono, *The Man Who Planted Trees* (Hartford, VT: Chelsea Green Publishing, 2007).

[6] T. Wright, *Reflecting the Glory: Meditations for Living Christ in the World* (Minneapolis, MN: Augsburg Fortress Publishers, 1998).

[7] W. Brueggemann, *Awed to Heaven, Rooted in Earth* (Minneapolis, MN: Fortress Press, 2002).

[8] Ibid., 3.

[9] W. May, *Beleaguered Rulers: The Public Obligation of the Professional* (Louisville, KY: Westminster John Knox Press, 2001), 265.

[10] Ibid.

[11] L. Veysey, *The Emergence of the American University* (Chicago, IL: University of Chicago Press, 1965).

[12] G. Marsden, *The Soul of the American University: From Protestant Establishment to Established Nonbelief* (New York, NY: Oxford University Press, 1996).

[13] J. Reuben, *The Making of the Modern University: Intellectual Transformation and the Marginalization of Morality* (Chicago, IL: University of Chicago Press, 1996).

[14] I Chronicles 12:32.

[15] A. Wolters, *Creation Regained: Biblical Basics for a Reformational Worldview* (Grand Rapids, MI: Wm. B. Eerdmans Publishing Company, 2005), 132.

[16]F. Rudolph, *The American College and University: A History* (Athens, GA: University of Georgia Press, 1991).

[17]W. Brueggemann, *The Creative Word: Canon as a Model for Biblical Education* (Minneapolis, MN: Fortress Press, 1982).

CHAPTER 3

The Saga of a Christian College

This essay was read to a small group of Geneva College faculty colleagues at an informal gathering at the Wooden Angel restaurant in January 2006.

Marilynne Robinson's Pulitzer Prize winning novel, *Gilead*,[1] is a book that you should read. The book might be described best as a long letter of 76-year-old preacher, John Ames, of Gilead, Iowa to his quite-young son. John Ames knows that he won't have the benefit of seeing his son grow very old because he himself is so old, but he wants him to know some very important things about life. So, he writes them down in this book. Here is the gist of what he says: In the joy and in the sorrow, in the bafflements and in the epiphanies, in its brokenness and in its wholeness, life is a splendid, mysterious delight because of the One who made it, moves within it, and ultimately fulfills it. Listen to Pastor John's words to his little son:

> I feel sometimes as if I were a child who opens its eyes on the world once and sees amazing things it will never know any names for and then has to close its eyes again.

I know this is a mere apparition compared to what awaits us, but it is only lovelier for that...And I can't believe that, when we have all been changed and put on incorruptibility, we will forget our fantastic condition of mortality and impermanence, the great bright dream of procreating and perishing that meant the whole world to us. In eternity this world will be...the ballad they sing in the streets...Oh I will miss the world![2]

I think that I had a little glimpse of this same sentiment in early October at the confluence of the Providence and Moshassuck Rivers in Providence, RI with colleague Eric Miller. We had just finished an invigorating Lilly Fellows conference, had parked our car near historic Brown University, walked down a very cool hill past the First Baptist Church of America (the very first, mind you), and plopped down on comfortable cement seats, right along the river. I know that "comfortable, cement seats" sounds like an oxymoron, but it wasn't. We came to find out that we were in the middle of Providence's annual WaterFire festival: large cauldrons of fire, burning brightly, right on the water, being stocked efficiently at regular intervals by teams of Rhode Islanders in old sturdy boats named for pagan gods. An eclectic assortment of music being piped in through speakers mounted permanently (we think) along the riverbanks; numerous booths and stages; people everywhere; eventually a fresh fish dinner outside at the Capitol Grille. What a night!

What we talked about throughout that evening was life— particularly at Geneva—life in a way that felt similarly to the way that Marilynne Robinson wrote about it in *Gilead*. And, we resolved that night that maybe it could be useful—perhaps even vitally important—for me to draft some thoughts about life at Geneva in the future. What follows is what I wrote.

Saga is not an unfamiliar word, though perhaps used relatively infrequently by many. In its most simple form, it refers to an account of events and experiences, successes and failures, as they unfold historically for a person or group of persons. In a more dramatic form, however, saga conjures up notions of adventure, the heroic, utopia, the romantic, and loyal devotion. For example, former Yale sociologist Burton Clark says of saga: "A saga is not simply a story but a story that at some time has had a particular base of believers...The element of belief is crucial, for without the credible story, the events and persons become history; with the development of belief, a particular bit of history becomes a definition full of pride and identity for the group."[3] Further, and most pertinent for the thoughts that follow, Clark suggests that saga may appropriately refer to organizations, including colleges and universities. Let me explain.

In the late 1980s, when I was in graduate school at Penn State, I came across a book called *The Distinctive College*, written by Burton Clark almost 20 years earlier in 1970.[4] In this book, Clark develops the idea of "organizational saga" based on his research at three, prominent, historically liberal arts institutions. He contends that these colleges were distinctive precisely because of their respective strong sagas; to be distinctive was to have a compelling saga. More specifically, the sagas of these distinctive institutions were characterized by:

- A commitment to eschew the "adaptive servicing of demand or [to] the fulfilling of roles dictated by higher authorities"[5] as the *raison d'etre* of the institution;

- The ability to make an institution's mission "total across a system in space and time;"[6]

- "Deep emotional commitment" in which "believers define themselves by their organizational affiliation, and in their bond to other believers they share an intense sense of the unique;"[7]

- "A feeling that there is the small world of the lucky few and the large routine one of the rest of the world;"[8]

- Expressions of saga throughout the institution—in "statues and ceremonies, written histories and current catalogues, even in an 'air about the place;'"[9] and

- A "strong, self-fulfilling belief."[10]

Clark goes on to say that saga is cultivated most easily in new institutions since they can invest in saga from the beginning and with intentionality, and without existing internal or external constraints, customs, and procedures. According to Clark, saga is also substantially realizable in two other types of institutions as well: struggling institutions and "established" institutions. Regarding the former, Clark notes that "crisis or decay" in an institution can pave the way for the development of a saga because "those in charge, after years of attempting incremental adjustments…realize finally that they must either give up established ways or have the organization fail."[11] Regarding the latter, Clark suggests that initiating a saga at established institutions is most difficult, particularly if they are not experiencing significant crises. Even in established institutions, however, nurturing saga is possible, particularly when a "self-defined need for educational leadership" exists.[12]

What does Clark's notion of saga as applied to colleges have to do with Geneva College? Allow me to make several observations. First, Clark's analysis prompts the elementary questions: When you think of contemporary Geneva, do you think of saga? Is Geneva a distinctive college? "Yes" is certainly a possible—if not complete—response to both of these questions. That Geneva is more than 150 years old, that Geneva is the *only* college in the world connected to the Reformed Presbyterian communion, that Geneva is one of *only* two handfuls of Christian colleges in the reformed tradition in North America, that Geneva was transplanted in Beaver Falls from Northwood, OH, that Geneva is the alleged birthplace of college basketball, that Geneva's mission statement has considerable campus recognition, that Geneva was invested in the Underground Railroad, that Geneva did not capitulate to intellectual and cultural naturalism but drafted instead the Foundational Concepts of Christian Education, that Geneva has persisted—albeit with fragility—in a river valley otherwise decimated by the collapse of industry—these and other characterizations make it reasonable to respond "yes" to the question, "Is Geneva a distinctive college?"

And yet, my sense is that some of us fairly quickly responded in our heads with a "no" to this question and that the "no" was based on a comparison. That is, "no," Geneva is certainly not a distinctive institution compared to Harvard, or to Reed, or to Alverno, or to the University of California—Monterrey Bay, or to Howard. Fair enough. However, while it might be conventional wisdom to think that Geneva is not distinctive compared to these or other institutions, is Geneva distinctive compared to Robert Morris? To Allegheny? To Waynesburg? To Chatham? To Grove City? To Messiah? To Calvin? To Wheaton? [13] Why or why not?

Clark's work is helpful in this regard because he suggests that distinctiveness or saga have more to do with palpable, intrinsic realities than with assumed external comparisons. More specifically, Clark contends that institutional distinctiveness consists of a clear and vibrant identity; forged intentionally over time *de novo* or in response to crisis, need, or opportunity; around which institutional participants have consensus and express loyalty; and, of which all institutional structures and practices routinely testify. With these specific characteristics now in view, I ask again, Is Geneva a distinctive college?

I do not think that it is too harsh to say that distinctiveness defined these ways currently eludes Geneva. Geneva's historic and contemporary uniquenesses somehow do not seem to be translating well into powerful, transformative, univocal educational experiences. I also do not believe that I am alone in this view. That is, a substantial number of voices[14] among us have emerged over the last five years that seem to indicate, at least in part, that Geneva has and is struggling to be distinctive:

- Shirley's (Kilpatrick) profession in a faculty meeting that "Geneva needs a new metaphor;"
- Pete's (Croisant) profession that "we have many departments and individuals doing good things but there isn't a sense of real unity binding us together;"

- Jim's (Gidley) profession that "we seemed to be locked into a PR mentality that makes it almost impossible for us to admit that the institution has flaws;"

- Eric's (Miller) profession that "our crisis of identity at Geneva may well be linked to the larger problem of the fragmenting of the common language and culture that has so disrupted the [larger] academy in recent decades;"

- Don's (Opitz) profession that "we have inherited and created an organizational culture that is wearing us down and tearing us apart. Thin vision and ambiguous priorities contribute to such a politicized culture."

- Dave's (Harvey) profession that "we all spend such energies sidestepping [the conflict between the liberal arts and the professional programs] that we are dysfunctional rather than professional and biblical in the way that we deal with this issue;"

- Mark's (Haas) profession that "If we as faculty are not interested or do not feel able to discuss philosophical issues, then are we not capitulating our God-given duty not to conform to the world or to be taken captive by worldly philosophies."

- Former Psychology professor Randy Bergen's profession that "our pedagogy will have to be demonstrably richer than it currently is...I think it unlikely that we will be competitive or successful if we continue to offer entry level courses to 180 students at a time in relatively unattractive classrooms."

- Leila's (Wallace) profession, largely in reference to technology but broader applications might be quite easily drawn as well: "Can we afford to be seen as a dinosaur?"

- Byron's (Curtis) profession that "spiritual pride significantly weakens our faculty community of its ability to discuss certain crucial matters in a useful, edifying way."

- Stanley's (Clark) profession that "We have an attitudinal problem, with spiritual roots; that we are afraid of change; that we are unwilling to make the tough decisions; that we are caught in a trust gap; and, that we have leadership problems (e.g., We are often unable to convince others of the right means and ends for the college)."

- Bob's (Copeland) profession that "Many people no longer feel that they are persuaded and inspired, but directed, distrusted, and micromanaged...It may sound melodramatic to say that 'there is a struggle going on for the soul of Geneva College,' but it is not far from the truth."

- Terri's (Williams) profession that "[Geneva's] recent approach has been to run screaming away from the prospect of change or to be bogged down with uncertainty and doubt. Little happens and people are demoralized and discouraged. Conducting business becomes drudgery. Pessimism rules the day."

- Dave's (Essig) profession that "For most of us developing a Christian perspective has not been a primary concern in our church experience or in our undergraduate and graduate work. It is not surprising that many of us feel that integration is [simply] not our job."

- Jack's (Delivuk) profession that "One of the problems facing Geneva College is that the boards of Corporators and the Trustees and the administration have not given the college a clear identity."

- Brad's (Frey) profession that "The Christian college can often seem as fragmented as the secular university. Attempts to find cohesion in the curriculum seldom get beyond the platitudes of 'the integration of faith and learning' and 'servant leadership,' or required Bible courses."

- Eric's (Miller) profession that "Apart from serious devotion to participation in Christian learning communities that are rooted in vibrant, mature Christian intellectual traditions, we as scholars and teachers will mainly replicate the sorts of practices, for better and worse, that we learned in the academy—whether we formally adhere to the 'Foundational Concepts [of Christian Education]' or not."

- Howard's (Mattsson-Bozé) profession that "[Geneva] is a respectable but mediocre institution in desperate need of leadership."

May I remind you that all of these voices were heard within the last five years. It is also important to note that these voices do not include any similar comments that were preferred—orally or in writing—within the context of discussions and/or written documents about the core curriculum, the "Blueprint for Diversity," the academic strategic plan, the Performa or the Crane data, Tim Russell's *Our Reformed Perspective* pamphlet, the summer reading groups, the "Wolterstorff talks" and subsequent responses to him, the Panel on General Education document, and more. Nor do these quotes nearly account for the multitude of comments on these issues that occur routinely around tables at the dining hall, via the faculty listserv or other email, within the confines of offices, in non-work settings, or under one's breath on the way home from school.

So, to reiterate my two-fold point: First, I sense that Geneva may not be a distinctive institution at least as Clark defines one and, second, I am not alone in this view. A clear and contagious identity that routinely orients and is reified throughout all dimensions of campus life and function, and that is shared with passion, articulateness, and loyalty by a vast majority of institutional participants currently seems to be missing at Geneva College.

These thoughts lead to a second observation, namely another question or two: Need Geneva be a distinctive college? Should Geneva even aspire to be or to become a distinctive college?

Well, if the only other option is "stable but fragile,"[15] I think that many may affirm "distinctive" or "saga-rich" as better monikers. It strikes me, however, that Clark's notion of distinctiveness or saga has significant affinity with Christian sensibilities. That is, as Christians, we underscore particular commitments that give meaning, purpose, and texture to all else in us and in the world, and that link us with others throughout the ages—both quick and dead—who also embrace these commitments. Further, Christians seek to fulfill these commitments loyally and creatively and communally and passionately and articulately, so that the One who beckoned us to those particular commitments in the first place will receive honor and glory, and until his commitments to us and to his kingdom-come-on-earth-as-it-is-in-heaven might arrive finally and forever. If Clark's view of distinctiveness boils down to clear institutional identity, a coherent expression of institutional commitments throughout an institution, and energetic consensus among institutional participants in support of institutional practices and hopes, then I think that it is reasonable that Christian colleges such as Geneva think seriously about pursuing distinctiveness.

Third, in terms of the particular institutional reality in which we find ourselves currently, in Clark's terms, Geneva is some combination of, first, a college "in crisis" and, second, a college with a "self-defined need for leadership." I think that the comments from our colleagues that I have already read reflect both of these institutional realities. More importantly, I believe that these two institutional contexts are significantly related. On the one hand, experiencing crisis may conjure up notions of incompleteness, of longing for clear purpose, of desire for something more and better, or of the [lamentable] triumph of the mundane or routine. On the other hand, expressing a need for leadership in no small way may represent heartfelt pleas to be relieved of these very same expressed crises: Show us the way! Help us to understand what most matters! Refocus our priorities! Teach us what to love! Bring refreshment to dry land and bones! Equip us for battle! Convince us that our labors are not in vain! Bring us word! Give us hope!

What I am suggesting, then, is that my colleagues' comments above, taken together with other voices that we have heard as well, seem to indicate the presence of institutional crises at Geneva but, at the same time, represent a call for resolution—we are having some troubles and we need some help! If this is a reasonable read of the situation, then a legitimate question may be: So what? Seen in one light, everyone has some troubles and needs some help. Maybe we should just get used to the way life is and stop grumbling so much about it. Although I am mindful of and, like you, regularly experience the ubiquitous incompleteness that attends life in an already-but-not-yet world, I simply cannot and will not resign myself to a worldview that emphasizes sober acquiescence; a "that's just the way things are" perspective and attitude must not be the best we can do or hope for.

How else may we respond? Here is what I will say, and what I am humbly asking you to help me to say best: Geneva needs a "project." Geneva needs a clear and compelling vision for how and to what end it will accomplish its God-given educational task. Geneva needs a "story" that will animate and interpret all that occurs here, a "story" that will hold all of the other stories together. Distinctiveness will remain beyond our grasp without a project.

So, what's the story? What is our project to be? We already affirm that the educational project at Geneva is rooted in and framed by a Christian view of life. The nature of this project in our day and for our day, however, needs a new wineskin. To that end, what follows are five, fundamental themes of a distinctive, Christian educational project for our times at our place. Plenty more might be said and should be said about each of these five themes but, for the purpose of brevity, I will attempt to represent each clearly albeit briefly:

1. The Educational Project at Geneva will be Theological, Anthropological, and Creational

Education at Geneva must affirm the centrality of God, humans, and the created order. These are the foundational components of our story. As such, we and our students must be significantly literate about each of them if we are to speak our story clearly in understanding and in living fundamental questions of existence such as: Where are we? Who are we? What's wrong? What, if anything, can remedy what's wrong? Likewise, education at Geneva must affirm the inseparability and mutual non-exclusivity of God, humans, and the created order. To omit or to devalue any of these three components is to truncate the story and the power and the scope of the story that we wish to tell, to have believed, and to be lived more fully. For example, to omit or to devalue God is to affirm naturalism as our story. Or, to omit or to devalue the created order is to affirm pietism as our story. It is only when we embrace all three together that, to change the metaphor a bit, our "song hits the right notes." The good news is that, to continue the metaphor, the song has been composed, has been sung, and is being sung—and we have the opportunity to participate in the chorus.

2. The Educational Project at Geneva will be Perspectival

Perspectives, stories, projects, worldviews, legitimating ideas, narratives, points of view—in most ways I am not concerned with exactly what word we choose to convey that a Geneva education must be perspectival. What I am most concerned about is that we help students understand that thinking and living have everything to do with the unavoidability, the centrality, and the richness of perspectives.

One implication of this theme is that our educational effort must appropriately exhibit both continuity and discontinuity with other colleges and universities. We have continuity with other institutions because we have many of the same subjects, we support many of the same departments, we use many of the same books, we discuss many of the same "facts," we prepare students for many of the same careers, we have residence halls and sponsor programs through them, we profess in things called classrooms, we field athletic teams, we have faculty development opportunities, and so on.

And yet, affirming that a Geneva education is fundamentally a perspectival education necessitates a discontinuity with other institutions in these regards as well. That is, a perspectival emphasis suggests that we do all that we do *particularly*—what we do is animated by and shaped by the point of view that we say is true and good and right. In the final analysis, I am suggesting that if students graduate from Geneva without understanding the fundamental perspectivalized nature of life, we have not delivered a distinctive education on our terms.

3. The Educational Project at Geneva will Emphasize Discernment

By their very nature, perspectives are discriminating—they limit, they make distinctions, and they precipitate appropriate judgments and actions. Perhaps another way to think of this is to say that perspectives provide a foundation for discerning what to make of things and ultimately how to live. Discernment might be described as the process by which we attempt to understand or to "read" the times—past and present. Discernment seems to have substantial affinity with what the Bible calls wisdom. It necessarily involves coming to terms with what we can affirm and what we must critique, and subsequently what all of that means for daily decisions and behaviors.

4. The Educational Project at Geneva will Signpost God's Kingdom

The sons (and daughters) of Issachar[16] understood the times, knew what to do, and...and, did it? Well, some did, and some did not. And they all did it imperfectly, sporadically, and incompletely. The Christian educational project at Geneva must take care not to frame its perspectival and discernment emphases as cognitive processes alone, for the Christian faith cannot be reduced simply to propositions, ideas, or "confessions." While thinking Christianly and understanding Christianly are certainly highly desirable outcomes in the educational project that I am proposing, without concerted efforts to help students also know how to do what we have taught them to know to do, we will fall short of the goal. The Bible makes clear that lights under bushels, that faith without works, that believing without following, that gifting without loving are all counterproductive to God's intentions for his kingdom. Thus, the Christian educational project at Geneva must strive to be, dare I say, "practical," in that we reach to teach and to model for students—in and out of classrooms, with regard to ideas and with regard to behaviors, in our personal relationships and in our structural processes— how they might enflesh Christian perspective and Christian discernments of the times and, in so doing, serve as signposts to God's kingdom for others. A glimpse of God's kingdom, you say? This way please!

5. The Educational Project at Geneva will Emphasize Calling/Vocation

Perhaps one of the most relevant means of assisting students to understand how to signpost Christian faith is to emphasize particular arenas to which God calls us by his grace to serve Him faithfully. Accordingly, the Christian educational project at Geneva will pay significant attention to calling/vocation; ours will be a vocational education. In being and doing so, however, we will eschew any suggestion that vocation equates solely and/or inappropriately to job or career. Instead—based on Christian theological, anthropological, and creational concerns—we will highlight a multiplicity of vocations that God calls us to consider, through which He calls us to serve, and within which He calls us to signpost His kingdom.

These five interdependent and mutually reinforcing themes, then, represent the heart of a vision for a distinctive, Christian educational project for Geneva College. As such, they serve as starting points both to develop and to measure all facets of our educational effort—in the classroom and out of the classroom. Core courses, courses in various majors, and electives would be created or modified to take on the particular accent of one or several of these central themes of our project.

Traditional undergraduate programs, non-traditional under-graduate programs, and graduate programs all would utilize these five themes as points of departure. The presence of both liberal arts fields and professional fields at Geneva would be ar-gued—I think more compellingly, by the way—from a constel-lation of these five themes. All Chapel programs, residence hall initiatives, and campus colloquia—to name a few co-curricular educational offerings—would proceed under the banner of some number of these themes; so would conversations about diversity, information literacy, and budgets. We would hire faculty and staff who were not only willing, but enthusiastic to participate in a project that trumpeted these themes. Outcomes statements would be revised to reflect a commitment to help students make progress toward each of these themes. In short, if by God's grace we might be so blessed to have our deepest hopes as expressed in these themes at least partially realized, Geneva would become a distinctive institution to the extent that these five themes de-fined, sourced, shaped, and brought coherence to our efforts, and simultaneously served as the foundations for a robust consensus among us.

In my view, the implementation of this project should begin with a revision of the core curriculum. More specifically, I pro-pose that these five themes be employed to construct a new core curriculum that bears the name Foundational Studies. My hope is that many or all of these courses be developed collaboratively, even interdisciplinarily; that they be taught in multiple sections with wise attention to pedagogical concerns and with freedom to utilize common meetings occasionally and/or when appro-priate; that they be writing rich; that they be diversity enhanced; and that they be team-taught, and accounted for as such with respect to faculty load. As you will see a bit later, my intention is not to restrict these elements to Foundational Studies courses alone, but it strikes me as crucial that they be included substan-tially in courses described as "foundational." The courses in the new Foundational Studies program, directly derived from the five central themes of the project, may look something like this:

An Introduction to College (3 credits)

Semester 1

This course uses the college context to introduce and explain the concept of worldviews and to highlight worldview formation as the centerpiece of all college education. It will focus on the contested terrain of knowledge, learning, and teaching, the relative "power" of education, a compare/contrast of the American higher education project in general with the Geneva project in particular, and, utilize examples/applications from various fields. It will also introduce the notion of academic faithfulness/the calling of student.

Tales of the Kingdom (3 credits)

Semester 2

This course is concerned front and center with the story of redemption. It will utilize both testaments of the Bible to frame the particular contours/distinctives of the Christian story. It is not a Bible survey course, but a course that employs biblical theology to tell the story on which we hang all that we are and all that is.

Understanding the Times (6 credits)

Two Semesters (e.g., Semesters 3 and 4)

This two-semester course takes its departure from the notion that faithfully discerning contemporary times is enhanced to the degree that one wisely understands previous times. As is the case with the Tales of the Kingdom course, these two courses are meant to provide interpretive historical frameworks for understanding, rather than to "pitch and catch" historical "facts" with students. It is unclear to me how these two courses could best be developed, but a couple of suggestions would be:

1. Focus on World History (as such) for one semester and American History (as such) for the other;
2. Use "intellectual history" or "epistemology" to frame both semesters and proceed either chronologically, thematically, or both;
3. Perhaps it would be instructive to integrate the story of

the church/Christian peoples within whatever approach is taken; and,

4. Theological, anthropological, and creational emphases could serve as general subtexts to whatever approach is taken.

Calling Studies (6 credits)

Two Semesters (Semesters 5 and 6; OR, any two semesters of 3, 4, 5, 6, 7, or 8)
Two courses will provide academic study of six areas of life in which God calls persons to serve him faithfully, independent of their major area of study. Both semesters will highlight three calling areas each, perhaps something like this:
One Semester: Church/Worship, Government/Politics, and Marriage/Family
Another Semester: Work/Careers, Play/Recreation/Leisure, and Economy/Buying and Selling

Engaging God's World (3 credits)

Semester 3, 4, 5, 6, 7, or 8
This course will be designed to help students understand and evaluate current social trends on their own terms and with a Christian view in mind. More specifically, students will study culture (including cultural diversity), technology, and popular media since they are so unavoidable and so central to contemporary life. They are also areas of life that many Christians far too easily imbibe and/or embrace uncritically. This course will seek to redress this problem.

The Good Life (3 credits; Capstone Course)

Semester 7 or 8
This course will capstone the foundations studies program by revisiting the central themes of a Geneva education. In many ways, this course may mirror the current HUM103 course.

Off-Campus Study Course (3 or more credits)

Semester 3, 4, 5, 6, 7 or 8

All students will be required to take a course that includes some off-campus study component. This course proceeds on the notion that such a requirement has great potential to fulfill many of the five central themes of a Geneva education. The fact that the extant research on off-campus study programs suggests that such courses are pedagogically powerful is an added and notable benefit.

Finally, I envision a Foundational Studies program that may include two department-based components. Nonetheless, including them as components suggests that, though they will vary by department, they are foundational and common to a Geneva education. These two components are:

1. A pro-seminar in one's major (1 credit; first year) that will introduce students to departmental expectations and the contours of the field, including central topics, primary literary sources, common research practices, and the like; and,

2. A capstone course in one's major (3 credits; final year) that will help students bring closure and coherence to studies in their chosen major as framed by the five central themes of a Geneva education, but accounting for the notion that capstone educational experiences may be accomplished in several ways.

It is probably an understatement to say that the foundational studies program that I have just envisioned is different than our current general education program. True enough. But let me be clear as to why. The foundational studies program that I presented is not different because of personal druthers. Rather, the foundational studies program that I presented is different because the five themes that I have presented as the bedrock of our educational project require appropriate expression. Stated another way, if you want *not* to like the foundational studies program that I have briefly discussed, please choose not to like it because it will not help us to reify the five central themes of the project that I am suggesting. Of course, if you do not like the five themes at all, then the game was over a long time ago. But you should also understand that if we have unclear, conflicting, non-operative, or no themes at all to animate and shape our efforts, then pretty much any curriculum will do, and any answer to any question on any topic will also do. I, for one, do not like that option...at all.

Another way to frame this issue is to affirm that when one makes a fundamental, all-encompassing commitment, it "changes everything." Using a well-known biblical imagery, we do not go back into the womb, but we do become new creations! Or, when we are no longer blind, but can see—well, that changes everything! Or, all of you have heard C.S. Lewis on this point: "I believe in Christianity as I believe that the Sun has risen: not only because I see it, but because by it I see everything else."[17] One big thing is the source for understanding all other things. I am arguing that such it is with educational commitments. Depending on the commitments that an institution makes, all else takes shape, has meaning, proceeds. So, in the same way that the five themes of the project require a general education program that complements and displays them "on the ground"—which I have taken a shot at above—it also stands to reason that the five themes would and should provoke other changes as well. Here are a few that come to mind for me, though I will not take time to comment on each:

1.   Limit the number of hours in a major—While embracing the five themes that I have proposed clearly and appropriately supports the continuation of majors at Geneva, it strikes me that the five themes ostensibly suggest that majors always must be in service to something beyond themselves. Stated another way, the function of a whole is to interpret the parts. I believe that one of the appropriate implications of the five themes is to see majors differently—not as wholes, but as parts. And, I

think one way to do that is to limit the number of hours in every major, acknowledging that professional degree programs could have a higher limit than traditional liberal arts degree programs. There is much more that may be said here, but suffice it to say two things: First, that if the general education program became smaller, as I have proposed, and the number of hours in majors were limited as well, the result would be that students would have more choice in their educational experience at Geneva. Frankly, I would count that as a very positive consequence, and, again, not because it is my druthers, but because I think there is something about the five themes that calls such an idea forth. And, second, all of this implies a significant and comprehensive curricular change effort. Though that is a scary proposition, the more important point is that if a saga unfolds and is sustained because those who live the saga are convinced that there is a pearl of great price to be won or lost, then it may stand to reason that all should be actively involved in the effort…even if it makes us all tremble.

2. Rethink curricular delivery—I have become sufficiently intrigued by the 12-3 curricular calendar at Hiram College in Ohio. Hiram touts itself as the only college in the country that uses this model. Each 15-week semester is split into 12 weeks and 3 weeks. During the 12-week session, students take courses that last 2 hours or more several times per week, depending on number of credits; during the 3-week session, students attend class every day during the week, or study off-campus. At first glance, I have to say that there is something about this model that might deliver our Christian educational project well. It certainly would make it so that the unfolding on our new educational vision was going to involve everyone.

3. Reconfigure faculty loads.

4. Reconfigure academic departments.

5. Significant bolster faculty development resources.
6. Develop an MA in Christian Studies program.
7. Thoughtfully and intentionally increase our international student population to at least 7% by 2010.
8. Ask every department to designate at least one lower level course and one upper level course as a writing-enriched course.
9. Ask every department to designate at least two courses as diversity-enhanced courses.
10. Ask every department to designate at least one course as an honors course, based on agreed-upon characteristics.
11. Create living-learning communities around undecided students, honors students, theme floors, and the like.
12. Develop a sophomore year co-curricular program focused on identity and calling.
13. Develop a Health, Physical Education, and Recreation undergraduate minor and/or major to address our historic and current overemphasis on athletics/sport rather than on whole health, life-long physical activity, and thoughtful Christian critique of athletics/competition/sport in American culture.

Two more comments and then I am done. First, a CliffsNotes version of what I have said is this:

1. A compelling, orienting saga that welds us together in common purpose and serves as the wellspring of our efforts currently eludes Geneva.
2. We need such a saga.
3. I offered one possible project in this paper, characterized by five, integrated themes.
4. Those five themes make demands on the heart of our subsequent educational efforts, namely the general education program, so I have taken a shot at what such a general education program—called Foundational Studies—might look like.

5. The central project represented by the five themes "changes everything," or, at least, informs and shapes everything else, and I have attempted to provide a few examples of this.

It strikes me that possible next steps, then, are a function of yours and others' relative buy-in to some number of these five propositions. Maybe you buy them all and want to work on further clarity and implementation. Maybe you only buy the first two propositions and think that I am wet with propositions three through five. Whatever the case, maybe this can be a point of departure for what, if anything, comes of this paper.

Notes

[1]M. Robinson, *Gilead: A Novel* (New York, NY: Picador, 2006).

[2]Ibid., 57; 115.

[3]B. Clark, "The Organizational Saga in Higher Education," *Administrative Science Quarterly*, Vol. 17, No. 2 (June 1972), 178-184; 178.

[4]B. Clark, *The Distinctive College* (Chicago, IL: Aldine Publishing Company, 1970).

[5]B. Clark, "The Organizational Saga in Higher Education," 56.

[6]Clark, *The Distinctive College*, 235.

[7]B. Clark, "Belief and Loyalty in College Organizations," in B. Clark, *On Higher Education: Selected Writings, 1956-2006* (Baltimore, MD: Johns Hopkins University Press, 2008), 65-79, 75.

[8]Ibid.

[9]Clark, "The Organizational Saga in Higher Education," 61.

[10]Ibid.

[11]Ibid., 57.

[12]Ibid.

[13]I selected these institutions because they many regarded them, at the time, as institutions to which Geneva compared itself.

[14]All of those included were faculty members at Geneva at the time, unless noted otherwise. These comments were excerpted from feedback retrieved at a faculty retreat.

[15]This was the way that Geneva's president at the time characterized the institution and, fortunately and unfortunately, it became a common way to refer to Geneva's fundamental institutional identity.

[16]I Chronicles 12:32.

[17]C.S. Lewis, "Is Theology Poetry?" in *The Weight of Glory* (New York, NY: HarperCollins, 2001), 140.

CHAPTER 4

Educating for [Godly] Wisdom in the Shadow of Empires

This essay was presented at the Symposium on Faith and Culture at Baylor University in October 2011.

Introduction

I want to focus my comments this afternoon on three ideas. First, I will suggest that all attempts at what might be called Christian faithfulness, including educating for wisdom, occur within the context of what Walter Brueggemann calls "empires."[1] Second, I will note that empires from without are not the only obstacles to overcome in the pursuit of educating for wisdom; that is, "the enemy" is us as well. And, finally, I will offer several suggestions and perhaps conversation starters for what educating for wisdom with a Christian accent may involve.

Educating for Wisdom in the Shadow of the Empires

In his book, *Texts That Linger, Words That Explode*,[2] Old Testament scholar Walter Brueggemann suggests that Israel's faithfulness was at risk of compromise or annihilation because it was—to use Brueggemann's phrase—"always in the shadow of the empire[s]." You will remember that the empires of this particular

period in Israel's history were Egypt, Assyria, and Babylon. Was
Israel able to exist within the shadow of these empires without
being "confiscate[d]"[3] by them? No. The "reach" of the empires
was unavoidable and inexorable, while the empires may have
provided certain opportunities and benefits, they also had the
power to misshape and misdirect Israel's strivings to be faithful,
and they did.

In the context of this conference, empires other than Christianity embrace visions and versions for educating for wisdom in
the 21st century. Alternative definitions of wisdom are afoot as
are other presumptions about and practices of educating. Such
visions and plans are enticing and winsome, offering promise
for one's future and one's hopes. Such visions and plans may not
seem overtly oppressive or onerous, much less dangerous. In
fact, such visions and plans may seem to offer life, liberty, and
the pursuit of happiness. But, such visions and plans also may
cast long shadows on the efforts of Christian educators and institutions to educate for wisdom, perhaps even to the point where
educating for wisdom with a Christian accent is unwittingly obscured, in captivity, domesticated, indistinguishable from the
empires that, without violence, have done it in.

What are some of these contemporary educational empires?
Let me briefly suggest four. First is the empire of "wisdom education is 'what I decide to make it' education." This empire is perhaps largely populated by college students who believe that the
satiation of their various appetites constitutes the wisest form of
education. It may also be at least partially embraced by colleges
and universities that are all too willing to oblige. Wisdom is simply doing what one needs to do, and not doing what one does not
need to do. Anya Kamenetz's new book *DIY U: Edupunks, Edupreneurs, and Coming Transformation of Higher Education*[4] may
have this version of wisdom just about right. The description of
the last chapter of the book explains that it offers "A four-part
guide for the student who wants to hack her own education."[5]
DIY U, by the way, stands for "do it yourself university." I suspect
that Mary Grigsby's findings that 70 percent of students consider

socializing more important than academics gives additional texture to this version of wisdom education (as quoted in Richard Arum and Josipa Roksa's book, *Academically Adrift*.)[6]

The second empire is "wisdom education is 'if it lands me a job' education." This empire is predicated on the idea that the wisest form of education is education that prepares one for employment; educating for wisdom is education that trains students for jobs. Accordingly, certain fields of study clearly do educate with this version of wisdom education in mind (e.g., business, education, and engineering), while others do not (e.g., philosophy, English, and sociology). This is not to suggest that some may believe that certain disciplines and courses may be important for students to take, though not for the sake of wisdom as such. "I have to take it" and wisdom development are two different things to students and to parents in particular. I suspect that suggesting that this empire has considerable power in the academy—including Christian colleges and universities—is anything but an understatement, exacerbated by the high and rising costs of postsecondary education.

The third empire is "wisdom education is 'cultivating the intellect' education." Ah, now we're talking! This empire emphasizes intellectual or rational development as the heart of wisdom education; if students learn the right things the right ways, they will come to think right. In turn, if they think right, they will do right. And, if they think right and do right, then they will be...well...wise. Echoing the tones of the eminent John Henry Newman, Robert Hutchins says it clearly: "An education that consists of the cultivation of the intellectual virtues, therefore, is the most useful education, whether the student is destined for a life of contemplation or a life of action...[and]...the intellectual virtues are habits resulting from the training of the intellectual powers."[7] If one could say that "if it lands me a job education" has substantial power among students and their parents, one might also posit that "cultivating the intellect education" is valued by faculty members in general, and by faculty members with appointments in the humanities in particular. I should probably add that David Patterson's book, *When Learned Men Murder*,[8] may provide some caution in adopting this view too hastily as the norm for wisdom education. He chillingly notes that "Of the fourteen men gathered at the 1941 Wannsee conference in Berlin to design and plan the Holocaust...eight held doctorates from some of Europe's most prestigious institutions."[9]

The fourth, and last empire that I will mention is "wisdom education is 'getting done what you're supposed to get done' education." This empire may be described as an institutional empire of sorts in which wisdom accrues to the extent that one simply follows particular procedures and fulfills particular obligations. "Have you completed a minimum of 120 hours, and do you have at least one major and a minimum GPA in your major and overall? Good. You have become wise." "Is our departmental curriculum in compliance with state regulations, accreditation standards, or both? Great, we can now deliver wisdom." "Have you become a specialist in your field? Super, you have attained wisdom." In short, wisdom consists simply of graduating.

Are any of these four empires altogether nefarious? No. In fact, in my view, there is considerable wisdom in allowing students freedom to explore, even if they make unwise choices, and it strikes me as wise that education has a preparatory quality to it. Similarly, education that does not have something to do with the intellect seems quite foolish to me and finishing what one starts has a certain ring of wisdom to it. The sage proverb, "A good dissertation is a finished one," comes readily to mind.

Suggesting, however, that each of the four empires that I identified has redeeming qualities is a far cry from believing or trusting the empire for life itself. Of course, this is the trick with faithfulness and with wisdom. How can one simultaneously affirm good aspects of otherwise misdirected empires while not becoming seduced by its enchantments that demand full allegiance? In my view, this is precisely what Christian wisdom involves, though I am quite aware that other Christians may disagree. For example, some Christians believe that bad empires are easy to spot and, once spotted, should simply be eschewed and rooted out. For example, in a provocative and, frankly, compelling essay, Robert Brimlow argues that Christian institutions should not have business departments because doing so represents "conflicting allegiances"[10] or, more pointedly, "serving two masters."[11]

Educating for Wisdom…Without Wisdom

Second, I must note that there is not only trouble outside river city, but within river city as well. That is, it is not as though the only threat to educating for wisdom with a Christian point of view comes from outside Christian educators and outside Christian institutions. No. There is trouble inside Israel as well. To put it the way that Augustine noted in *The Confessions*, Christians and Christian institutions can "become a vast problem" to themselves, "pursu[ing] the empty glory of popularity ambitions for the applause of the audience."[12] Or, perhaps another internal problem is that Christians and Christian institutions have not developed sophisticated theological moorings to guide their efforts, as numerous scholars have opined, such as Mark Noll, Doug Henry and Bob Agee, Robert Benne, and Julie Reuben.[13] Or, still another angle on an eclipse of wisdom is rooted IN some versions of Christian theological systems. For example, in their book, *Divided by Faith*, Michael Emerson and Christian Smith suggest that "Because evangelicals view their primary task as evangelism and discipleship (at least discipleship of a certain kind)…they most consistently call for changes in persons [but] leave the dominant social structures, institutions, and culture intact…[As a result] evangelicals' views…conform to the socio-economic conditions of their time."[14] My point here is to ensure that, to the extent that the pursuit of godly wisdom in higher education is compromised in some way, such compromise may be as much the result of the inadequacy of one's understanding of Christian faith as it is the seduction of counterfeit and/or confounding external empires.

Educating for Wisdom with a Christian Accent

Third, and finally, what might educating for wisdom from a Christian point of view suggest? Let me offer several things.

First, Christian educators and Christian institutions should be known for their commitment to wisdom development. I do not think that educating for wisdom is simply what comes naturally for Christian educators and Christian institutions, nor do I believe that educating for wisdom is self-evident to Christians, requiring no further explanation and no serious, ongoing investments. However, I do believe that educating for wisdom is precisely the educational vision for which Christian educators and Christian institutions should be known.

Second, Christian educators and Christian institutions should recognize that educating for wisdom is a perspectival undertaking. If educators at colleges and universities of all kinds across the land were asked, "Do you think that we should help college students develop wisdom?" I believe that most would quickly respond, "Of course." Then, how do we explain that neither the purposes nor the practices of higher education are uniform across the educational landscape? In my view, it is because educating for wisdom is not a monolith. Instead, educating for wisdom goes forward predicated on fundamental commitments or values or anchors that frame what it means, the ends to which it aspires, and strategies for being successful. Christian educators should not only be at the forefront of knowing and promoting such perspectivalism, but should work devotedly to develop and hone the theological and biblical scaffolding that animates their particular versions of educating for wisdom.

Third, Christian educators and Christian institutions may benefit from using Walter Brueggemann's work on wisdom in general and his work on Christian education in particular, particularly as found in his book, *The Creative Word*.[15] Brueggemann suggests that the structure of the Old Testament canon, in addition to the actual words or substance that comprise it, provide sound advice for wise educating. More specifically, he suggests that the Torah's (Priests) emphasis on identity and tradition, the Prophets' emphasis on critique and debunking and change that most often includes struggle and suffering, and the

Kingly emphasis on discernment and exploration and discovery offer a compelling framework for a Christian understanding of educating for wisdom. Brueggemann summarizes:

> There have always been those who preferred the To-rah of certitude from the scribe or the freshness of the word from the prophet or the hunch of counsel from the wise… It is the invitation of canon to educators that we should have a varied repertoire of both mode and sub-stance, and that we should have a keen sense of which season requires which part of the canon.[16]

What might it mean to have the entire educational enterprise constructed around this tripartite, but inextricably interrelated and coherent, model? I suspect that some may think that such a model is already in place, at least in the so-called core curric-ulum. Well, maybe. I suspect it will depend on what an institu-tion's core curriculum looks like. If an institution's core curric-ulum has little relevance beyond itself, its importance imagined only in the minds of its own priests, then I suspect that the kind of wisdom education that Brueggemann has in mind is missed. Further, it may be fair to say that, for all intents and purposes, academic majors are the core educational undertaking. Such an approach, at least to the extent that I understand Brueggemann, also would not qualify as an educating for wisdom strategy. To believe Brueggemann, educating with wisdom in mind from a Christian point necessitates that all aspects of the learning proj-ect are inextricably related.

Fourth, Christian educators and Christian institutions may benefit from tapping particular biblical injunctions as starting points for exploring educating for wisdom with a Christian ac-cent. Allow me to provide one example of what I mean here. In the Old Testament, the sons of Issachar are described as those who "understood the times and knew what to do" (I Chronicles 12:32ff). It seems reasonable to me to suggest that the sons of Issachar were wise; their wisdom consisted on a blend of under-standings and actions. In our current day, what would it look like to help students understand the times and know what to do? What are the particular "times" we must help them to understand? What does understanding mean? Does understanding have anything to do with discerning good and bad? Will knowing what to do have something to do with understanding? What are the particular places in which they will do what they know they must do? In addition to these types of questions, does education for wisdom Issachar-style shed any light on the relationship between liberal arts types and professional arts types? Does it suggest a different way to think of learning and majors and pedagogy altogether? What if it did?

Finally, Christian educators and Christian institutions must not overlook structural considerations for the educating for wisdom enterprise. Benjamin Bloom[17]—of educational taxonomy fame—argued that institutions must identify clear educational objectives—educating for wisdom, for example. Bloom also believed that unless an institution carefully developed particular educational offerings to emerge from and to cultivate these objectives, and unless an institution carefully arranged these educational offerings in an appropriate order and sequence, the attainment of the educational objectives would be jeopardized. I agree. So, Christian educators and Christian institutions wish to educate for wisdom. Good. Is the best way to "get there" to have the process last four years? Is the best way to get there to have some classes last 50 minutes and others 75 minutes? Is the best way to get there to have general education, majors, and elective curricula? Is the best way to get there to take four or five courses simultaneously? Is the best way to get there to require off campus study and internships and practica? Is the best way to get there to learn balkanized disciplines? Is the best way to get there to have co-curricular programming? Is the best way to get there to require capstone experiences? Is the best way to get there to have required chapel? I suspect that you get the point. However, there are two specific ramifications that I want to emphasize. First, á la Brueggemann, the *structure and delivery* of an education for wisdom approach says as much about what counts as wisdom as the *mission* of education for wisdom itself. To what extent do the current structures of and delivery strategies for our educational programs correspond with our beliefs about Christian wisdom? And, second, since most Christian educators and Christian institutions seem to have the exact same educational programs, including the structure of those programs *and* the delivery of those programs, is it fair to say that we all simply are already "educating for wisdom" from a Christian point of view? Said another way, should we be concerned that all of our programs for educating for wisdom look pretty similar, including pretty similar to our secular postsecondary counterparts?

Conclusion

This notion of "faithfulness in the shadow of empires"—from without and from within—strikes me as helpful in its simplicity: faithfulness matters and it is also contested, from without and from within. I hope that we have the courage both to name and face regnant empires that may be at work in our midst, and to understand what educating for godly wisdom may mean…even if it means tweaking, renovating, or radically refurbishing what we currently do personally and institutionally.

Notes

[1] W. Brueggemann, *Texts That Linger, Words That Explode: Listening to Prophetic Voices* (Minneapolis, MN: Fortress Press, 1999).

[2] Ibid.

[3] Ibid., 82.

[4] A. Kamenetz, *DIY U: Edupunks, Edupreneurs, and the Coming Transformation of Higher Education,* (Hartford, VT: Chelsea Green, 2010).

[5] Ibid., iii.

[6] R. Arum and J. Roska, *Academically Adrift: Limited Learning on College Campuses* (Chicago, IL: University of Chicago Press, 2011), 59.

[7] R. Hutchins, *The Higher Learning in America* (New York, NY: Routledge, 1995), 63.

[8] D. Patterson, *When Learned Men Murder* (Arlington, VA: Phi Delta Kappa International, Inc., 1996).

[9] G. Bogue and J. Aper, *Exploring the Heritage of American Higher Education: The Evolution of Philosophy and Policy* (New York, NY: Rowman and Littlefield Publishers), ix.

[10] M. Budde and J. Wright (eds.), *Conflicting Allegiances: The Church-Based University in a Liberal Democratic Society* (Ada, MI: Brazos Press, 2004).

[11] R. Brimlow, "Who Invited Mammon?: Professional Education in the Christian College and University," in M. Budde and J. Wright, eds., *Conflicting Allegiances: The Church-Based University in a Liberal Democratic Society* (Grand Rapids, MI: Brazos Press, 2004).

[12] Augustine, *The Confessions* (New York, NY: Oxford University Press, 2009), 52.

[13] M. Noll, *The Scandal of the Evangelical Mind* (Grand Rapids, MI: Wm. B. Eerdmans Publishing Company, 1995); D. Henry and B. Agee (eds.), *Faithful Learning and the Christian Scholarly Vocation* (Grand Rapids, MI: Wm. B. Eerdmans Publishing Company, 2003); R. Benne, *Quality With Soul: How Six Premier Colleges and Universities Keep Faith with their Religious Traditions (Grand Rapids, MI: Wm. B. Eerdmans Publishing Company, 2001)*; and J. Reuben, *The Making of the Modern University: Intellectual Transformation and the*

Marginalization of Morality (Chicago, IL: University of Chicago Press, 1996).

[14]M. Emerson and C. Smith, *Divided By Faith: Evangelical Religion and the Problem of Race in America* (New York, NY: Oxford University Press, 2001), 21-22.

[15]W. Brueggemann, *The Creative Word: Canon as a Model for Biblical Education* (Minneapolis, MN: Fortress Press, 1982).

[16]Ibid., 12.

[17]B. Bloom, *Taxonomy of Educational Objectives, Handbook 1, Cognitive Domain, 2nd Edition* (Boston, MA: Addison-Wesley Longman Limited, 1956).

CHAPTER 5

Christian Higher Education and the Challenges of Postmodern Individualism

(Or, Explaining Reality, Including Three Average Examples)

This essay was given as part of Grove City College's 125th anniversary celebration and Vision 2025 proceedings in November 2001.

But the mere survival of colleges and universities is not enough. If their attention is completely absorbed by the pressures of maintaining operational viability, if their freedom to imagine better possibilities is rendered impossible by the tasks of coping with horrendous necessities, if their behavior only encourages an attitude of material aggrandizement but never the yearning to think or dream, our culture will lose the leaven crucial to hope, and will descend into an age of sophisticated nihilism.[1]

Introduction

On an exam that I gave about a month ago, I asked students to choose one of three essay questions that were listed in the final section of the test. As I was grading the exams, I noticed that one student had penciled in a fourth question, below the other three, that read: "Explain reality. Include three good examples." He explained to me later that he thought that the question he had added was comparable to the other three. Perhaps my essay questions tend to be broad.

Today I find myself sympathizing with this student's sentiments because the subject that I have been asked to tackle is "Christian Higher Education and the Challenges of Postmodern Individualism." I have taken the liberty to subtitle my paper "Explaining Reality, Including Three Average Examples," as the subject before us strikes me as extraordinarily large and complex and my time to offer comment quite modest and fleeting. Thus, the approach that I have taken in this paper is of necessity broad-brushed and partial. First, I will briefly describe the term postmodern individualism, which I believe to be a primary animating worldview of contemporary American society. Second, I will offer some snapshots of the impact of postmodern individualism on three particular arenas of life: religious expression, socio-cultural life writ large, and finally higher education. Then, I will conclude with some implications of postmodern individualism for the business of an institution such as Grove City College with the hope that they might serve as somewhat of a prelude for today's second presentation.

Let me note two things before I begin. First, it is critical for Grove City to include such a topic as this in its anniversary proceedings. Higher education and American society have always been inextricably related, from the unmistakable import of the earliest colleges for colonial life, to the establishment of land grant institutions in the mid-19th century, to the differentiation and massification of American higher education in the 20th century, to linkages between the federal government and universities' basic science research efforts. Clark Kerr goes as far as to say, "As society goes, so goes the university; but, also, as the university goes, so goes society."[2] The historic relationship between colleges and universities and American society is anything but bubble-like, although I realize that sometimes it feels that way, particularly to students. Thus, it is imperative to consider the society-college dynamic, and I applaud Grove City College for including it as an important part of Vision 2025's look forward.

This leads to a second consideration, namely, that as an institution interested in honoring Christ, Grove City is obliged to be appropriately responsive to its socio-cultural contexts. From my perspective, biblical injunctions to "discern the times," "to seek wisdom," "to be in the world but not of it," and so on, are as applicable to institutions who wish to be faithful to the Lord as they are to persons who wish to do likewise. Seen in this light, Grove City's interest in exploring its current social setting and in being responsive to this setting via the continued planning and implementation of its entire educational experience now and over the next 25 years, can be and should be construed as a matter of Christian faithfulness.

The Influence of Postmodern Individualism

My paper proceeds from the notion that a dominant influence within the contemporary American cultural landscape in which Grove City College is situated is what might be called postmodern individualism. Let me assure you that my intent is not to philosophize incomprehensibly about postmodernity or individualism as such. I am simply persuaded by people like Andrew Delbanco[3] who suggest that our society is currently organized around the idea of Self, having earlier been predominantly shaped by the ideas of God and Nation in succession. More specific to the college-society relationship, James Burtchaell[4] suggests that colleges (and society) have developed from being animated by Christian pietism, to an uneasy pietism, to an indifference to pietism, to—finally—postmodernism, whereby individual realities, preferences and aspirations supplant allegiance to any external, overarching purposes or goals. Isaiah Berlin's creative essay juxtaposes two animals—the hedgehog and the fox—to illustrate the same point.[5] The hedgehog "relate[s] everything to a single central vision" while the fox "pursue[s] many ends, often unrelated and even contradictory." The hedgehog touts law, order, unity, and certainty while the fox embraces freedom, serendipity, multiplicity, and uncertainty.

Perhaps a specific college-related example better illustrates this notion of postmodern individualism. The scene is a commencement ceremony within the last decade at one of the most prestigious institutions in the land, at which an honored graduating undergraduate stated: "Among my classmates...I believe that there is one idea, one sentiment, which we have all acquired at some point in our Harvard careers; and that, ladies and gentlemen, is, in a word, confusion." That same year, an honored graduating graduate student made these remarks to the assembled crowd: "They tell us that it is heresy to suggest the superiority of some value, fantasy to believe in moral argument, slavery to submit to a judgment sounder than your own. The freedom of our day is the freedom to devote ourselves to any values we please, on the mere condition that we do not believe them to be true."[6] Notice the disregard for a sense of a grand story or for meaning beyond self-referential understanding or personal choice. It is little wonder that within several years of the addresses that a story in *The Chronicle of Higher Education* coined the term "absolutophobia" to describe the American college scene.[7] Perhaps sociologist David Lyon's sense that American culture has moved from Providence to Progress to Nihilism[8] is more true of the contemporary scene than we would like to admit.

Let us turn now to examine how what I have called postmodern individualism takes shape in three realms of contemporary American life, beginning with its impact on religious expression.

The Impact of Postmodern Individualism on Religious Expression

As you may be aware, there is currently much being written about subjects such as character, morality, and religious expression in American culture. News magazines, professional journals, and university press books seem to feature these types of topics with increasing regularity. Let's look at a few examples. University of Virginia social philosopher James Hunter (a convinced Christian believer who is a graduate of Gordon College) opens his most recent book, *The Death of Character*, with a chilling three-page "Postmortem" that begins with these words:

> Character is dead. Attempts to revive it will yield little. Its time is passed…The social and cultural conditions that make character possible are no longer present and no amount of political rhetoric, legal maneuvering, educational policy making, or money can change that reality. Its time has passed.[9]

Tom Beaudoin is less dour in his recent book about Generation X's "irreverent spiritual quest."[10] According to Beaudoin, "religion still matters" among the younger generation, but the ways in which it matters are vitally important to understand. That is, the proverbial "search for God" and/or spiritual understanding are important to young people today, but such a search takes place under the rubric of four important themes: 1) institutions are suspect; 2) personal experience is fundamental; 3) suffering and alienation are unavoidable starting points; and 4) ambiguity is central.[11] If you are roughly my age or older, your response to religious expression that proceeds from these themes is likely to be something like, "These people need psychotherapy!" After all, we were raised to trust institutions, to acquiesce to external authority, to downplay the sensual, to "go tough when the going got tough," and to believe that ambiguity was a sign of weak-mindedness. Of course, we did not have the benefit of being incubated in the "amniotic fluid" of the popular media and boundless technology. And, we would quickly add that "we're better off for it. These young whippersnappers might be searching for some weird spirituality thing, but they certainly can't be interested in the Christianity that I believe in."

There's the rub, right? Today's students can, in fact, be Christians but their Christianity may not be expressed in the same ways that "ours" is. A Christian faith that is shaped by the ethos of 21st century postmodern individualism will look differently than a Christian faith shaped by the ethos of a 20th century modern individualism. Perhaps this helps to make sense of why today's traditional student population, according to Richard Cimino and Don Lattin, are most interested in finding meaningful "personal religious experiences" in "downsized" and "decentralized" local congregations, in pursuing short-term outreach opportunities to less fortunate populations, and in utilizing electronic media to create and sustain linkages with other believers.[12] When Self is a primary reference point for Christian faith, particularly in a context in which grand stories are personally suspect in some degree, Christian faith certainly can be authentic, but it may not look like the Christian faith that 50-year-old Christians—or 125-year-old Christian colleges—embrace. Listen to the way that Robert Wuthnow puts it:

> At the start of the twentieth century, virtually all Americans practiced their faith within a Christian or Jewish framework. They were cradle-to-grave members of their particular traditions…Organized religion dominated their experience of spirituality, especially when it was reinforced by ethnic loyalties…Now, at the end of the twentieth century, growing numbers of Americans piece together their faith like a patchwork quilt. Spirituality has become a vastly complex quest in which each person seeks in his or her own way.[13]

Wuthnow goes on to explain that, over the last 50 years, a change has occurred in which faith, spirituality, or religious expression has shifted from an emphasis on dwelling to seeking. Dwelling faith emphasizes a secure, situated, temple religion. Seeking faith stresses a fleeting, sojourning, tabernacle religion. Dwelling faith emphasizes constancy, seeking faith stresses transition. Dwelling faith is about residence and membership; seeking faith is about homelessness and search for meaningful connections. Social identity is ascribed or achieved in dwelling faith; in seeking faith, social identity is created and negotiated. Dwelling faith emphasizes denominations as safe havens of sacred space; seeking faith sees mainline denominations as constricting old wine-skins. In short, the faith of our day, framed as it is within the context of what I have called postmodern individualism, reflects an "insistence that the sacred cannot be known fully" and that individuals are simply responsible to "work hard to figure out their own lives."[14]

Perhaps Wuthnow's observations provide some insight into national survey data. According to recent Gallup Polls, fully two-thirds of surveyed Americans have made a personal commitment to Jesus Christ...although only 41% of them said that they are absolutely committed. Moreover, over 80% believe that the Bible is the inspired Word of God, even though only 17% read it daily, almost 50% rarely or never read it, 40% said that it is too hard to understand, a whopping 84% couldn't even "hazard a guess" as to what was meant by the "Great Commission," and 63% had no clue what John 3:16 referred to.[15] In any case, the spirituality of the 21st century, alive and well—even thriving—as it may be, presents some significant challenges to institutions such as Grove City that wish to engage students in understanding the implications of a gracious King and a here-and-coming kingdom.

The Implications of Postmodern Individualism on Socio-Cultural Life

One of the best-selling books of the 1980s was a book called *Habits of the Heart*.[16] In it, Robert Bellah and friends chronicled (but nevertheless lamented) that individual fulfillment had become one of the most important socio-cultural values in America. In a follow-up book a number of years later, called *The Good Society*, Bellah, et al. took their argument further by explaining that the rise of individualism has been accompanied by a growing absenteeism in public life.[17] According to the authors, many Americans, having drunk deeply from individualism, consider the institutions of public life—politics, community organizations, the economy, organized religion—either as restraining, hostile, irrelevant, or simply "over their heads." Content to be

self-content and self-absorbed, these folks no longer "pay attention to" or are "mindful" of the larger realities much less needs
of socio-cultural life in America.

More recently, Robert Putnam's bestseller, *Bowling Alone*,
picks up Bellah's concern by providing chart after chart representing downward trends in American social life. For example,
between the mid-1970s and the mid-1990s, the percentage of
Americans who served as an officer of a club or organization
dropped 42%; the percentage of Americans who worked for a
political party dipped 42%; the percentage of Americans who
served on a committee for some local organization declined
39%; the percentage of Americans who attended a public meeting on town or school affairs dropped 35%; and, the percentage
of Americans who wrote a letter to a senator or member of congress fell by 23%.[18] Putnam concludes:

> Active involvement in clubs and other voluntary asso-
> ciations has collapsed at an astonishing rate, more than
> halving most indexes of participation within barely a
> few decades...Americans have been dropping out in
> droves, not merely from political life, but from orga-
> nized community life more generally.[19]

Of course, according to Putnam, technology ostensibly offers
some short-cuts for those who want to be socio-politically active "from a distance." Mostly with disgust, he recounts a recent
advertisement that read:

> If you care...you can do something...easy! www.ifnot-
> now.com Be a full-time citizen activist...for 5 minutes a
> week! Over a dozen of the best social advocacy groups
> provide the information—you read the alerts, send let-
> ters, get responses, and monitor results—all at the click
> of a button. It's a one-stop shop for staying involved. We
> want to make it easy for you to make a difference! Make
> your voice heard! www.ifnotnow.com Sign up for a free
> trial now![20]

The downward trend in socio-cultural American life due to individualism is exacerbated to the extent that the future is perceived
to be overly unpredictable or unstable. For example, according to
Clark Kerr, progress has always been assured in American culture
until very recently. However, according to Kerr, considerable "apprehension" currently exists in contemporary America: "We fear
the nuclear bomb, environmental deterioration, the population
explosion, the manipulation of DNA, the possibility of atomic
and biological terrorism, and much else."[21] And, Kerr's book was
out a number of months before the terrorist attacks on September 11, 2001! If postmodern individualism has gradually contributed to a declining trend in social commitments, apprehension
about the future will only further support such disengagement.

Perhaps one of the brighter spots of socio-cultural life in
America is the institution of the family. Even Bellah was sanguine about the role that families can and do play in helping its
members understand and establish patterns of commitment and
involvement.[22] And, yet, as psychologist David Myers reports
in his recent book, for each year in the 1990s, the 2.4 million
marriages are accompanied by 1.2 million divorces; since 1960,
the percentage of divorced adults has quadrupled. Moreover,
more Americans are marrying later if at all, and the overall pro-
portion of unmarried American adults has increased to almost
41% nationwide.[23] Presumably, individualism is playing a role in
family life as well.

To turn to another aspect of family life, how are American
children doing? This is truly one of the most agonizing aspects
of American socio-cultural life to read about. Permit me to focus
on American adolescents as a subset of all children. The news
is chilling. Based on her extensive ethnographic research on
American adolescence, Patricia Hersch concludes that the primary descriptor of adolescents is that they are alone. She writes:

> A clear picture of adolescents, of even our own children,
> eludes us—not necessarily because they are rebelling, or
> avoiding or evading us. *It is because we aren't there.* Not
> just parents, but any adults. American society has left

its children behind as the cost of progress in the work-
place...Meanwhile adolescents are growing up with no
adults around, a deficit of attention, and no discussion
about whether it matters at all.[24]

Without even counting the effects of broken homes, Hersch
contends that today's adolescents are confused regarding what
constitutes healthy development, find it difficult to identify role
models, experience few—if any—rites of passage, have more
information than they know what to do with but little sense of
how to understand it, and seemingly boundless license to de-
termine where they will go and what they will do at any giv-
en time. If Hersch is right, it seems a reasonable question for
many American colleges and universities to ask, "How will we
respond to students who will arrive on our campus and find
out that we offer more supervision and accountability than they
ever received at home?"

The Impact of Postmodern Individualism on Higher Education

Teaching in postmodern America can be an eye-opening experience, says Peter Sacks in a recent book. He remembers receiving the following feedback on his teacher evaluation form early
in his career:

I hated this class and found it hard to get up in the
morning to get here. I would have dropped it except that
I am graduating in June. You must understand that we
are beginning college writers and not graduate students.
Your attendance grading is "BS" because we pay for our
school and should be able to choose whether to attend
or not...If I don't get a decent grade because of your
critical attitude, I will be speaking to your superiors.[25]

This is a voice from what Sacks calls "the entitlement society"
to which large numbers of today's traditional-aged students
confidently belong. They are interested in being gratified—even
quickly—in and out of the classroom. And, if they are not, they
may express that they have been victimized unfairly—like the

student in the previous quote. To use Neil Postman's images, they are beholden to the god of Economic Utility (that tells them that they are what they do for a living) and to the god of Consumership (that tells them that they are what they accumulate).[26] In service to either god, college is a necessary rite of passage. But it is also clear that such students are fundamentally *in* college to be *out* of college earning a "decent wage," so that they can be *up* to creating a "decent life." Of course, college fortunately offers them an action-packed and fun-filled training ground for the hustle-and-bustle corporate worlds that they cannot quite get to fast enough. So says an oft-cited *Atlantic Monthly* article of almost one year ago that characterizes today's students as "the organization kids."[27]

Seen in another light, Levine and Cureton[28] report that the most commonly mentioned adjective that today's undergraduates use to describe themselves is "tired." If some of the observations that I have been citing from various sources are fair representations, being tired makes some sense, doesn't it? After all, many students come to college convinced—even if subconsciously—of a self-referenced world in which absolutes seem mostly irrelevant, and they have observed such a world by virtue of growing up largely alone in relation to parents and other adults. Add to this the idea that they, as Levine and Cureton further elucidate, are trying to figure out whether they should be mostly hopeful or mostly fearful of the future, but in the meantime have been convinced by their self-referencing worldview that what matters is individual choices, lived experiences with friends and by oneself, and personal satisfaction and comfort now and into the future. To hold all of that together would be, well, tiring.

Lest you think that I disparage today's college students too vociferously, allow me to add quickly that postmodern individualism has also done a number on faculty members and on postsecondary institutions. The apotheosis of academic professionalism in the academy has created disintegrated institutions. In our efforts to be "good scholars," we have given all to disciplines and departments and atomized knowledge. And, in our wake goes curricula—even general education curricula—that barely hold together, pedagogical isolationism, and inexorable bickering over resources and promotions and rights and small-potatoes fine points. In many institutions across the country, faculty members have little to say to one another. And, if students are getting a unified curricular experience, they must be tireless geniuses, because it certainly is not because the institution planned it that way. In short, faculty members—and many colleges and universities across this land—are tired too. Personally, I am reminded of our opening faculty workshop at the beginning of the fall semester in which our speaker suggested that ours was becoming a culture of exhaustion.

Conclusion

In concluding, allow me to return to a comment I made at the outset: As an institution interested in honoring Christ, Grove City is obliged to be appropriately responsive to its socio-cultural context. It strikes me, then, that the critical question as the next 125 years are christened is this: What is Grove City College's educational response amidst a culture that may take its cues from postmodern individualism? To be more specific: What is and will Grove City do in its curriculum to challenge, critique, and offer biblically reasoned alternatives to the hegemonic influence of postmodern individualism? What is, and will Grove City do curricularly, pedagogically, and co-curricularly to emphasize and model the coherence of learning and knowledge that is suggested by a Redeemer who holds all things together (cf., Colossians 1)? What is and will Grove City do in and out of the classroom to minister to students who have been alone, fearful, without hope, self-absorbed, bigoted, or clueless? What is and will Grove City do to assist and support faculty and staff in capturing a vision of their callings and the requisite skills and attitudes not only to redress the emptiness of postmodern individualism in students' lives, their own lives, and in the world, but to offer convincingly a New Way to see and live life rooted in grace, service, justice, and peace? What is Grove City doing, and *will* Grove City do to help students sustain a Christian *metanoia* that eschews postmodern individualism when they leave the pines and columns growing and head into a society that exudes postmodern individualism?

My view is that responses to these types of questions constitute the very fabric of Grove City College's institutional faithfulness in the years ahead. May the Lord soften and strengthen it for this critical task.

Notes

[1]E. Long, Jr., *Higher Education as a Moral Enterprise* (Washington, D.C.: Georgetown University Press, 1992), 220-221.

[2]C. Kerr, *The Uses of the University, Fifth Edition* (Cambridge, MA: Harvard University Press, 2001), 194.

[3]A. Delbanco, *The Real American Dream: A Meditation on Hope* (Cambridge, MA: Harvard University Press, 1999).

[4]J. Burtchaell, *The Dying of the Light: The Disengagement of Colleges & Universities from Their Christian Churches* (Grand Rapids, MI: Eerdmans, 1998). See Chapter 8 for a helpful summary.

[5]I. Berlin, *The Hedgehog and the Fox* (New York, NY:: Simon & Schuster, 1953), 1-2.

[6]As cited in R. Bellah et al., *The Good Society* (New York, NY: Vintage Books, 1991), 43-44.

[7]R. Simon, "The Paralysis of 'Absolutophobia,'" *Chronicle of Higher Education* (June 27, 1997).

[8]D. Lyon, *Postmodernity* (Minneapolis, MN: University of Minnesota Press, 1999).

[9]J. Hunter, *The Death of Character: Moral Education in an Age Without Good or Evil* (New York, NY: Basic Books, 2000), xiii.

[10]T. Beaudoin, *Virtual Faith: The Irreverent Spiritual Quest of Generation X* (San Francisco, CA: Jossey-Bass, 1998).

[11]Beaudoin commits the entire central section to his book on further illustrating these characteristics. See pp. 49-142.

[12]R. Cimino and D. Lattin, *Shopping for Faith: American Religion in the New Millennium* (San Francisco, CA: Jossey-Bass, 1998). In particular, see Chapter 6.

[13]R. Wuthnow, *After Heaven: Spirituality in American Since the 1950s* (Berkeley, CA: University of California Press, 2000), 2.

[14]The first chapter of Wuthnow's book provides clear insight into the differences between "dwelling" and "seeking" faiths.

[15]As discussed in W. Romanowski, *Eyes Wide Open: Looking for God in Popular Culture* (Grand Rapids, MI: Brazos Press, 2001), 26-27.

[16]R. Bellah, et al., *Habits of the Heart* (Berkeley, CA: University of California Press, 1985).

[17]R. Bellah, et al., *The Good Society*.

[18]R. Putnam, *Bowling Alone: The Collapse and Revival of American Community* (New York, NY: Simon & Schuster, 2000). These data excerpted from pp. 45.

[19]Ibid., 63-64.

[20]Ibid., 173-174.

[21]Kerr, 206.

[22]Bellah, et al., *The Good Society*.

[23]D. Myers, *The American Paradox: Spiritual Hunger in an Age of Plenty* (New Haven, CT: Yale University Press, 2000), 40.

[24]P. Hersch, *A Tribe Apart: A Journey into the Heart of American Adolescence* (New York, NY: Ballantine Books, 1998), 19.

[25]P. Sacks, *Generation X Goes to College: An Eye-Opening Account of Teaching in Postmodern America* (Chicago, IL: Open Court, 1996), 154.

[26]N. Postman, *The End of Education: Redefining the Value of School* (New York, NY: Alfred A. Knopf, 1995). The first two chapters lay out the "gods who fail" and include the two gods that are mentioned above. All of the four gods that Postman mentions can be easily linked to what I have been referring to as postmodern individualism.

[27]D. Brooks, "The Organization Kid," *Atlantic Monthly* (Volume 287, No. 4, April 2001).

[28]A. Levine and J. Cureton, *When Hope and Fear Collide: A Portrait of Today's College Student* (San Francisco, CA: Jossey-Bass, 1998).

CHAPTER 6

The 'R-Word' and its Alleged Relevance to the Academic Enterprise at Geneva College

This essay was presented at a faculty luncheon on October 12, 2000 at Geneva College.

I am here today by default. When I originally asked John Cruzan about having one of the faculty luncheons each semester devoted to "church-relatedness," my idea was to invite in someone from the outside. Even when I gave him a title for the presentation I thought, "Ah, I'll be able to get someone to do that, no problem." However, as the semester has blurted forth, finding a speaker became lost in the cosmos. Thus, you're going to have to endure me rather than a Mary Stewart Van Leeuwen, or a Doug Sloan, or a Jim Bratt. Sorry about that!

Notwithstanding my default status, I am genuinely interested in the topic, and I have been for some time. I went to graduate school taken by the concept of the secularization of church-related higher education and have continued to enjoy thinking, reading, talking, and writing some about it since. My current participation in the Rhodes Consultation on the Future of the Church-Related College allows me to be a kid in a candy store.

In Parker Palmer's terms, the subject of church-related colleges
has truly invited me in.[1]

I am pleased that the church-related conversation seems to
be growing some at Geneva, too. The last two fall faculty conferences have included some concern about "the r-word" (i.e., reformed), the Rhodes conversations are underway once a month,
various faculty committees invoke the r-word for this and that,
and, of course, there is the somewhat common lingo of "big R
and little r"[2] around campus, even though there is no requirement to know what either means.

This may be an appropriate place to begin, although I want
to move pretty quickly here simply because, to me, the most important part of the discussion is the relevance of the r-word to
the academic enterprise. What does the word *reformed* refer to
here at Geneva? In historical context, it is fair, albeit simplistic,
to say that big-R Reformed typically refers to the churches and
the particular theology that emerged as a result of the Protestant Reformation in the 16th century and beyond. In contrast,
little-r reformed often refers either to an attempt to understand
the broader cultural relevance and implications of the gospel or,
as it seems often to be used here, an in-house though somewhat
vacuous shorthand for all who confess Christ and seek to live
faithfully. More existentially, may I suggest that the meaning
of the word "reformed" at Geneva is largely in the eye of the
beholder. Some use it synonymously with the Reformed Presbyterian Church of North American (RPCNA); some use it
synonymously with Christian; some use it to refer to a historic
tradition; some use it to summarize our "Foundational Concepts
of Christian Education;" some use it simply as code for "Geneva's perspective;" some don't understand it; some understand it
more fully than others; some think that they understand it; some
are confused by it; some are angered by it; some are impassioned
about it; some believe it; some criticize it; some think of it as no
instrumentation and exclusive psalmody in worship, and sab-
bath observance;[3] some think of it as TULIP;[4] some think of it as
stupid; and some consider it as combinations of these and other

things. What you will hear today is one person's perspective on it and his hope that discussion and actions about it will increase in the days and years ahead.

Let me ask a series of questions. I do not intend them as rhetorical in any way. Rather, I use them collectively as a heuristic that may shed some light on our path as we seek to be a college shaped by the reformed tradition. First: Can a college be Christian without being reformed? And the answer is...*yes*. If you think about CCCU[5] institutions alone, the vast majority are Christian colleges but without reformed marching orders.

Second question: Can a college be Christian without being an institution affiliated with the RPCNA? And the answer is... *yes*! Again, if you look through the list of 90+ CCCU institutions, there is only one institution that would claim RPCNA-edness (i.e., Geneva College). Third question: Can a college be reformed without being affiliated with the RPCNA? And the answer is... YES! Once again, if you look through the list of 90+ CCCU institutions, you will find colleges that define their identities within the context of the reformed tradition, but are not affiliated with the RPCNA—Calvin, Dordt, Trinity Christian, Whitworth, King's, Belhaven, Northwestern, and Redeemer come to mind.

A fourth and final question: Can a college be affiliated with the RPCNA without being reformed? And the answer is...*maybe*! More specifically, I wonder if Geneva may be such a college. I suspect that some of you will quickly and heartily agree. And, you will offer as explanation/lamentation that Geneva is affiliated with the RPCNA but may be not reformed because not all of its faculty are members of the RPCNA, or because not all of its students are members of the RPCNA, or because not everyone believes in irresistible grace, male headship, God's sovereignty, Christ as Lord of nations, closed communion, exclusive psalmody, supralapsarianism, a literal seven-day creation, to name a few topics that may be representation of the reformed tradition. For those who eagerly agree that Geneva may be a college that is affiliated with the RPCNA but not reformed for these kinds of reasons, I caution: "Be careful." To do so suggests that to be

affiliated with the RPCNA or to think RPCNA-ishly is to be reformed. I think that that is potentially faulty logic.

I wonder if Geneva may be an RPCNA college without
being reformed for a different reason, namely, that Geneva and
the RPCNA have drunk deeply from two of the three wells that
supply the reformed tradition, but have left largely unsampled
the waters of a third well that equally sources the reformed tradition. What in the world am I talking about? Let me explain
these mysterious "wells" before I return back to this statement.
Notre Dame historian and Christian George Marsden posits
three historic and contemporary strands of the reformed tradition as follows: 1) doctrinalist, 2) pietist, and 3) culturalist.[6] The
doctrinalist strand of the reformed tradition emphasizes—surprise—doctrinal issues. Those who embrace this strand define
faith in terms of central as well as ostensibly peripheral doc-
trines, theological correctness is paramount, saying the right
things in the right way is essential, and, the local church is absolutely vital in the effort to maintain right theology, right worship,
and right thinking.

The pietist strand of the reformed tradition emphasizes lifestyle or behavioral issues. Those who embrace this strand define
faith in terms of behaving in appropriate ways, that is, in ways
that testify clearly to the hope that is within. You can probably
think of examples that emerge within this particular emphasis:
routinized family patterns of worship (sometimes twice a Sunday), family devotions, keeping Sunday "set apart," giving sac-
rificially to Christian causes, avoiding the appearance of evil
such as might occur if one attends the theatre or casino, or if
one smokes, chews, swears, or dances. The pietist strand of the
reformed tradition is sometimes unfortunately, but perhaps ac-
curately, referred to as a faith of "dos and don'ts." Once again,
the role of the local church is vital as a point of encouragement,
resource, and correction for what might be referred to as "proper
or righteous living."

Finally, the culturalist strand of the reformed tradition emphasizes the principled but wholehearted engagement of culture.

Those who embrace this strand define faith in the context of worldview. Christianity is "a way to see" and live in the world that is predicated on the theological motif of creation, fall, redemption, and consummation. Other emphases on the Kingdom of God, vocation and calling, common grace, normativity, and so on provide the contours for engaging all of culture with a spirit of wonder, exploration, critique, and possibility. Again, the role of the local church is vital in cultivating sufficient theological underpinnings and lots of encouragement and support to help believers to be in the cosmos, for the cosmos, of the cosmos (in the sense we are created by God and for His honor), critical of the cosmos, but not duped or seduced by the cosmos.

So, these are the three strands that comprise the reformed tradition. In the vernacular, perhaps they could be referred to as strong biblical theology (doctrinalist), godly character and behavior (pietist), and fearless engagement of culture (culturalist). From my perspective (and others as well), the reformed tradition is at its best when these three strands exist in a dynamic and mutual triad; that is, when an easy harmony is struck among them in which together they inform, shape, and mediate God's truth in one's life for life.

However, I believe that sometimes one of the strands of the reformed tradition can overshadow or eclipse the others. If this occurs, I think that a kind of a mutant reformed tradition emerges. For example, without the contributions of godly character and behavior and the fearless engagement of culture, strong biblical theology can become pharisaical dogmatism, or what Francis Schaefer referred to as dead orthodoxy. Similarly, without the contributions of strong biblical theology and fearless engagement of culture, godly character and behavior can become vapid moralism. And, without the contributions of strong biblical theology and godly character and behavior, fearless engagement of culture can become unbounded secularism.

Now it is time to revisit a statement that I made some minutes ago, namely, that Geneva may be an RPCNA college without being reformed, in that it has drunk deeply from two of the three wells that supply the reformed tradition, but have left largely unsampled the waters of a third well that equally sources the reformed tradition. Stated more explicitly, I wonder if Geneva emphasizes the strong biblical theology and godly character and behavior strands of the reformed tradition, but not the fearless engagement of culture strand. Moreover, I wonder if Geneva emphasizes the strong biblical theology and godly character and behavior strands of the reformed tradition, but not the fearless engagement of culture strand because its sponsoring denomination—the RPCNA—emphasizes the strong biblical theology and godly character and behavior strands of the reformed tradition, but not the fearless engagement of culture strand.

Let me be even more explicit. If it is true that the RPCNA emphasizes strong biblical theology, then does that help us to understand why we have a college with particular requirements for the president, for the chair of the Bible department, and for the political science faculty position? If it is true that the RPCNA emphasizes strong biblical theology, then does that help us to understand why we have a college that, in the hiring process, asks candidates doctrinal questions about the substitutionary atonement of Jesus, the historicity of Adam and Eve, and the inerrancy of the Scriptures? If it is true that the RPCNA emphasizes godly character and behavior, then does that help us to understand why we have a college that requires chapel? If it is true that the RPCNA emphasizes godly character and behavior, then does that help us to understand why we have a college that attends to policies that govern activity on Sundays? If it is true that the RPCNA emphasizes *both* strong biblical theology *and* godly character and behavior, then does that help us to understand why we have a college that differentiates between "sorta worship" and true worship? If it is true that the RPCNA emphasizes *both* strong biblical theology *and* godly character and behavior, then does that help us to understand why we have a college that requires faculty to be active members in evangelical churches?

Let me proceed yet further. If it is true that the fearless engagement of culture is not emphasized in the RPCNA, then does that help us to understand why we have a college that struggles with a lack of conversation about, much less a lack of understanding of, the integration of faith and learning? If it is true that the fearless engagement of culture is not emphasized in the RPCNA, then does that help us to understand why we have a college that struggles with a lack of conversation about much less a lack of understanding about a biblical view of knowledge? This is Sloan's critique that I mentioned at the fall faculty conference.[7] If it is true that the fearless engagement of culture is not emphasized in the RPCNA, then does that help us to understand why we have a college that, in the hiring process, considerably overlooks what a candidate thinks about her subject in favor of what she thinks about the atonement. As long as she can show "evidence of ability to articulate the Christian faith," she will not have to worry about showing evidence of ability to critique her discipline from a Christian perspective? If it is true that the fearless engagement of culture is not emphasized in the RPCNA, then does that help us to understand why we have a college that downplays a faculty candidate's understanding of the relationship between Christian faith and his preferred pedagogical practices? If it is true that the fearless engagement of culture is not emphasized in the RPCNA, then does that help us to understand why we have a college that views the writing of the integrative paper more as a performance measure than as a faculty development opportunity? If it is true that the fearless engagement of culture is not emphasized in the RPCNA, then does that help us to understand why we have a college that has a curriculum that substantially was and is developed like, looks like, and is delivered like the curricula of most secular institutions? If it is true that the fearless engagement of culture is not emphasized in the RPCNA, then does that help us to understand why we have a college that experiences internal conflict because it requires chapel even though the reformed tradition has historically eschewed "required worship?" Frankly, I wonder if, more often than we may like to admit, we fit Arthur Holmes lamentable description of a Christian college that "offer(s) a good education plus biblical studies in an atmosphere of piety."[8] I submit that his description should not characterize a Christian college in the reformed tradition.

In closing, I am convinced that the reformed tradition has an incredible contribution to make to Christian colleges like Geneva. To my mind, no other tradition—given its three strands—contributes more to an understanding of what a Christian college is and does, what it should be and what it should do. That is why I also would like to suggest that perhaps Marsden's tripartite description of the reformed tradition could serve us well at Geneva. For example, could we use the three strands to help us revise our mission statement, review academic programs, modify the core curriculum, and reinvent the Learning and Transition course? Could the three strands be the foundation upon which we re-evaluate all that we do here, from how we put together a syllabus, to how we enact a faculty development program? From how we might differently construe "religious affairs" on campus to the appropriateness of a discipline-oriented academic structure? From the proper roles of athletics, bible studies, and honors programs to the development and implementation of financial aid strategies? And the list goes on! Moreover, if it is true that the healthiest way to embody the reformed tradition is when a balance is struck among the three strands, and if it is also true that the RPCNA currently does not equally emphasize the culturalist (fearless engagement of culture) strand, then couldn't part of the appropriate mission of the college in relationship to its affiliated church be discussing ways and developing strategies that help it become more healthily reformed?

Needless to say, none of this is easy, even if it is right. But if our college needs to "get healthier" by achieving a better balance among the three strands, then it should do so. If what I have said has any merit at all, to do otherwise is to remain in the reformed tradition that pays too little attention to the culturalist strand and, at certain times on certain days in certain ways, may end up looking more than it should like a church, a bible college, or a Catholic university.

I know that, by this time, some may consider me to be loony, others heretic, and others strident. I think it is also fair to say that some may think me exclusively a cultural Calvinist, well on my way to secularism. While it is the case that I drink beer and wine on occasion, swear here and there, have mowed my grass, grocery shopped, and played tennis and golf on Sunday, attend and teach Sunday school at a PCUSA (read "apostate") church, significantly favor Meredith Kline's take on the creation account,[9] have some dear Christian friends who are also Catholic, and am substantially persuaded by the countercultural, alternative society, anabaptist rhetoric, let me assure you that I am honestly and diligently striving to be a faithful servant of Immanuel who, in the words of Abraham Kuyper, is our "skin-draped point of fellowship with the Father."[10] His in-the-flesh testimony as well as the scriptural testimony of God's redemptive work in history, lead me to believe with all of my heart (with all that I am) that such striving always occurs under his past, present, and future grace and in the context of understanding more fully a strong biblical theology, a godly character and behavior, and a fearless engagement with culture.

Notes

[1] This is an allusion to Parker Palmer's book *The Courage to Teach: Exploring the Inner Landscape of a Teacher's Life, 20ᵗʰ Ed.* (San Francisco, CA: Jossey Bass, 2017), particularly the idea that learning, at its best, is neither teacher-focused nor student-focused, but rather subject-focused; the subject invites both teachers and students to explore.

[2] This nomenclature represents a largely intramural conversation among those in the reformed tradition, including some—likely few— at Geneva College. This essay briefly examines a possible distinction between Reformed (i.e., "big-R Reformed") and reformed (i.e., "small-r reformed"). This conversation occurred in the context of Geneva College's particular historic and current identity as an institution with strong affiliation with the Reformed Presbyterian Church of North America (RPCNA).

[3] These are particular characteristics of the Reformed Presbyterian Church of North America (RPCNA), and would have been known to those in attendance at the luncheon in which I made this presentation, whether they were members of the RPCNA or not.

[4] TULIP is an acronym sometimes used to summarize Reformed theology in which T represents the total depravity of humanity, U represents God's unconditional election, L represents limited atonement (cf., universal atonement), I represents God's irresistible grace, and P represents the perseverance of saints.

[5] This is a reference to a membership organization called the Council for Christian Colleges and Universities, of which Geneva College is a member.

[6] G. Marsden, "Introduction: Reformed and American," in D. Wells (ed.), *Reformed Theology in America: A History of Its Modern Development* (Grand Rapids, MI: Wm. B. Eerdmans Publishing Co., 2009), 1-12.

[7] This is a reference to Douglas Sloan's book *Faith and Knowledge: Mainline Protestantism and American Higher Education* (Louisville, KY: Westminster John Knox Press, 1994).

[8]A. Holmes, *The Idea of a Christian College, Revised Edition* (Grand Rapids, MI: Wm. B. Eerdmans Publishing Co., 1987), 5.

[9]See J. Duncan III, et al., *The Genesis Debate: Three Views on the Days of Creation* (Irvine, CA: Crux Press, 2000).

[10]A. Kuyper (James Schaap, Adapter), *Near Unto God* (Sioux Center, IA: Dordt College Press, 2008), 53.

CHAPTER 7

Leading Academe

A substantially different and significantly shorter version of this essay was published with the same title in a 2015 book titled Ernest L. Boyer: Hope for Today's University.

Introduction

Michael Fullan and Geoff Scott report that when they told a colleague that they were compiling "a book on turnaround leadership in universities, he responded in a nano second, 'It will be easier for Obama to turn around the U.S.'"[1] I have experienced a similar sentiment at times in drafting this essay: Can a person who completed his career in higher education before the economic, social, political, and technological complexities of the 21st century—even a person who many construed to be an education guru—really have any wisdom to address the contemporary challenges, even crises, of leading academe? To avoid any suspense or undue stress, my response is simple: Yes, Ernest Boyer seems to have plenty to offer our current moment with respect to higher education leadership.

This essay explores ostensible crises in the academy and then examines some of Boyer's salient contributions. More specifically, this essay consists of three interrelated sections. In the first section, I consider four possible current crises in leading academe. In the second section, I summarize some of relevant and arguably timeless contributions that Boyer offered with regard to educational leadership. And, in the brief third section, I suggest several ways that Boyer may have directly responded to leadership in the academy in the current day. In the end, I hope that readers will not express the incredulity of Fullan's and Scott's colleague, but rather be deeply appreciative of Boyer's wisdom and, more importantly, motivated to lead, as Boyer believed, "from a sense of purpose and from knowing that the cause for which you work is truly worthy."[2]

Crises in Leading Academe?

Whether or not a specific issue warrants the designation of crisis may ultimately be in the eye of the beholder. Is planet earth experiencing an environmental crisis? Is the United States in the midst of an economic crisis? Does China have a population crisis? In a similar fashion, what counts as crises in American higher education leadership is likely a matter of perspective.[3] Moreover, opinions regarding the presence of crises in leading academe may concern both a more "local" context (i.e., one's own institution), more system-wide contexts (e.g., state systems), or more social contexts (e.g., national economy), as well as any particular aspect of postsecondary life (e.g., ratio of full-time and part-time faculty, tuition discounting policies, balance of teaching and research, level of state appropriations, support for technology, and so on). How one defines crises in leading academe may also be related to the particular role that one occupies within or outside of a college or university (e.g., president, faculty member, student, parent, policy analyst).

These are relevant considerations to mention at the outset of this section of the essay because I have no doubt that some readers simply will disagree that one or more of the particular issues that I include rise to the level of crisis. Others will opine that my inclusion of a particular issue is due to my role as a full-time faculty member at a small, private institution. And, still others will be distressed that I omitted altogether whatever it is that they believe to be the most vexing crisis facing leadership in the academy. I readily admit these and, I suspect, other limitations to my approach, perspective, and choices. I nonetheless hope that what I have included below will provide an occasion to consider several concerns and challenges with regard to leading academe, generate curiosity in identifying particular troubles related to leadership in the academy in local and broader contexts, and encourage significant resolve in detecting, rectifying, and preventing crises of educational leadership in the days ahead.

Crisis 1: The Crisis of Presidential Succession

According to the American College Presidents Study (ACE, 2007),[4] the average age of college presidents was 60 in 2006, and the percentage of college presidents that are 61 years old or older has risen from 14 percent in 1986 to 49 percent in 2006. These data lead Susan Pierce to posit that a majority of college presidents—and even "a fair number" of their successors—will be retired by the year 2020.[5]

While some, no doubt, may applaud the departure of specific college and university presidents, Pierce is concerned with these trends for two reasons. First, her research indicates that the group of professionals historically most likely to pursue college presidencies (i.e., chief academic officers) is demonstrating an increasing lack of interest in seeking presidential roles. Richard Ekman, the president of the Council of Independent Colleges, agrees, noting that presidential responsibilities are "largely unattractive" to many chief academic officers, particularly because of "the increasingly external orientation of presidential duties."[6]

The second reason that Pierce expresses reservations about presidential leadership trends is because the boards of postsecondary institutions are becoming more willing to hire heretofore nontraditional candidates. That is, more boards are beginning to pursue "external" candidates who have no experience in the academy, but do have substantial experience as creative entrepreneurs, venture capitalists, wealthy businesspersons with good connections to potential funding sources and a commitment to "strategic dynamism."[7]

For both reasons, Pierce is concerned that colleges and universities have something significant to lose if growing numbers of presidents have little or no understanding of academic life— its culture, its purposes, its curricular strategies, its operations, its social roles, and the like. She also acknowledges, however, that attracting and hiring presidents who are intimately familiar with the academy because of direct and/or significant experience within it provides no guarantee that they will provide capable, effective presidential leadership. Stated another way, a crisis in leading academe may occur when the "wrong" person is hired to be the president, whether that person is identified from within the academy or from without.

Crisis 2: The Crisis of Wrongheaded Leadership

More than a few argue that the crisis in leading academe is what might be called *wrongheaded leadership*. Although authors use various designations to describe such wrongheaded leadership, many contemporary critics seem to be particularly concerned that educational leaders are business-fying the academy, that those leading colleges and universities are profaning the acropolis with the principles and practices of the agora.[8] Pejorative descriptions that reflect this type of institutional leadership abound: academic capitalism,[9] the all-administrative university,[10] the corporate university and the new managerialism,[11] market-model U,[12] the commercialization of higher education,[13] the McDonaldization of higher education,[14] and college for sale.[15] Although she writes with public research universities particularly in mind, Gaye Tuchman provides just one strategy of the corporatized institutional leadership model, a strategy that she refers to as the "audit society":

> The "audit society" enables "coercive accountability" carried out in the guise of transparency, trust, and public service... It entails both forced and voluntary surveillance, as individuals as organizations audit themselves and subject themselves to audit by others... The coercive accountability associated with both an audit society and its culture helps to constitute an *accountability regime* [emphasis hers]—a politics of surveillance, control, and market management disguising itself as the value-neutral and scientific administration of individuals and organizations.[16]

One might be tempted to place the blame for this crisis of wrongheaded leadership squarely and solely on the shoulders of an institution's administrative leadership. And yet, the relative power and scope of this presumed crisis is that many college and university faculty may also be entranced by the commodification of higher education.[17] For example, Mark Edmundson wonders if in their obsession and rush to market themselves and their work, many faculty are unconcerned with and inarticulate about the purpose of higher education. Edmundson goes as far as to say that "sometimes [he thinks] that there are more *potential* [emphasis his] intellectual idealists among the administrators than among the faculty."[18] Likewise, Kenway, Bullen, and Robb lament that many university faculty gladly construe themselves as "technopreneurs" that purposely combine and hone "networking skills, a techno-scientific orientation and an entrepreneurial sensibility" in service to "accommodate[ing] the interests of industry both at the level of content and mode of delivery, and when it is funded in a way that maximizes competition and hence the opportunities for investment and private gain." In these authors' view, many faculty researchers have, in effect, surrendered knowledge discovery and production as a "tradable commodity."[19] Even Gaye Tuchman, quoted above in reference to the audit society, suggests that many faculty have capitulated to the commodification "regime," sometimes willingly, sometimes by default, sometimes to avoid or prevent further administrative incursion, and sometimes to tout their own work (e.g., the assistant professor who emails friends and asks, "Can you like my new book on Facebook?" with the hopes that he can use these data to garner merit pay, to contribute to promotion, or both).[20]

Faculty may also demonstrate obeisance to corporatized higher education by their lack of leadership to the contrary. For example, Gary Rhoades contends that a majority of faculty may be altogether unaware regarding "the scope and significance of the restructuring that is ongoing in higher education,"[21] choosing instead simply to assert their professional autonomy, including from the developments that are occurring in the social sector in which they work. Further, Frank Donoghue expresses concern that some faculty blithely "accept the erosion of their working conditions as an unpleasant fact of life,"[22] which is exacerbated in institutional settings in which the percentage of part-time instructors is significant. Jennifer Geddes offers an apt conclusion:

> If professors can't articulate what they do or why it matters in terms not beholden to the market, then who can? What resources are there for re-envisioning and re-articulating the purposes of higher education in a way that responds to the rapid and far-reaching cultural changes taking place in our world today and that resists the commodification of knowledge, scholarship, attention, and reflection?[23]

Crisis 3: The Crisis of Leadershiplessness

Books and essays written on leadership are legion, and the lexicon continues to grow. And for good reason. In increasingly multifaceted, contentious, and complex settings—including the academy—many want to continue to believe that leadership matters, even acknowledging different paradigms of leadership, different styles of leadership, and different strategies of leadership. For example, Heifetz, Grashow, and Linsky begin their recent book by stating that "build[ing] a sustainable world in an era of profound economic and environmental interdependence" is "a tall order."[24] But, of course, if we embrace "adaptive leadership"[25] or "Level 5 leadership"[26] or "transformational leadership"[27] or "transactional leadership"[28] or "turnaround leadership"[29] or "servant leadership"[30] or "principle-centered leadership"[31] or "exemplary leadership"[32] we will meet the challenges effectively and ultimately succeed. To paraphrase an Archimedean [and Senge-ian[33]] principle, "If you give leaders a lever long enough, they shall move the world."

But will they? Could a crisis in leading colleges and universities be that leadership is not really preferable or even possible? Does the academy have a crisis of leadershiplessness? That is, given the nature, complexity, and scope of the internal and external realities that colleges and universities face, and if particular educational ends may be unclear or unimportant except for marketing purposes, perhaps believed yet unspoken mantras of "live and let live," "whatever," or "just do it" are sufficient and even motivating for a majority of an institution's administration, faculty, staff, and students. When "all we have to do is survive, see you again tomorrow" is enough, is leadership of any flavor or style necessary save managing particular details and meeting certain deadlines? Garland says it this way:

> Public higher education is an unhappy family...Unhappy families are blind to the truth about themselves, even though that truth may be obvious to others. The family members blame each other for their problems, refuse to admit their shortcomings, lash out at critics, and react hostilely to suggestions for change...In the end, they accept their present state of misery instead of taking responsibility for their destiny and doing things differently.[34]

What may fuel the leadershiplessness crisis even more is that not only do educational "leaders" "accept their present state of misery," many may not think the present situation miserable at all. While there may be regular aggravations, a few significant hurdles to clear, and perhaps even an occasional inconvenient institutional truth to which to respond, things just seem to work. Day in and day out, good things occur, and satisfactions are obtained. This "is what it is" leadershiplessness mentality both reflects and spurs higher education's historic ponderous response to change; knee-jerk overreactions are anathema to those leading academe—perhaps even as Rome is burning. For example, according to Christenson and Eyring:

> The current crisis in today's universities is real…In the spirit of honoring tradition, universities hang on to past practices to the point of imperiling their futures. When reduced budgets force them to cut costs, they trim but rarely make hard tradeoffs. Nor do they readily reinvent their curricula to better prepare students for the increasing demands of the world of work. Paradoxically, they respond to economic downturn by raising prices. From a market competition standpoint, it is slow institutional suicide.[35]

One wonders if persistent economic hardships will retard or reverse the leadershiplessness crisis. These troubles are real and, likely, will get worse. For example, according to Dennis Jones, the president of the National Center for Higher Education Management Systems (NCHEMS), by FY2015, all 50 states will experience structural deficits in funding higher education, from a projected 2.1% decrease to a projected 10.9% decrease.[36] William Zumeta adds:

> In the present economic doldrums, which I expect to last in some form for at least half a decade, it should be getting clearer to those in higher education that it is in their interest to rethink long-standing assumptions about how to educate more students with the resources they have, because it is unlikely that we will see much if any growth in per-student revenues for the foreseeable future.[37]

If economic woes are inadequate to attract the attention of the leadershipless, perhaps technology may. In his book *Abelard to Apple: The Fate of American Colleges and Universities*, author Richard DeMillo recounts a conversation with a faculty colleague at a large, land-grant institution in which they were discussing what the 21st century university would look like. His colleague's response was terse: "It will not look like us."[38] Others, like Andrew Rosen, agree, arguing that, given the inexorability of technological advances and technology-dependence,

> Mobile learning will [eventually] become superior to face-to-face learning…[making it] harder for parents to justify the cost of shipping their sons and daughters off to a resort for four years…By 2036, it's a virtual certainty that many students…will be purchasing education separately from the socialization experience of today's college…[and] no longer [with the expectation] to acquire all of their education from the same provider.[39]

The crisis of leadershiplessness apotheosizes business-as-usual-react-as-is-necessary-tomorrow-is-the-same-as-today "leadership," responding to changes if reasonable and/or convenient, and even then, only incrementally and at the margins of institutional life. To the extent that this crisis is real, the perceived stability of many American colleges and universities may be on the verge of compromise if not imperilment.

Crisis 4: The Crisis of Confusion Regarding the Goals of Higher Education

Robert Hutchins wrote, "The most striking fact about higher learning in America is the confusion that besets it."[40] That was over 75 years ago. More recently, Hacker and Dreifus suggest that:

> Universities have become multiversities, staffed by casts of thousands and dedicated to everything from esoteric research to semi-professional athletics…higher education has much in common with the nation's medical system…or, more truthfully, the absence of anything systemic…In neither sphere does it seem possible for anyone to shout Stop!—whether it's installing another

MRI or when a college decides to shift an athletic team
to a more costly division...[41]

Neither Hutchins in 1936 nor Hacker and Dreifus in 2012 were
enthusiastic about what they observed regarding American colleges and universities. And they are not alone. The history of
American higher education is replete with those who expressed
deep concerns with respect to its purposes. More often than not,
critiques that posit confusion about the goals of American higher education distill to disagreement regarding its most appropriate goal. For example, Hutchins lamented the confusion of
American higher education because its only appropriate end—
the cultivation of the intellect—was being obfuscated by institutions' insatiable love of money (which led them to do anything to
attract students, donors, and the favor of state legislatures), rampant vocationalism (at both undergraduate and graduate levels),
isolating and balkanizing professionalism (among faculty), and
a dead-wrong vision of progress (because it was rooted in the
hegemony of the research ideal which, for Hutchins, was "science without philosophy"—and thus "bad"). Likewise, Hacker
and Dreifus express serious concern that higher education "has
lost track of its original and enduring purpose: to challenge the
minds and imaginations of...young people, to expand their understanding of the world, and thus of themselves."[42]

This is not to say that other educational leaders fully support
what might be called an "all things to all people" mission for
colleges and universities. For example, soon after the American
Civil War ended, Andrew White, as the first president of Cornell, marketed it as an institution that would have "something
for everyone." By the move into the 20th century, William Rainey
Harper's University of Chicago had been dubbed "Harper's Ba-
zaar" because of its extensive—rather than monolithic—curricular commitments. And then, one century after White's nascent
model at Cornell emerged, Clark Kerr's "uses" of the university
made it clear that the defining strength of the American university was its multiple identities. Drawing on William James'

notion of a "pluralistic universe,"[43] the glory of Kerr's multiversity vision was precisely because of its commitment to:

> Having several purposes, not one; in having several centers of power, not one, in serving several clienteles, not one. It worshiped no single God; it constituted no single, unified community; it had no discretely defined set of customers. It was marked by many visions of the Good, the True, and the Beautiful, and by many roads to achieve these visions.[44]

One should not underestimate or overlook Kerr's multiversity model, for it symbolizes an "academic revolution"[45] that has since attained prominence. That is, not only is the multiversity model operational in research universities, it also is the standard by which other colleges and universities measure their relative success. To be clear, despite continuing rhetoric that a clear, central mission is important, the vast majority of those leading American colleges and universities know that pursuing multiple purposes with multiple constituencies in multiple ways—while privileging the research ideal if only marginally[46]—is simply normal. This is exactly why Kerr believed that the most effective educational leaders in the 21st century would be "foxes" rather than "hedgehogs." In contrast to a hedgehog leadership approach that "relate[s] everything to a single central vision...in terms of which alone all that they are and say has significance," a foxlike leader "pursues many ends, often unrelated and even contradictory...moving on many levels, seizing upon the essence of a vast variety of experiences" without being concerned about the extent to which their multifaceted efforts may or may not hold together around a central mission.[47] From Kerr's perspective, the sheer volume and complexity of the issues that educational leaders face in the 21st century necessitates that they "explore opportunities and create solutions"[48] unencumbered by an animating central purpose. In his last postscript, written in 2001, Kerr agreed with comments made earlier by Ernest Boyer and Fred Hechinger that higher education was adrift. But, Kerr added, "I agree that [higher education] is now adrift, but it may be at the vital center of a society adrift."[49] And, for Kerr, only foxlike leaders had the capacity to lead adrift institutions in an adrift American culture.

If Kerr is correct, does the confusion regarding the purposes of the academy constitute a crisis? I suspect that hedgehog leaders may respond quickly in the affirmative. Fox leaders, however, may not see the multiplicity of ends to be pursued and constituencies to serve as well as the complexity of internal and external environments as confusion at all, but simply as "the way things are," even embracing "the parts" as "the whole." Perhaps another option is one posited by George Keller,[50] who suggests that the various segments of American higher education do best when they clearly define the type of institutions that they wish to be. For example, institutions that desire to be all things to all people would do so, and institutions that wish to embrace a central vision that drives all else would do so. In either case, what is most important to Keller is that all institutions improve the quality of their efforts, and that all institutions be willing to collaborate with other institutions as they pursue their distinctive contributions otherwise. DeMillo suggests a largely similar approach, arguing that institutions should "define their value," and, then, "become architects" toward those ends.[51] Like Keller, DeMillo believes that clarifying "one's own brand" and then working creatively and collaboratively toward operationalizing that brand with excellence is best for colleges and universities and for the public.

Boyer's Contributions to Leading Academe

Perhaps a helpful way to summarize Boyer's thinking on leading academe is to consider it in the context of two interrelated categories. The first category is what Boyer referred to in a book that he was preparing on leadership as the "qualities of a leader."[52] These qualities of leadership provide insight into particular traits that Boyer believed were crucial to leading academe effectively. He believed that effective leadership was simply inseparable from one's personal qualities or values.

A second category may simply be called *leading academe*. It represents an attempt to consider several explicit priorities to which Boyer believed postsecondary education leaders must be committed. That is, Boyer thought that educational leaders should lead with certain things in mind to be emphasized, pursued and accomplished; being a faculty or administrative leader must not be separated from particular things that they should be "up to" for the sake of excellent education. In the pages that follow, I will summarize some of Boyer's contributions in each of these two categories. As readers peruse this section, I encourage them to imagine how Boyer may respond to the crises of leading academe identified in the previous section.

Qualities of a Leader

At the time of his death, Boyer was working on a book that he had named *Everyone Can Lead: Qualities of Effective Living.*[53] In the table of contents for this book, Boyer proposed seven qualities of a leader. What I hope will be clear from exploring this list of traits—particularly when taken within the larger context of Boyer's life and work—is that Boyer believed that good leadership and good life were inextricably connected. The very title of Boyer's book-in-process suggests precisely such a linkage as does one of its early chapters: "The qualities of good leadership are the qualities of good living."[54] For the purposes of the continuity of this essay, in the brief descriptions of Boyer's "qualities of a leader" below, I have taken the liberty to list these qualities in a slightly different order than he may have had in mind.

Living by Convictions

It is impossible to evaluate Boyer's efforts without concluding that he was a person rooted in and animated by particular convictions. In contrast to the knee-jerk pragmatism and anomic opportunism that may characterize at least one of the crises identified earlier (i.e., the crisis of leadershiplessness), Boyer observed: "Somehow we have deluded ourselves into believing that we can be responsible people without ever taking sides [or] without expressing firm convictions about fundamental issues."[55]

A particular poignant testimony to Boyer's emphasis regarding the importance of convictions for effective leadership comes from a comparison that he draws between his role as the academic dean of the then tiny and now defunct Upland College and his subsequent leadership role within the United States Office of Education. Regarding the former, he says:

> I am convinced that the rewards of leadership come... from a sense of purpose and from knowing that the cause for which you work is truly worthy...As I look back to those days of innocence, I recall that we were enthusiastic,...because we had convictions about the goals we shared...there was on that campus a spirit which I can only describe as "moral unity."[56]

And, regarding the latter, he laments: "People in the federal bureaucracy have lost their zest for living, at least between the hours of 9 to 5. Not because they are evil, but because the system does them in."[57] To be sure, systems—governmental and educational alike—can and do "do people in." But, to be clear, is "the problem" that Boyer was describing in this speech that leaders are absent convictions, or that they have misguided convictions? The intention of Boyer's speech was not to address this specific question. Based on Boyer's other writings, including some that will be included later in this essay, I believe that Boyer was concerned both with the absence of convictions and with wrong-headed convictions. His inclusion of "living by convictions" as a component quality for educational leaders to possess, then, is his attempt to emphasize the importance of convictions, the importance of "appropriate" convictions, and "living by" and leading from these convictions.

Putting People First

According to Boyer, "There is no such thing as an organization apart from people."[58] Whether it involved inaugurating a yearly, week-long summer retreat with the presidents of the SUNY system, or relinquishing the podium to go into a student protest to

meet face to face with students, or his regular and frequent admonition to recognize and reward faculty members, Boyer man-
ifested his belief that colleges and universities "move[s] ahead
not by paper, but by people."[59] Boyer writes:

> As I reflected on the larger picture, I concluded that
> there was no such thing as SUNY—except as people
> "think it." You cannot touch it, you cannot feel it, it is
> only in our heads. And the question that administrators
> must concern themselves with is this: "What signals are
> we generating in people's heads?" No college or univer-
> sity is any greater than what people think about the in-
> stitution. And it is the obligation of leadership to start
> making the moves to create the right kinds of visions.[60]

Boyer's "people first" moniker was, at least in part, a response
to the creeping routinizing of American colleges and universities in the 1980s, from both external and internal forces. Boyer was not opposed to planning, management, and evaluation
processes in the pursuit of excellent education. Rather, he was
concerned that such processes would not become the master to
be served at all costs. From his perspective, allegiance to such a
master results in dire consequences:

> The ever-increasing role of outside agencies in campus
> matters is gradually wearing down the men and women
> who occupy the internal governance structures at col-
> leges and universities in the United States. As leadership
> is diminished, power and initiative flow even more rap-
> idly to outside bureaucracies. Under such circumstanc-
> es, administration too often means simply responding
> to an impersonal system, flowing along on a ceaseless
> tide of forms, reports, and computer printouts.[61]

If Boyer were alive today, I suspect that he may conclude that his
"people first" exhortation has been obscured. Various contemporary authors suggest the same, arguing that a "new managerialism"[62] emphasizing technique, control, efficiency, standard-
ization, and centralization has supplanted more collegial models

of higher learning. At the same time, I wonder if it still may not be too late to heed Boyer's clarion call: "The greatest enemy of leadership is the inclination to be more preoccupied with competence than with caring…effective leadership must mean focusing more on the needs of people than on process and procedures."[63]

Engaging in Good Communication

If "putting people first" is a fundamental quality of good leadership from Boyer's perspective, it makes sense that he is also interested in emphasizing effective communication as well. Boyer recounts a story in which, as the chancellor of the State University of New York (SUNY) system, he was about to speak to gathered faculty from across the system as well as to its trustees, when a group of over 300 SUNY students took over the meeting, demanding the immediate release of some other students who had been arrested the previous night for breaking into the president's office on the Buffalo campus. Boyer and the students jockeyed back and forth, in heated debate. Then, Boyer records the following:

> After about an hour, I concluded we weren't listening to each other, and the meeting was in shambles. Even worse, I concluded that I was talking not to people, but to a faceless mob. More in desperation than inspiration, I left the platform and walked into the crowd [of students]. I began talking to a single student. I asked her name, I asked about her family. Soon several others joined us and to make the story short, the session ended, [and] a compromise was reached.[64]

Even though Boyer joked that, after this experience, he "occasionally glance[d] toward the door to see if students [were moving] in,"[65] he admitted that it taught him that "leadership will certainly erode when communication stops, or when a leader tries to tell each separate audience what he or she thinks it wants to hear."[66] Moreover, this experience convinced Boyer that "almost any struggle can be negotiated successfully, [and almost] any difficulty can be overcome" at least to the extent that "good leadership means good communication and candor."[67]

Keeping Problems in Perspective

Boyer's recollection above of his dealings with a large group of unsettled students dovetails nicely with his conviction that one of the qualities of leadership means keeping problems in perspective. Numerous professional gatherings asked Boyer to speak about the future of education in light of the present and the past. And, he gladly and deftly obliged. Sometimes he recounted critical moments in the history of higher education to suggest that the academy had always faced significant challenges and that change—even fundamental change—was inexorable. Sometimes he identified particular difficulties that were afoot among colleges and universities during a certain period of time. In each case, however, Boyer was intent on doing what he said was critical to do: Keep problems in perspective.[68]

To be clear, Boyer did not underestimate, trivialize, or ignore the problems facing the colleges and universities of his day. Nor did he doubt the urgency in addressing them. He also did not seem to be discouraged or undone by them, caving in to what one of his colleagues referred to as a "nattering nabob of negativism."[69] Rather, his was an honest, courageous, and collaborative approach: Challenges are significant, complex, and ubiquitous...but they are not insurmountable...and the learning leaders of each college and university must work together to respond to them diligently, thoughtfully, creatively, and based on one's convictions and vision of higher education.[70]

Boyer's balanced leadership approach is poignantly seen in a speech entitled *Education 2000: New Wine, New Bottles*,[71] in which he acknowledged the presence of "the chronic doomsayers" that announce that "we may be foreclosing the possibility of life on earth—or so narrowing it that a paralysis of the human spirit is just as likely as an Armageddon war."[72] And then Boyer intoned this question: "And what does all of this have to do with education in the year 2000?" In his remarks that follow, Boyer developed a rhetorically powerful response to this question that details a perspective that educational leaders must embrace. This perspective involved both "[extricating] ourselves from those preoccupations of the moment that loom so large" and "alerting our students to the larger contours of their world, of helping them see the broader ramifications of their actions and of conveying the urgent need to marshal all our resources as we confront the critical choices of the future."[73]

One final comment is well worth making about this particular quality of leadership. In the introductory paragraph to Boyer's qualities of leadership, I mentioned that Boyer believed that good leadership and good living were inextricably connected. This principle is clearly in view here as well. More specifically, Boyer believed that keeping problems in perspective "at the office" was related to keeping their own lives in perspective. Boyer writes:

> [Leaders] must put institutional victories and defeats in their proper place...Too often, in the heat of battle, our priorities are tragically misplaced. We sacrifice our health, and those we love, believing that somehow the endless obligations of the job are always more important or that somehow, if we become totally consumed, our leadership will be enhanced. Nothing could be further from the truth.[74]

Staying Well-Informed

Although much of Boyer's professional life was lived before "the information age," he nonetheless considered being informed an essential component of good leadership. Further, his work and writings seem to testify not only to being informed, but also to being facile with information in making an argument or illustrating a point. For example, in one speech,[75] he used compelling rhetoric about world hunger, global population issues, the OPEC oil crisis, the Cuban Missile Crisis, genocide, and power outages to clarify the challenges that Americans faced at the time. In another speech,[76] he reviewed the role of the professoriate from the founding of Harvard to the 1980s—succinctly and clearly! In short, the examples that he included in his writings—from Mayan jungles to PTAs; from Carnegie reports to the Socratic method; from John Amos Comenius to Clifford Geertz to Oliver Twist; from Sputnik to the Smith-Hughes Act—suggest that Boyer was a studious observer and purveyor of information. Perhaps most importantly, however, Boyer was an expert at synthesizing information to understand the times and to frame particular objectives and strategies.

Taking Time to be Creative

Boyer believed that "academic leadership means having a modest agenda of [one's] own."[77] From Boyer's perspective, the creativity of leaders was always in jeopardy. It could be compromised by the sheer volume of demands on one's time; or, creativity could be snuffed out when critical and desirable changes were a long time in coming, were denuded of their influence because of their incremental adoption, or never occurred at all. Boyer reflects on his strategy for sustaining creativity:

> The academic leader must be able to see where yardage can be gained and then move aggressively to claim new turf. You'll never have a winning touchdown every day, but I'm convinced that modest openings always can be found. Absent that ability, linebackers will drop you back yard by yard every single day. Leadership means having a strategy of your own. The only thing that got me out of bed for every job I've held is to know that tucked away there was a little yardage that was mine alone—an idea that I could work around the edges. If I thought that I was there simply to respond to the strategy of others, I'd stay in bed.[78]

Of course, one of the clearest examples of a "little yardage" for Boyer was Empire State College (ESC). In the Foreword to Richard Bonnabeau's handsome history of ESC written just days before his death, Boyer laments the imitative nature of American colleges and universities, that, in spite of claims to the contrary, they are "busily engaged in cloning one another."[79] Boyer's lament led him to pursue "a modest agenda of his own"—the creation of an innovative institution that we now know as Empire State College. From the outset, ESC emphasized student-centered learning based on written and signed educational contracts[80] and in partnership with "master teachers"[81] who served as mentors to the process. In addition, the ESC involved the development of "Learning Access Centers" throughout the state of New York, most often in existing buildings, to minimize the costs of new construction. The founding of ESC, in its own right, is not an important component of Boyer's considerable legacy. It is also, however, a quintessential example of Boyer's emphasis on the importance of creativity for those who lead academe.

Having an Inspired Vision

As the conclusion of one of his speeches, Boyer borrowed some lines from the American poet, Vachel Lindsay, as follows:

> *It is the world's one crime, its babes "grow dull"*
>
> *Not that they sow, but that they seldom reap*
>
> *Not that they serve, but have no God to serve*
>
> *Not that they die, but that they die like sheep.*
>
> *The tragedy of life is not death.*
>
> *The tragedy is to die with commitments undefined,*
>
> *convictions undeclared, and service unfulfilled.*[82]

Leaders with undefined commitments, undeclared convictions, and unfulfilled service are not good leaders from Boyer's point of view. Quite to the contrary. Even though I have included this as the final quality of leadership, in Boyer's list, it was at the top of the list. For him, "having an inspired vision" [83] was the wellspring of good leadership and, in turn, of excellent higher education. As early as the 1980s, Boyer said it this way: If the learning leaders of America's colleges and universities are not animated by "transcendent purposes, our campuses will be viewed as academic shopping malls where students come in, pick up what they want, and leave with their little bag of credential goodies."[84] The connection for Boyer was crystal clear—to the extent that colleges and universities are first and foremost (and perhaps only)

credentialing stations, the source of the problem is a lack of vision and/or the absence of a proper vision among those leading
the academy. Stated another way, Boyer's perspective on leading
academe was inextricably related to his belief that the commodification of higher education was wrongheaded; when colleges
and universities are simply shopping malls, academic leaders
are little more than store managers who ensure that "the trains
run on time" in service to the effective marketing and timely
sale of the commodities.

There seems to be clear sense in Boyer's mind that the
calling and challenge of college and university leadership was
to prevent such an "education as commodity" approach, and
that the means of doing so was a devoted embrace and dogged
pursuit of a tangible, educational vision. In the next section, I
will highlight a few of the characteristics that comprised such a
vision for Boyer.

Leading Academe

What seems most critical for understanding Boyer's perspective
on leading academe is that, for him, leading academe was not
to be disembodied from an educational vision for colleges and
universities. And, to be clear, such a vision was not a corpora-
tizing approach that seems regnant in the current day, but one
that was, at its heart, directly concerned with fundamental *educational* questions such as: What are the desired ends of higher
education, both during the college experience and beyond it?
What is a curriculum, and how might curricular programs be
designed and delivered to maximize progress toward hoped-for
ends? What are the appropriate roles of faculty members in the
pursuit of these ends? What must characterize the relationship
between higher education and contemporary social life?

Thoroughly exploring Boyer's mind and work in addressing these questions is well beyond the pale of this essay. What
I do wish to do, however, is to highlight and briefly summarize
several explicit aspects of Boyer's educational vision. In effect,
the eight themes that follow reflect some of the responses that
Boyer may have offered to the question, "Leading academe with

regard to what?" As I intimated earlier, these themes are significant to consider in juxtaposition to the crises of wrongheaded leadership, leadershiplessness, and confusion regarding the goals of higher education portrayed in the first part of the essay. That is, much of Boyer's thinking reflected in what follows may be viewed as correctives or preventatives to these crises. In the final analysis, what I hope to convey is that Boyer believed that the possession of leadership qualities, by itself, was insufficient for leading academe effectively. From his perspective, educational leadership must include a content—or vision—as well, about which they were articulate, for which they advocated, and that which they pursued both earnestly and doggedly.

Curricular Coherence

Curricular coherence is a central theme in Boyer's educational vision and one, about which, he wrote extensively.[85] The chapter on general education in this volume,[86] for example, provides testimony to the critical importance that Boyer placed on this theme.[87] Boyer laments the fragmentation of higher education curriculum, a fragmentation that is nourished by balkanized academic departments[88] rather than by what he calls "the human agenda."[89] The troubling result of such fragmentation, according to Boyer, is that students graduate from college but "…fail to see…connections that would give them a more coherent view of knowledge and a more authentic, more integrated view of life."[90]

Some may find Boyer's advocacy for curricular cohesion old-fashioned or irrelevant, particularly in a century characterized by diversity, complexity, and change. And yet this is precisely why Boyer believed that an emphasis on coherence or "connections"[91] was critical. From Boyer's perspective, meeting these challenges depended in an inordinate way on integrating "vocational and humanistic traditions"[92] in service of the common good. To do otherwise was potentially to fall prey to what Boyer dubbed "the Boesky Syndrome."[93] This is a reference to American investor, Ivan Boesky, who utilized his financial training and expertise to accumulate millions of dollars via insider trading in the mid-1980s. Boesky is even purported to have given a 1985 commencement address in which his main point to those assembled was that "greed is healthy."[94] Boesky was eventually heavily fined and imprisoned for his...well, for his *expertise*.

Boyer's notion of the Boesky Syndrome is to suggest that expertise that is detached from virtues rooted in the humanist tradition and isolated from service of the public good may compromise human and social flourishing. When "students [become] competent in a special field, but they're not... asked to consider...competence to what end,"[95] the Boesky Syndrome is activated, leading Boyer to lament:

> At a time when values should be shaped and personal priorities sharply probed, what a tragedy it would be if the most deeply felt issues, the most haunting questions, the most creative moments were pushed to the fringes of our institutional life. What a monumental mistake it would be if students, during the undergraduate years, remained trapped within the organizational grooves and narrow routines to which the academic world sometimes seems excessively devoted.[96]

Accordingly, Boyer believed that academic leaders must ensure that "general and specialized education [are] blended during college—just as they [are] blended during life."[97] But, as important, academic leaders must utilize this coherent curricular model to "help students go beyond their private interests, gain a more integrative view of knowledge, and relate their learning to the realities of life."[98]

Educating for the Common Good

Related to the previous theme, Boyer's call to educational leaders to embrace and deliver an "education for the common good" is unmistakable; though higher education certainly resulted in personal benefits to faculty and students alike, its primary purpose, promise and power lay with its enriching impact on human welfare. His publications and speeches are replete with some version of this refrain, most often referring to it as "the scholarship of engagement." This form of scholarship directly links the efforts of colleges and universities with the "most pressing social, civic, economic, and moral problems"[99] of America and the world. For Boyer, simply acquiring knowledge is inadequate, whether such knowledge is the product of a faculty member's research or symbolized by a student's completion of an undergraduate degree. Instead, "If the human species is to survive on this planet—with civility—knowledge must be directed toward humane ends."[100]

Boyer specifically and routinely commented that American colleges and universities must become "staging grounds for action" as they resolve to address and seek to rectify problems in America concerning children's poverty and health care, the public schools, and national urban life. But he also suggested that American higher education must devote energies to responding thoughtfully and effectively to global issues related to populations, food and water supplies, energy distribution, and the security/safety of one's homeland. In short, Boyer posited that educational leaders "simply must do a better job of alerting our students to the larger contours of their world, of helping them see the broader ramifications of their actions and conveying the urgent need to marshal all [of] our resources as we confront the critical choices of the future."[101] Needless to say, doing so will require the leaders of academe to embrace this vision and to develop facility in mobilizing curriculum, co-curriculum, and colleagues to these ends.

Teaching Excellence

One of Boyer's seminal works—*Scholarship Reconsidered*[102]—makes clear that the scholarship of teaching is a primary component of his strategy for leading academe effectively. According to Boyer,

> When all is said and done, the quality of undergraduate education must be measured not just in the dining halls and dorms, but most especially in the classrooms, as students and professors interact authentically with each

> other. The simple truth is that the work of the professoriate becomes consequential only as it is understood by others, since teaching is…the highest form of understanding. It is absolutely clear that a high quality of undergraduate education will be accomplished only when the university gives more dignity and more stature to the essential act of teaching.[103]

Boyer thought that good teaching was characterized by "command of the material to be taught, a contagious enthusiasm for the play of ideas, optimism about human potential, the involvement of one's students, and…sensitivity, integrity, and warmth as a human being."[104] One will quickly notice in this list that Boyer's notion of effective academic leadership combined intellectual curiosity and pedagogical expertise with what might be called interpersonal style. For him, leading academe necessitated faculty members' commitment to both content and character, teachers who "not only knew their subjects, but knew their students, too."[105] Perhaps this is why he was quick to add that "the most important teaching may go on outside the classroom"[106] though not in a "paternalistic fashion."[107] Simply stated, Boyer firmly believed that faculty members were indispensable for establishing the overall quality of the students' entire educational experience.

Institutions offer recognition, incentives, and rewards for those things that they most value; one's heart and one's treasures are inseparable. During much of Boyer's career, research and writing was most prized in much of the academy; recognition, incentives, and rewards likewise followed. From Boyer's point of view, however, "Good teaching is at the heart of the undergraduate experience."[108] As a result, those who would provide effective leadership for the academy must redouble their efforts to improve and incentivize teaching and to recognize and reward excellent teaching. Boyer concludes: "If, in the days ahead, undergraduates are not stimulated by great teachers, and if good teaching is not rewarded, then all the talk about excellence will be simply a diversion."[109]

Strong Campus Community

Cultivating and sustaining vibrant institutional communities is an essential component of Boyer's work. Another chapter in this volume offers specific and robust testimony to the six principles that characterize the campus communities that Boyer had in mind. In the context of this essay, however, three particular points stand out. First, Boyer believed that nurturing strong campus communities was endemic to the leadership of colleges and universities. All of an institution's leaders must be committed to an educational project that privileges and extends academic purposefulness, principled honesty, justice, discipline, caring, and routinely celebrates community accomplishments.[110] Strong campus communities both reflect and further spawn these critical values, and institutional leaders are at the forefront of such efforts.

Second, and relatedly, the academy's leaders must redouble their efforts to suppress and eliminate extant campus cultures that conflict with Boyer's vision of vibrant campus life. More specifically, he sensed that students on many campuses experienced "an overregulated academic world and...an under-regulated social and civic world."[111] Boyer continues: "We treat them like children when it comes to getting in their papers and deciding how many units they need...But on a social and civic side, it's sort of 'Do your own thing and figure it out.'" To address this problem, Boyer suggested that college and university leaders create a "post-*in loco parentis* theory of campus governance" that represented a "better blend [of] the academic and the civic...in which we would give students more freedom educationally and perhaps more responsibility socially and civically."[112]

And, third, Boyer was chagrined that what he called "little loyalties"[113] would overshadow and eventually come to dominate college and university campuses. These little loyalties took a variety of forms from self-interested student subpopulations to balkanized academic departments to isolated administrative functions to external, bureaucratized agencies. It is not that Boyer believed that parts were to be consumed by the whole, or that diversification was to be sacrificed to unity. Rather, Boyer was convinced that strong campus community was compromised when a campus was simply the sum of its constituent parts. For him, "larger loyalties" were the *sine qua non* to strong campus communities because such loyalties emphasized connections and cohesion among parts in service to common values and goals, while still preserving the importance and integrity of the particular parts of the campus. Stated another way, Boyer affirmed the one *and* the many and their inextricable relationship. As important for Boyer, a fundamental responsibility of those charged with leading academe was a continuous, clear, winsome, negotiating, clarifying, and communicating of this relationship between larger loyalties and little loyalties. Institutional leaders unwilling or unable to do so jeopardized the attainment of strong campus community and, in so doing, threatened the quality of the educational experience for all.

Equality of Opportunity

As a concluding challenge in a 1991 speech, Boyer asked the audience: "Do we still believe in quality education for all of our students and not just for the most advantaged?"[114] In this and other writings, Boyer was clear that higher education should welcome non-traditional-aged students, noting that college should not "be viewed as a four-year pre-work stage of life, but as a continuing process to be pursued from sixteen to eighty-five."[115] But, in this same speech, the particular focus of his comments regarding equality of opportunity was made very clear: higher education must not be "limited to those of the 'right' gender, the 'right' color, the 'right' income, and the 'right' religion."[116] Perhaps the following quote best captures the seriousness of this issue for Boyer, as well as his considerable passion for it:

> The truth is that the face of young America is changing, and by the year 2000 over one-third of all students in the public schools will be black or Hispanic. And these are precisely the young people with whom our schools and colleges have been least successful. I say with strong

urgency that equity and democracy are inextricably interlocked, and if this nation is to remain secure, our colleges and schools must reaffirm their commitment to opportunity for all. And if we fail here, we will have failed altogether for the future.[117]

Boyer's voice joined numerous others in the latter portions of the 20th century in calling for equal access to higher education, a call that has achieved substantial success. Boyer's championing of equal access was also coupled with his passion for a high-quality learning experience for all students, independent of their gender, race, socio-economic status, religion, or age. He writes:

If…we do not find creative ways to challenge prejudice on the campus, if we can't begin to heal the tragic racial and ethnic divisions in our culture, if we do not build bridges between the old and the young, I'm convinced that the very future of the nation is imperiled. Simply stated, the task we face is to strengthen community and define our commonalities while offering diversity, as well.[118]

Equality of opportunity—including with respect to participating in excellent learning opportunities—and a strong campus community were interrelated for Boyer. In fact, Boyer seemed to indicate that colleges and universities can and must serve as a model to other arenas of American society (i.e., schools, neighborhoods, churches, and organizations) for how best to operationalize simultaneous commitments to access and quality, and unity and diversity. And, once again, the success of colleges and universities in doing so depends on the resolve and skill of those leading academe toward these ends.

School/College Collaboration

Although this volume celebrates his contributions to American postsecondary education, Boyer was equally interested in the quality of America's schools. Moreover, he believed that the success of the former was closely linked with the success of the latter, noting that "the future of higher learning can be no stronger than the nation's schools."[119] Because of this partnership, Boyer believed that collaborations between colleges and schools must be a priority on the agendas of academe's leaders. Some of the specific ideas that Boyer mentioned are as follows:[120]

- Colleges and universities should sponsor fellowship programs for local teachers during the summer in which postsecondary faculty and elementary and secondary teachers gathered to discuss current research in the field, effective pedagogical methods, curricular innovations, and continuity between pre-collegiate education and postsecondary education (which may include jointly developed proficiency examinations that ensure that elementary and secondary school students are mastered particular skills in preparation for college; or, may include a jointly developed, eight-year—four years of high school and four years of college—general education sequence).

- Colleges and universities should collaborate with local schools to identify and begin recruiting future teachers from the ranks of junior high school students. Further, colleges and universities should provide full scholarships to the top 5% of entering students who desire to teach in public schools.

- Colleges and universities should require every incoming first-year student to write a letter to the most influential teacher (or two) that they had in elementary and/or secondary school and ensure that the letters are actually sent. The purpose of these letters is simply to thank these former teachers for their commitment to excellent learning.

- Colleges and universities should establish ways to recognize and honor excellence teaching in local schools (e.g., honorary degrees) and/or being done by their alumni (e.g., distinguished alumni award for school teaching).

- Colleges and universities should make their facilities, including laboratory equipment, available to local teachers and their students.

- Colleges and universities should seek external funding for joint school-college projects. Boyer laments: "Why is it that whenever we want to improve teaching in the school, we give the money to professors in the college?"[121]

- Colleges and universities, in partnership with schools, should develop what Boyer called "residential academies" that maximize the utilization of physical and human resources at both schools and colleges, and focus on instruction and preparation in particular fields (e.g., math/science, language studies, fine arts) for academically-gifted students.

- Colleges and universities should engage in regular conversations with local school districts regarding what constitutes "good" education, including clearly identifying expectations for high school and college graduates, and effective strategies for achieving continuity between learning expectations at both levels of education.

Collaborations between schools and postsecondary institutions do not occur by themselves. For this reason, the clear implication from Boyer's thinking is that school/college collaboration is an important aspect of the leadership that college and university educators must undertake.

Proper Use of Technology

Boyer had no doubt that colleges and universities would and should embrace technology. He likewise had no doubt that technology could be "used as teacher"[122] in the nation's colleges and universities. But he had his apprehensions as well. For example, he presciently predicted that technology would eventually result in a "global information commons—where information is owned by everyone."[123] But he simultaneously believed that "technology with all of its sophistication and with all of the illusion it creates, deals with reality in a very superficial and impressionistic way."[124]

The way forward in responding wisely to the inexorable expansion of technology in colleges and universities was for institutional leaders to ensure the proper use of technology. He had several particular things in mind. First, and not surprisingly given the centrality of this theme in his thinking, Boyer believed that technology must be used to foster coherence. In 1994, Boyer referred to the Internet as "a dazzling gold mine of information."[125] But, he was keenly aware that access to increasing amounts of information may be counterproductive to a cohesive knowing and integrated living.

Boyer's first point is strongly connected to a second consideration. Boyer asks: "Is it possible that we can have classrooms where students acquire not just the knowledge through technology, but perhaps the wisdom to interpret it as well."[126] Boyer's interest is to make clear that obtaining more knowledge because more information is readily available (i.e., via technology) does not guarantee that one gains wisdom. His view was crystal clear: "Technology can instantaneously transmit information all around the world. But technology, with all of its dazzling effects, cannot convey wisdom. For this we need educational institutions that help students of all ages become more discerning, teaching the capacity to separate the shoddy from that which is elegant and enduring."[127] He quickly adds that "for this to be accomplished we need, above all else, gifted and inspired teachers."[128]

A third point that Boyer makes regarding the proper use of technology is perhaps the one for which he has the most concern: "I'm convinced that the first and most compelling challenge we confront in any discussion of technology and the public interest, is to assure that the new technology will close, rather than widen, the gap between the privileged and the disadvantaged."[129]

Once again, Boyer's abiding interest in equality and quality of opportunity and educational experience is clear. And, given the relative power that he believed would continue to accrue to technology in higher education, Boyer was deeply concerned that technology—though it held immense promise for improving student learning and understanding—may also produce the unintended consequence of widening educational gaps rather than narrowing them or eliminating them altogether.

Boyer often concluded his comments on technology and higher education by referring to a statement made by E. B. White in 1938 regarding the impact that television would have on American culture, namely that television "would become either 'saving radiance in the sky' or an 'unbearable disturbance.'"[130] In Boyer's view, the same might be said about technology in higher education. Clearly, Boyer was "for" technology because of its capacity to augment the "radiance" of students' learning experience. Boyer also believed that avoiding technology becoming an "unbearable disturbance" to colleges and universities would require the principled and wise oversight of those charged with leading academe.

Governance

One final theme that Boyer considers critical for educational leaders to address is governance. More specifically, Boyer believed that the critical question of "who's in charge" had become not only confusing but increasingly contentious as well. He was particularly concerned about the impact of external entities (e.g., state and federal governments; professional and regional accrediting bodies; business and industry) on the ability of colleges and universities to offer excellent, coherent educational experiences. Boyer summarizes: "As I look down the next ten years and sources of intervention and control sometimes for economic purposes, and sometimes for social constitutional purposes, those in college and university administration are going to find that one of our most vexing problems is deciding 'who's in charge.'"[131] At the same time, he conceded that governance problems existed internally as well, particularly with respect to disagreements regarding institutional purposes, the nature of faculty work, and shared governance. Exacerbating these tensions—irrespective of their source being external or internal—were seemingly ubiquitous environmental pressures such as deferred maintenance, energy costs, shrinking fiscal resources, and increasing competition.

Responding well to these challenges was neither simple nor easy from Boyer's perspective. But leading academe effectively required a response to be sure. The best response, according to Boyer, involved being keenly informed of external and internal issues while simultaneously being unequivocally clear about institutional purposes, nurturing coherent curricular, co-curricular, and research programs sourced by such purposes, and cultivating collaboration and consensus around these same institutional purposes. Boyer called all educational leaders to embrace these governance efforts; otherwise, according to Boyer, institutional constituents will simply "carry on their work in isolated pockets," institutional "purposes will be blurred," and, "the unity of the enterprise…[will be] lost."[132] In short, college and university education of the first order is compromised when those involved in leading academe fail to lead or to lead well.

Notes

[1]M. Fullan and G. Scott, *Turnaround Leadership for Higher Education* (San Francisco: John Wiley & Sons, Inc., 2009), 149.

[2]E. Boyer, "Academic Leadership: Some Personal Reflections" (Academic Renewal Conference, Ann Arbor, MI, 1983), 1.

[3]George Kuh poses a similar question in his brief response to Mark Taylor's *Crisis on Campus: A Bold Plan for Reforming our Colleges and Universities* (New York, NY: Knopf, 2010) as part of a Review Forum organized by Todd Ream in the *Review of Higher Education*, 34, (4)(Summer 2011), 692-693.

[4]American College Presidents Study, (Washington, D.C.: American Council on Education, 2007).

[5]S. Pierce, *On Being Presidential: A Guide for College and University Leaders* (San Francisco, CA: Jossey Bass, 2011), 141.

[6]R. Ekman, "The Imminent Crisis in College Leadership" (*The Chronicle of Higher Education*, September 19, 2010), retrieved from: https://www.chronicle.com/article/The-Imminent-Crisis-in-College/124513.

[7]See V. Stoyanova, *David Teece's Dynamic Capabilities and Strategic Management: Organizing for Innovation and Growth* (The Macat Library, 2018); R. Burgelman, A. Grove, and P. Meza, *Strategic Dynamics: Concepts and Cases* (McGraw Hill/Irwin, 2005); and K. Warren, *Strategic Management Dynamics* (Hoboken, NJ: Wiley, 2008). Of course, this "strategic dynamism" also figured prominently in the aftermath of the firing (and eventual reinstating) of President Teresa Sullivan at the University of Virginia in June 2012.

[8]R. Zemsky, *Making Reform Work: The Case for Transforming American Higher Education* (New Brunswick, NJ: Rutgers University Press, 2009), 71. Zemsky does not necessarily view the tensions between the acropolis and the agora as a crisis, but rather as a relationship that must be "[more] accepted and [further] explored" (71). In fact, in a book that he wrote with G. Wegner and W. Massy he suggests that the way forward necessitates colleges and universities becoming more adept at being "market-smart and mission-centered." *Remaking the American University: Market-Smart and Mission-Centered* (New Brunswick, NJ: Rutgers University Press, 2005).

[9]S. Slaughter and G. Rhoades, *Academic Capitalism and the New Economy: Markets, State, and Higher Education* (Baltimore, MD: Johns Hopkins University Press, 2009).

[10]B. Ginsberg, *The Fall of the Faculty: The Rise of the All-Administrative University and Why it Matters* (New York, NY: Oxford University Press, 2013). It comes as no surprise that Ginsberg uses the term "administrative blight" to describe the crisis.

[11]G. Tuchman, *Wannabe U: Inside the Corporate University* (Chicago, IL: University of Chicago Press, 2011). Tuchman's emphasis may easily be described as the commodification of colleges and universities. According to her, in 2009, 60% of Americans agreed with the statement: "Colleges today are like most businesses and care mainly about the bottom line."

[12]J. Washburn, *University, Inc.: The Corporate Corruption of Higher Education* (New York, NY: Basic Books, 2005). Washburn's perspective is unmistakable given the subtitle of her book.

[13]D. Bok, *Universities in the Marketplace: The Commercialization of Higher Education* (Princeton, NJ: Princeton University Press, 2004).

[14]D. Hayes and R. Wynyard, *The McDonaldization of Higher Education* (Westport, CT: Praeger, 2002).

[15]W. Shumar, *College for Sale: A Critique of the Commodification of Higher Education* (New York, NY: Routledge, 1997).

[16]Tuchman, 12.

[17]I am choosing to focus the crisis of wrongheaded leadership around the theme of the commodification or corporatization of the academy. However, I should note that A. Hacker and C. Dreifus (*Higher Education? How Colleges are Wasting Our Money and Failing Our Kids—and What We Can Do About It*, [New York, NY: Times Books, 2011]) contend, in part, that wrongheaded leadership takes the form of the unwillingness of administrative and faculty leaders to address the fragmentation and autonomy that characterizes the academy; in fact, they may be construed to say that the very nature of wrongheaded leadership is that it continues to perpetuate fragmentation and autonomy. Also, with respect to the wrongheadedness of the faculty in particular, some suggest that spoiled, self-aggrandizing faculty members who hide behind tenure represents a "real" crisis. See: N. Riley, *The Faculty Lounges and*

Other Reasons Why You Won't Get the College Education You Paid For (Chicago, IL: Ivan R Dee, 2011).

[18]Mark Edmundson, "Under the Sign of Satan: William Blake in the Corporate University," *The Hedgehog Review*, Spring 2012, 8-16.

[19]J. Kenway, E. Bullen, and S. Robb, "The Knowledge Economy, the Techno-Preneur and the Problematic Future of the University," In S. Marginson's (ed.), *Prospects of Higher Educations: Globalization, Market Competition, Public Goods and the Future of the University* (Rotterdam: Sense Publishers, 2007), 123-137; 129; 125.

[20]See G. Tuchman, "Pressured and Measured: Professors at Wannabe U," In *The Hedgehog Review*, Spring 2012, 17-28.

[21]G. Rhoades, *Managed Professionals: Unionized Faculty and Restructuring Academic Labor* (Albany: State University of New York Press, 1998), 4.

[22]F. Donoghue, "Do College Teachers Have to be Scholars?" In *The Hedgehog Review*, Spring 2012, 29-42, 37.

[23]J. Geddes, "The Corporate Professor," In *The Hedgehog Review*, Spring 2012, 6-7.

[24]R. Heifetz, A. Grashow, and M. Linsky, *The Practice of Adaptive Leadership: Tools and Tactics for Changing your Organization and the World*, (Boston, MA: Harvard Business Press, 2009), 3.

[25]Ibid.

[26]J. Collins, *Good to Great: Why Some Companies Make the Leap...and Others Don't* (New York, NY: HarperBusiness, 2001).

[27]B. Bass and R. Riggio, *Transformational Leadership, 2nd Edition* (Mahwah, NJ: Lawrence Erlbaum Associates, Inc., 2005).

[28]E. Bensimon, A. Neumann, and R. Birnbaum, *Making Sense of Administrative Leadership: The "L" Word in Higher Education, ASHE-ERIC Higher Education Report* (Washington, D.C.: School of Education, George Washington University, 1989).

[29]Fullan and Scott.

[30]R. Greenleaf, *Servant Leadership: A Journey into the Nature of Legitimate Power and Greatness* (Mahwah, NJ: Paulist Press, 1977).

³¹S. Covey, *Principle-Centered Leadership* (New York, NY: Fireside Press, 1992).

³²J. Kouzes and B. Posner, *The Leadership Challenge, 3ʳᵈ Edition* (San Francisco, CA: Jossey Bass, 2002).

³³P. Senge, *The Fifth Discipline* (New York, NY: Doubleday, 1990).

³⁴J. Garland, *Saving Alma Mater: A Rescue Plan for America's Public Universities* (Chicago, IL: The University of Chicago Press, 2009), 107.

³⁵C. Christensen and H. Eyring, *The Innovative University: Changing the DNA of Higher Education from the Inside Out* (San Francisco, CA: Jossey-Bass, 2011), xxii-xxiii.

³⁶W. Zumeta, "What Does it Mean to be Accountable? Dimensions and Implications of Higher Education's Public Accountability," *The Review of Higher Education*, Fall 2011, 131-148, 141.

³⁷Ibid.

³⁸R. DeMillo, *Abelard to Apple: The Fate of American Colleges and Universities* (Boston, MA: Massachusetts Institute of Technology, 2011), 285.

³⁹A. Rosen, *Change.edu: Rebooting for the New Talent Economy* (New York, NY: Kaplan Publishing, 2011), 181-182.

⁴⁰R. Hutchins, *The Higher Learning in America* (New York, NY: Routledge, 1995), 1.

⁴¹Hacker and Dreifus, 4.

⁴²Ibid., 8-9.

⁴³William James, *A Pluralistic Universe* (New York: Longmans, Green, and Company, 1909).

⁴⁴Kerr, 103.

⁴⁵C. Jencks and D. Riesman, *The Academic Revolution* (New York, NY: Routledge, 2001).

⁴⁶Examples of this may include an institution pursuing university status; the adoption of a college model for academic governance; faculty culture that—even tacitly—places a higher value on research, publication, and

professional conference presentations than on teaching and advising and institutional service.

[47]C. Kerr, *The Uses of the University, 5th* Edition (Cambridge, MA: Harvard University Press, 2001), 208.

[48]Ibid., 229.

[49]Ibid., 210.

[50]G. Keller, *Higher Education and the New Society* (Baltimore, MD: Johns Hopkins University Press, 2008).

[51]See DeMillo, 269ff.

[52]E. Boyer, "Everyone Can Lead: Qualities of Effective Leading." This document is simply one page in length, representing Boyer's rough outline of a book that he had in mind to write. He crafted this "one-pager" close to the time of his death in 1995.

[53]Ibid.

[54]Ibid.

[55]E. Boyer, "Leadership: A Clear and Vital Mission," The Isabella Cannon Leadership Program, Elon College, February 18, 1991, 39.

[56]Boyer, "Academic Leadership," 1.

[57]Ibid.

[58]Ibid., 3.

[59]Ibid.

[60]Ibid.

[61]E. Boyer, "Rebirth of Leadership From the Ashes of Bureaucracy," March 16, 1984.

[62]Tuchman, 69-87. See also, Christensen and Eyring, 2011; Ginsberg, 2011; Slaughter and Rhoades, 1998; Washburn, 2005.

[63]E. Boyer, "Leadership: A Clear and Vital Mission," 23-24.

[64]E. Boyer, "American Education at the End of the Twentieth Century," Speech on July 21, 1989, 3.

[65]Boyer, "Academic Leadership," 4.

[66]Ibid., 5.

[67]Ibid.

[68]As noted at numerous other places in this essay, this is a recurring theme in Boyer's speeches.

[69]E. Boyer, "Education 2000: New Wine, New Bottles," 6.

[70]The "balance" mentioned here appears in many Boyer speeches. The following speech is simply one example: E. Boyer, "Trends and Issues in Higher Education," speech delivered at the Ohio College Association.

[71]E. Boyer, "Education 2000: New Wine, New Bottles."

[72]Boyer, "Education 2000," 6.

[73]Ibid., 7.

[74]Boyer, "Academic Leadership," 5.

[75]E. Boyer, "Education 2000."

[76]E. Boyer, "The Responsibility of the Faculty for the Undergraduate Experience."

[77]Boyer, "Academic Leadership," 4.

[78]Ibid.

[79]R. Bonnabeau, *The Promise Continues: Empire State College, The First 25 Years* (Virginia Beach, VA: The Donning Company/Publishers, 1996), 6. I am indebted to Richard for sending me a copy of this handsome volume, based on our meeting at Messiah University in April 2012 to inaugurate the Boyer Center.

[80]These learning contracts were a large part of the learning innovation that Boyer and his colleagues had in mind. Eschewing more traditional pedagogical methods of lecture and seminar, learning contracts placed students in command of learning, and at his or her own pace. Bonnabeau includes this description of learning contracts based on a 1991 interview with William Dodge, the acting dean for continuing education at SUNY at the time of the founding of ESC: "Any kind of instructional material that was organized and appropriate both in complexity and level of learning should be grist for the

mill of a contract…All we knew was that there was a lot of learning materials in libraries, in colleges, in universities, at work, in cultural organizations, and in government…The contract was an organizing structure for marshaling these resources within the community, both academic and social and governmental and cultural" (Bonnabeau, 26).

[81]Bonnabeau, 26.

[82]Boyer, "American education at the end…," The name of Vachel Lindsay's poem is "The Leaden-Eyed," originally published in 1912. Boyer's inclusion of it in this particular speech is slightly incomplete and slightly incorrect. Lindsay's sobering poem reads as follows:

> *Let not young souls be smothered out before*
> *They do quaint deeds and fully flaunt their pride.*
> *It is the world's one crime its babes grow dull,*
> *Its poor are ox-like, limp and leaden-eyed.*
> *Not that they starve; but starve so dreamlessly,*
> *Not that they sow, but that they seldom reap,*
> *Not that they serve, but have no gods to serve,*
>
> *Not that they die, but that they die like sheep.*

[83]Boyer, "Everyone Can Lead…" As I mentioned at the outset of this section, I placed this quality of leadership at the end of the list as an appropriate segue to the next section of the essay.

[84]E. Boyer, "Reflections on Higher Education in the 1980s," 6. Speech given in 1979..

[85]Boyer is clear: "I am convinced that the search for a larger more integrative view of education means first that colleges should develop a curriculum with coherence," E. Boyer, *Selected Speeches, 1979-1995* (San Francisco, CA: Jossey Bass, 1997), 58.

[86]This is a reference to the book that was published on Boyer, mentioned at the outset.

[87]In the short book entitled *Quest for Common Learning: The Aims of General Education* (San Francisco, CA: Jossey Bass, 1991), Boyer and co-author Arthur Levine provide a particular—and compelling—example of a cohesive, integrated curricular approach that is animated by what they call

"the human commonalities" rather than by the orthodoxies of academic disciplines/departments.

[88]Boyer was emphatic in his disdain for such fragmentation, noting that "I'm convinced that in our fragmented academic world this task of integration becomes more urgent every single day. Of course, let's keep the academic departments to manage the essential administrative functions. But, in the coming years, let's create new interdisciplinary forums to investigate the larger, more integrative questions," E. Boyer, "Critical issues in higher education," given at the 125th Anniversary Symposium at the University of Kansas on April 19, 1991.

[89]E. Boyer, Excellence in Education: Challenges for the Nineties," 4. Speech given in Albany, NY on January 15, 1991.

[90]Boyer, "American Education at the End," 1.

[91]Boyer draws from Comenius' allegory entitled *The Labyrinth of the World and the Paradise of the Heart* and laments the irony of "learned" doctors who were "so interested in the patient's anatomy that a patient dies" and "learned" lawyers who developed "new ways to take someone else's property." The point of Boyer's use of Comenius' allegory is clear—learning that privileges detached (i.e., from all else) specialization at all costs is dangerous to the welfare of persons and society. In contrast to this vision for higher learning, Boyer makes clear a vision for colleges and universities that academic leaders must guard and further: "The most essential and most neglected goal of American education is best expressed by the simple word 'connections'" Boyer, "American Education at the End," 1.

[92]Boyer, "Reflections on Higher Education in the 1980s," 4.

[93]Boyer, "Critical Issues," 7.

[94]http://invest.yourdictionary.com/boesky-ivan-f-abbv.

[95]Boyer, "Critical Issues," 7.

[96]E. Boyer, *College: The Undergraduate Experience in America* (New York, NY: Harper and Row, 1987), 283.

[97]Boyer, "Critical Issues," 7.

[98]*Selected Speeches*, 68.

[99]Ibid., 82.

[100]Boyer, "American Education at the end," 5.

[101]Boyer, "Education 2000," 7.

[102]E. Boyer, *Scholarship Reconsidered: Priorities of the Professoriate* (San Francisco, CA: Jossey Bass, 1987).

[103]Boyer, "The Responsibility of the Faculty," 4.

[104]Boyer, *College*, 154.

[105]Boyer, "Critical Issues," 8.

[106]Boyer, *College*, 157.

[107]Boyer, *College*, 158.

[108]Boyer, *College*, 159.

[109]Boyer, "Critical Issues," 9.

[110]These six principles are discussed originally in E. Boyer, *Campus Life: In Search of Community* (San Francisco, CA: Jossey Bass, 1990).

[111]Boyer, "Trends and Issues," 7.

[112]Ibid.

[113]Ibid.

[114]Boyer, "Excellence in Education," 6.

[115]Boyer, "Education 2000," 3.

[116]Ibid., 2.

[117]E. Boyer, "Meeting the Education Needs of America: A Look Ahead to the 21st Century", 8. Delivered at The Presidents Forum at the Waldorf-Astoria Hotel in New York City on December 2, 1986.

[118]Boyer, "Critical Issues," 5.

[119]In this particular speech to the Ohio College Association, Boyer implores those gathered that their own concerns regarding financial resources should not overshadow their sensitivity and support for schools. The longer, and more poignant, quote from which I drew the quote included in the text is worth including: "I prayerfully hope that the leaders in this country will understand that helping little children is at least as important as bailing out the

savings and loans and sending troops to the Persian Gulf. If we do not understand that the battle for the future lies without our cities, and most especially relates to the children of this country, I believe we will have neglected the essential foots of the educational and civic and moral future of this nation. How then can we in higher education participate in a civil and thoughtful way in the debate for our own resources while still being wonderfully understanding of the need to strengthen schools? I hope that this will not be a trade-off in which we will somehow pit one against the other. Because, in the end, the future of higher learning can be no stronger than the nation's schools," E. Boyer, "Trends and Issues," 1.

[120]These ideas are a recurrent theme in Boyer's speeches and writing, and are culled from many of the sources included in this essay including "A Partnership: The Schooling of the Teacher," *Selected Speeches*, 95-105.

[121]Boyer, *Selected Speeches*, 104.

[122]E. Boyer, "An Agenda for Educational Leadership," 5.

[123]Boyer, "New Technologies," 2.

[124]Boyer, "Reflections on Higher Education," 5.

[125]*Selected Speeches*, 140.

[126]Boyer, "An Agenda for Educational Leadership," 5.

[127]Boyer, *Selected Speeches*, 142.

[128]Ibid., 141.

[129]Ibid., 138-139.

[130]Ibid., 141.

[131]Boyer, "Reflections on Higher Education," 2.

[132]Boyer, *College*, 246.

CHAPTER 8

Profiling and Prompting our Professional Persona and Practice

This essay was presented as the opening plenary address for the Association for Christians in Student Development annual conference at Calvin University on June 1, 1998.

Introduction

Over a year ago, I sat with 8–10 colleagues in a room not too far from here honing the theme and emphases for the conference that you now "see" before you. Much has changed since that day. I no longer work at Calvin, I am now mostly a faculty member rather than mostly an administrator, and I now am the father of a precious baby girl. What has not changed since that day is the resolve of ACSD's conference committee to fashion a conference that would stand as a signpost for professional faithfulness. A committee report that it sent to the ACSD Executive Committee put it this way: "Our sense is that the Lord calls us to respond to His enduring faithfulness by considering our roles as student affairs professionals as places in which we strive to approximate—in continuing, less-than-perfect, fits-and-starts-ways—what God may have in mind."

The conference committee envisioned that the opening address for the conference would provide some "targets"—provocative "targets"—at which to aim throughout our few days together, not only in dining hall conversations, but in workshop sessions as well. As you will see as I proceed tonight and as the conference proceeds via other plenary addresses and workshop sessions, the "targets" that the conference committee envisioned include our professional identity, purposes, performance, organizational structures, approaches, partnerships, and the like. And that is as it should be. For these are exactly the arenas in which our relative faithfulness and/or unfaithfulness to God's call upon our professional lives takes shape.

So, here is what I would like to do tonight. First, I will identify several characteristics that I believe ACSD professionals share. I think it is vital to remember that which we have in common as we undertake a conference that is not only ambitious, but also seeks to be honest about who we are, what we do, why we do what we do, and where we are going. Second, I will examine various ways that ACSD professionals differ. Because I believe that in our differences potentially lies untapped strength, I will suggest that we do well to talk more openly about them. Third, I will present some areas in which we as Christian professionals and ACSD as a professional organization may have some blind spots or, at least, some further work to do. In this regard, I pick up on some general themes, both from my "preliminary manifesto" and from Bob Reed's "Happy Flies and Sour Grapes" that appeared in successive *Koinonia* magazines.[1] Finally, I will offer several recommendations that I deeply desire—along with my comments on commonalities, differences, and blind spots—will foster continuing conversations throughout the conference and into the days ahead. So, let us begin.

What We Have in Common

First, members of ACSD share a belief in and a commitment to Jesus Christ. We are Christians; in fact, it is even fair to say that members of ACSD are what is often referred to as "evangelical Christians." It may come as a surprise to some of you that ACSD's Constitution[2] includes a doctrinal statement, and that members of the association are described as those who "subscribe unreservedly" to it. More specifically, to be a member of ACSD means to believe in a Triune God, an authoritative scripture, the deity of Jesus—His virgin birth, sinless life, miracles, vicarious death, efficacious atonement, bodily resurrection, ascension into power, and triumphant return—the fallenness but redeemableness of persons, the work of the Holy Spirit personally and corporately, a bodily resurrection of both believers and non-believers, and the inherent evilness of dancing. Made you look! That last one is not included. In short, we have in common something that is distinguishing and distinctive, namely, that we are an association of Christians who work in the student affairs profession.

Second, members of ACSD attempt to connect "the faith thing" with "the work thing." Most of us if not all of us have done at least some thinking about the relationship of Christian faith to professional service, even if the extent to which our efforts have been manifest is in opening every meeting with prayer. To some degree if not to a large degree, we are again obliged to consider the confluence of faith and work according to ACSD's Constitution, as it identifies one of the purposes of the organization as: "to integrate the use of scripture and the Christian faith in the student development profession."

And, third, members of ACSD are united in their enjoyment of the college setting. Perhaps a primary reason that we like the college setting is because we have a common concern for and commitment to those who attend our colleges, namely students. We love them, don't we? We could not do, and we would not do what we do without them. To be sure, the college in which we work and the college students with whom we work can wipe us out, make us mad, frustrate us, and disappoint us. For the most part, however, we want to be in no other place doing no other thing than working with our colleagues to the end that the students with whom we work would aspire to the important outcomes that our institutional mission statements delineate so boldly.

Two weeks ago, Geneva College's valedictorian urged her fellow graduates to honor the Lord in all areas of life by using Abraham Kuyper's powerful words that "there isn't one square inch of the creation about which Jesus doesn't say, 'This is mine!'" Her words were a reminder to me that, after a year that had its share of disillusionments and distractions, the college setting is the place to be and that our collective efforts with and on behalf of these sometimes upsetting and sometimes delightful people called students are truly worth it!

Where We Differ

First, members of ACSD differ with respect to various theological issues, styles of worship, denominational preferences, moral issues, socio-cultural practices, and the like. Some of us emphasize God's sovereignty and some of us human freedom; some of us enjoy more spontaneous worship styles and some of us enjoy more scripted worship styles; some of us attend Baptist churches and some of us attend Methodist churches; some of us resonate more with a pacifist approach to war and some of us resonate more with a just war approach to military conflict; and, some of us drink alcohol and some of us do not. In the same way that Hughes and Adrian in their book, *Models for Christian Higher Education*,[3] convincingly present a case for the non-existence of a monolithic Christian higher education, I likewise suggest that there is no such thing as a "typical" ACSD member. Furthermore, I believe that the extent to which we seek to uncover, discuss, and understand the ways that we are "different," we will strengthen our efforts both within our association and with respect to the association's presence within the larger student affairs profession.

Second, members of ACSD who work at Christian colleges and universities have different views regarding how to "do" Christian higher education. For example, some of our institutions require faculty, staff, and students to sign pledges and other of our institutions do not; some of our institutions exist largely to prepare students for missions and traditional ministry roles and other of our institutions offer an assortment of areas of study, such as in the liberal arts and sciences; and, some of our institutions stress the necessity of denominational affiliation and other of our institutions are equally eager to be identified as non- or interdenominational.

Given institutional differences such as these, it should come as little surprise that members of ACSD differ with respect to understanding and enacting the relationship between their faith in Jesus Christ, on the one hand, and their work within the field of student affairs on the other. For example, some of us may prohibit movies on campus altogether, others of us may only show so called "Christian" movies, others of us may show any movie if it complies with various pre-determined criteria, and still others of us may place the emphasis on discussing the agendas/world views of movies rather than on preempting or sustaining their viewing based on varying criteria related to subject matter. Or, with respect to residence life, some of us may operate a residence life program that only requires its RAs to lead floor Bible studies and mete out discipline when violations occur, others of us may operate a residence life program that trains RAs to plan academic and vocational programs for their residents because the literature of the field says it is important to consider the whole person, and others may operate a residence life program that challenges RAs to work in all of these areas and more and, at the same time, provides input regarding how to do such work based on a Christian view of persons and life.

To reiterate, my point here is not simply to state the obvious. Rather, by identifying some of the differences that exist among us with respect to how our Christian faith informs our professional identity and practices, I hope to prompt discussions among us that may help us understand one another better and more deeply as we consider other, "honest" perspectives regarding who we are, what we do, and why we do it. In so doing, we may also be able to articulate more clearly to our colleagues who do not profess Christian faith just exactly what we're up to and how we are "different."

And, third, members of ACSD differ with respect to position and giftedness. We are truly blessed as an organization to include persons who represent the spectrum of common responsibilities within the student affairs profession. Such a mixture helps to provide a visible reminder that the chief student affairs officer cannot say to the multicultural director, "Get lost!" Nor can the resident hall director say to the director of student activities, "What in the world are you doing?" Nor can the new hire say to the 18-year veteran, "You' re all washed up, you old fart!" I hope that during these next few days, we take advantage of the marvelous diversity of position and longevity of position that exists among us.

Likewise, and perhaps more importantly, we represent an amazing assortment of giftedness. Some of us are gifted conflict resolvers; some of us are gifted administrators; some of us are gifted in hospitality; some of us are gifted with discernment; and the list goes on and on. Of course, the trick is to have a "good match" between position and giftedness. And, likewise I would certainly like to think that longevity of service has some positive effect on giftedness, and vice versa. During the next few days, I hope that the diversity of our giftedness will be highlighted as we recount to one another the glories and glitches from the past year and challenge one another to examine the "match" between position and gifts. And, lest we forget, be sure to offer God the praise for being the Gift-Giver and Vocation-Caller.

Our Blind Spots

In the epilogue to the brand-new book (that all of us should read) edited by Nancy Evans and Christine Phelps Tobin called *State of the Art of Preparation and Practice in Student Affairs*, author Robert Young creatively uses *Alice's Adventures in Wonderland* as a commentary on the contemporary student affairs profession. Listen to some of the conversation between Alice and the Caterpillar:

"Who are you?" said the Caterpillar. This was not an encouraging opening for a conversation. Alice replied, rather shyly, "I—I hardly know, sir, just at present—at least I know who I was when I got up this morning, but I think I must have been changed several times since then." "What do you mean by that?" said the Caterpillar sternly, "Explain yourself." "I can't explain myself, I'm afraid sir," said Alice, "because I'm not myself, you see..." The Caterpillar had heard enough. "Enough," he said. "Do you mean to tell me that you are interested in student leadership and all such stuff?" "Oh no sir," Alice responded, "I would not go that far. All I know is that these days I seem to be just about anything that people want me to be." "If you cannot explain yourself, you cannot find yourself," said the Caterpillar. "Go on your way." "But which way, sir?" said Alice. "Every which way, since that seems to be where you are heading...But, oh bother, just follow one of the signs. Perhaps you will find someone out there to help you," the Caterpillar replied.[4]

The first potential blind spot: Are we settled, are we at peace with who we are, what we are up to, and why we are up to it at our respective institutions? Stated another way, if you were asked to appear before a team of faculty, administrators, and board members at your institution, could you articulate the particular nature of your role, why that role is integral to the larger mission of the college, and then demonstrate how everything you do resonates with why you exist and why you do what you do?

My sense is that we vary with the extent of our peace on these issues. For example, Calvin's Student Life Division has a remarkable effort in this regard, as I am sure other student affairs programs represented here have as well. It has drafted a document that explains its mission and vision, its role within the institution, a blueprint for intra-divisional relationships and connections, and a programming calendar that attempts comprehensively to concretize its aspirations through various programs. Moreover, it seems to be driven by an appropriate commitment to student learning and strives to do so in a way that accounts for a Christian view of life. You should ask to see it while you are here.

I am also fairly confident, however, that others among us have less peace about these questions of identity, mission, and reflective practice. Should we mostly be about providing services to students? After all, the "servant thing" sounds pretty Christian. Or, maybe student-affairs is most appropriately a branch of the campus ministry, Bible, and security departments, whereby our job is largely about helping students grow in their Bible knowledge, moral integrity, and overall spirituality outside of the classroom in deference to not being able to have each student's pastor make a daily or weekly visit? Or, maybe we have been persuaded by conversations and treatises within the larger student affairs profession and are attempting to redefine our tasks within the context of student learning, with a view toward recognizing that how we define the principles and goals of student learning cannot be disassociated from our Christian starting point.

Three comments are worth noting here. First, as I said as I began the last paragraph, some among us may honestly be struggling with our professional and institutional posture. Second, I sense that we have each of the three views that I have just mentioned present among us, as well as other approaches and combinations of approaches. And, third, notwithstanding that I believe that student learning is the appropriate context for our work, I lament that we have talked so little about it within this association. Insofar as we do not know much about the student learning movement much less consider it to be the focus of our efforts—being careful to note that we must provide particular nuance to it given our Christian faith—I think we are missing an opportunity for greater faithfulness in our professional capacities. And, if we continue to ignore the primacy of student learning for our work, perhaps we are more deserving than I thought of the derisive "fun and games" label that our academic affairs counterparts sometimes attribute to us.

The more important point, however, is that the conference this year is fashioned to provide good and abundant opportunities to talk about these issues with one another. They are absolutely central to developing and sustaining a clearer sense of who we are, what we do, and why we do it. In the same way that some scholars are promoting the idea of "teaching circles," where faculty within and across departments come together to talk informally but honestly about what to teach and how to teach, may I suggest that during this conference and beyond, we form "student development/student learning circles" (or whatever you would call them) to examine what, how, and why we do what we do with students outside of the classroom. Perhaps, as the Caterpillar advised earlier, we stand to benefit from the various "signs" that we may notice throughout this conference as we become resources for one another and as we "disciple" one another at this conference and on our respective campuses toward greater faithfulness in our important profession.

This leads me to a second potential blind spot: the relative strength of our ongoing professional development. While I feel fairly confident that the Chief Student Development Officers of the Council of Christian Colleges and Universities institutions provide some, if not significant, ongoing professional stimulation for one another within their cohort, I am less sanguine about the extent of professional growth opportunities for many of the rest of us...excluding on the job training day after day. Further, to be honest, I think that ACSD, including its conferences, publications, and chatline, heavily emphasizes, to borrow from its constitution again, "provid[ing] opportunity for Christian fellowship and exchange of ideas," and ostensibly downplays the first part of this first stated purpose, namely, "to promote professional growth."

Although there may be some among us that are less than convinced that professional development opportunities have any relevance much less impact on professional practice, I remain concerned that we receive some—if not significant—training for and about our efforts via this association and our respective institutions. In fact, given that we are Christians in the field, I might argue that we have twice as much work to expend in this regard since we must "translate" information and resources that we take in through a Christian lens. Are we aware of, if not systemically reviewing, relevant journals and/or magazines in our field? Do we have any exposure to professional associations besides ACSD? Are we connected electronically or otherwise to professional networks for the sharing of perspectives, practices, and programs? Are we relatively current with larger issues within the postsecondary field and do we have ready resources that we depend upon to provide such currency? Are we networking with colleagues to assist us in day-to-day tasks regarding philosophical foundations, policy formation, professional practice, and the like? And, finally, regarding each of these questions, do we have strategies in place to help us wrestle with these articles, books, case studies, presentations, experiences, practices, and the like from a Christian point of view? If we do not have affirmative and affirming responses to these kinds of questions, we are simply Christians working in jobs at colleges. Similarly, if we have affirmative and affirming responses to the former questions but not an affirmative and affirming response to the latter question, we are Christian professionals working in the field of student affairs, but we are neglecting to explore the possibility of a "Christian student affairs" or, stated another way, of "doing student affairs Christianly."

Perhaps the virtual absence of our "voice" within the larger student affairs profession, the relative lack of substantive conversations among ourselves regarding professional foundations and practice, and the dearth of dialog and resources within our association about "doing the profession Christianly" stand as signs that our ongoing professional development has been wanting. Consider the following: 1) ACSD has been silent on the student learning conversations within the profession, personally and organizationally; 2) last year at the ACSD conference at Asbury College, many, if not a majority of, conference participants decided to forego a scheduled panel discussion, about which I am not alone in believing was one of the most important sessions in ACSD history; 3) the book, *Student Affairs Reconsidered: A*

Christian View of the Profession and its Contexts,[5] has provoked relatively little conversation, has generated even less usage, and some—maybe many—are not aware of its existence, despite the fact that it is written by eight ACSD members and represents the *only* book that examines a thoughtful, Christian view of student affairs and student learning; 4) the new book that I mentioned earlier, *State of the Art of Preparation and Practice in Student Affairs* does not mention ACSD in a listing of student affairs-related professional associations; and 5) there has not been one, single comment—positive, negative, stupid, or brilliant—on the ACSD chatline relating to either Bob Reed' s article or my article in the last two *Koinonia* publications. At the expense of having to agree with my good friend Bob Reed, perhaps his words contain more truth than I originally hoped—he is worth quoting at length:

> Too many of us have become intellectually lazy, unwilling to grapple with difficult concepts...Christian student development people...have a responsibility to think and think and think. [We] have been poor stewards of [our] vocation by ignoring significant research and ideas that explain reality in ways that can make [us] much better at [our] craft...And, in some cases, perhaps many, Christians in student development have not even wrestled with what it means to be just that: a Christian in the field of student development.[6]

One final blind spot before I move on to several recommendations. This last blind spot has something to do with what I call "the enigma of the ACSD member who works at a secular institution." These "mutants" confuse us, and we are not quite sure what to do with them. We certainly allow them to come since they meet the basic membership requirements and we create space for them to be a subset of the organization. But we desperately hope that they will not ask the association how they should go about pursuing the second purpose of the organization on their campuses, namely, "to integrate the use of scripture and the Christian faith in the student development profession."

Herein, the blind spot is revealed: Our identity as Christian student affairs professionals "works" provided that we are Christians and work at Christian colleges. Stated another way, our distinctiveness as "Christian student affairs professionals" is determined through a simple formula: "we are Christians" + "we work at Christian colleges" + "we work in student affairs" = "we are Christian student affairs professionals." In this sense, we use the adjective Christian more as a descriptor of us personally and of our colleges institutionally rather than as the wellspring from which we understand and enact our vocation as student affairs professionals. Thus, because those who work at secular institutions do not work at Christian colleges, this particular ACSD organizational purpose of "integration" makes little sense; as it is stated, the purpose seems to be possible only if one is a Christian at a Christian college. I would also argue, however, that it ostensibly has little meaning for those who work at Christian colleges beyond reminding us that Christians use scripture and have faith. Because we place the greatest emphasis of the organization on what one believes and where one works and concomitantly downplay the possibility of seeing what we do and how and why we do it within the framework of a comprehensive Christian worldview, we not only do not know exactly what to do with those weird folk who work at secular institutions, but we also are not completely sure how the "Christian thing" and the "work thing" relate in our own work at Christian colleges.

Several Recommendations

As I close, then, I offer several ideas for us to consider, as departments of particular campuses and also as an organization. Several suggestions for our respective departments: First, if you do not already have one in place, draft a mission statement for your department. A few hints along the way: It should be complementary to your institution' s mission statement, it should resonate with the larger learning enterprise of the institution, it should be clear about being a distinctive Christian approach, it should include comment about the collaborative nature of work intra-departmentally and inter-departmentally, and it should be "doable."

Second, if you do not already have it in place, add criteria to your staff review processes regarding two things: first, a rationale for and the extent to which each staff member's efforts are learning-oriented; and, second, an explanation of the ways in which his or her efforts are shaped by a Christian point of view. Further, perhaps in the same way that faculty members at many of our institutions are required to submit an integration paper for promotion and/or tenure proceedings (i.e., a paper detailing how he/she understands faith-shaped learning *vis-à-vis* his/her discipline), perhaps we should require one another to draft integration papers as well, outlining how it is that our work has not only been learning-centered but distinctively Christian, too.

Third, we should be more engaged more regularly in the literature about our field and beyond. Simply being a subscriber to the *NASPA Journal* and *The Chronicle of Higher Education* does not get either of them read. Likewise, simply reading the *NASPA Journal* and *The Chronicle* without any attempt to relate them to our work or to interpret them within a Christian framework does not strengthen either our professional expertise or our resolve to do our work Christianly. And, if you don't know what the *NASPA Journal* and *The Chronicle* are, in the words of the immortal Gomer Pyle, "shame, shame, shame."

And, fourth—and related to the third—we must simply talk more with one another regarding our work around questions such as: What have you been reading lately related to your work? How would you critique this article from a Christian perspective? Can you help me to figure out how to implement this useful idea? How are Christian student affairs professionals alike and/or different from their counterparts who make no such claim to the Christian faith? What is our appropriate connection to faculty on campus? How might we work more and better together? As I stated earlier, in the same way that faculty members are being challenged to form "teaching circles" to discuss pedagogy and more, perhaps, on our campuses and over the next few days, we should consider the development of "student affairs circles" or, more particularly "residence life circles," "student activities circles," and "counseling circles."

Now, just a few recommendations for us as an organization. First, ACSD should review its mission statement contained in the Constitution with an eye toward clarity and amplification. While some words and phrases contained therein are relatively self-evident and generally "happen" among us—such as "Christian fellowship," "exchange of ideas," and the provision of "various services"—other words and phrases in the mission statement are substantially less clear and may not be operationalized as much as we like, the way that we like, or at all! Moreover, as I mentioned earlier, perhaps the document should better account for how things such as "promot[ing] professional growth" and "integrat[ing] the use of scripture and the Christian faith in the student development profession" are differentiated, relative to whether a person works at a Christian college or some other kind of college. At the very least, and perhaps most important, I believe that more simply needs to be said in the document regarding what is actually intended by these apparently important but, as currently written, arcane purposes.

Second, ACSD should consider drafting a "Principles of Christian Professional Practice" statement to include in the Constitution. To include a doctrinal statement but not a professional practice statement, to my mind, makes ACSD more of a para-church organization than a Christian professionals association. Then again, perhaps the presence of a doctrinal statement but the absence of professional practice statement provides a clue as to why we feel more comfortable about, do better with, and more to say with respect to fellowship and membership services compared to student learning and faith/work integration. Whatever the case, from my perspective, a statement such as the one that I am suggesting, that identifies our distinctiveness with respect to professional persona and practice would go a long way toward helping us define ourselves as well as helping others outside of the Christian faith understand who in the world we are.

Finally, ACSD, as an organization, should become part of the national conversation about student learning. As I stated in my recent article in *Koinonia*, in the midst of what many consider a redefining moment, a Christian voice should not be silent. Rather, ACSD should seize this opportunity to offer a Christian perspective on student learning. Such an initiative, if developed, not only would provide a rallying point for members of the organization, but also may help to reduce the confusion among our non-Christian counterparts regarding who it is that we are and what it is that we do.

Conclusion

In the introduction to the book that several ACSD colleagues and myself worked on over the last three or four years, I wrote about our two deepest hopes in writing it, as follows:

> First, that both Christians and those unfamiliar with Christian faith will recognize...that Christian faith involves more than Sunday service; rather it is a viable wellspring of thoughts and actions, in both public and private spheres, and is clearly within our work as educators. And, second, that those familiar with Christian faith who are also involved in higher education may become more engaged and empowered to undertake their efforts with the understanding that programs offered, classes taught, discipline dispensed, committees formed, counseling offered, friendships nurtured, policies framed, colleagues hired, and so on, are the very arenas in which Christian faith must take shape by God's grace and for God's glory.[7]

I hope that the conference that Calvin has planned and in which you are participating will challenge us mightily in these regards, as individually and organizationally we make strides toward professional faithfulness for Jesus' sake.

Notes

[1]*Koinonia* was the magazine/newsletter of the Association for Christians in Student Development professional organization.

[2]ACSD continues to have a Constitution and Bylaws. However, they have been revised eight times since I made this presentation. As a result, references in this document may not correspond with the most recent version, which can be found at the ACSD website (http://www.acsd.org/).

[3]R. Hughes and W. Adrian, *Models for Christian Higher Education: Strategies for Survival and Success in the Twenty-First Century* (Grand Rapids, MI: Wm. B. Eerdmans Publishing Company, 1997).

[4]R. Young, "Epilogue: A Heretical Bit of Whimsy," in N. Evans and C. Tobin (eds.), *State of the Art in Preparation and Practice in Student Affairs* (Lanham, MD: University Press of America, 1998), 239-249; 239-240.

[5]D. Guthrie (ed.), *Student Affairs Reconsidered: A Christian View of the Profession and its Contexts* (Lanham, MD: University Press of America, 1997).

[6]Back issue of *Koinonia* unavailable for reference.

[7]D. Guthrie, "Introduction," in D. Guthrie (ed.) *Student Affairs Reconsidered: A Christian View of the Profession and Its Contexts* (Lanham, MD: University Press of American, 1997), ix-xii; xi-xii.

CHAPTER 9

What Matters in Student Development?

For my friend, Bob Reed, who helped me to understand the hand with which I write best.
This essay was presented as the opening plenary address for the Association for Christians in Student Development annual conference at Messiah University on June 8, 2010.

Introduction

I am deeply honored to be here. My sincere thanks to the ACSD 2010 planning committee for their kind invitation to me to participate. I must admit to some reticence to offer my remarks since I haven't been in a student affairs role for 13 years now; I am a student affairs has-been. If it is any consolation, I would like to think that students' development has nonetheless been central to my efforts for those same 13 years.

I am going to suggest four things that must matter to student affairs professionals. I realize that, on any given day, all kinds of things matter to us—all kinds of things are on our to-do lists. But, at least for right now, I am less interested in rudimentary to-do lists than I am in what I consider to be four things that must shape and guide our to-do lists. The big four are: students, our institutions, the profession of student affairs, and Christian faith. Listen and see what you think.

Students

Students must matter to us as student affairs professionals. They are the particular focus of our efforts in the academy. We want them to come to our institutions, and we want them to graduate from our institutions; we want them to learn and we want them to mature; we want to befriend them, we want to nurture them, and we want to challenge them; we want them to conform to the image of Christ more and more, and we want them to sign-post the kingdom of God in the world for Jesus' sake. Oh, yes, students matter to us. You might say that they are "what we're about." You might say that we want them to become our glory!

What I would like to suggest this morning, however, is that we invest in understanding the students at our institutions more fully. I offer this suggestion for two reasons. First, investing in understanding students at our institutions more fully may assist us in conceiving and enacting intentional co-curricular strategies. And, second, investing in understanding students at our institutions more fully may offer us an opportunity to engage our faculty colleagues in a more productive, mutually beneficial way.

What do I mean by investing in understanding students at our institutions more fully? Well, just this: I think that we would do well to examine some literature written about college-aged persons on a regular basis. In turn, based on what we read and what we make of what we read, our ongoing work with and on behalf of students would chart particular courses. Let me explain by using four fairly current books, each of which is a study of contemporary young adults, the very folks with whom most of us spend considerable time. The four books are: *Souls in Transition* by Christian Smith[1]; *The First Year Out* by Tim Clydesdale[2]; *The Narcissism Epidemic* by Jean Twenge and Keith Campbell[3]; and, *The Dumbest Generation* by Mark Bauerlein.[4]

In *The Dumbest Generation*, author Mark Bauerlein laments the stupefying of young adults as they become more and more intoxicated with the wonders of the digital age. Bauerlein notes:

> The bedroom [or the dorm room?] is no longer [just] a sanctuary, it's a command center. E-mails, text messages, blog postings and comments, phone calls, tweets, feeds, photos, and songs pour in...and if kids don't respond, they fall behind...Even when logged off and disconnected, they sense that a buddy...may be talking about them, passing around an image, setting a rendezvous, amplifying gossip, or leaving a message...Peer contact never ends, and digital tools are as essential and ordinary as food and air and sleep.[5]

The ubiquity of digital technology available to and regularly used by young adults also involves what might be called collateral damage. For example, I cannot imagine that our faculty colleagues would jump for joy in knowing that, according to Bauerlein's research, 55% of high school students spend one hour or less reading or studying per week, and, that 54% of first year college students report that they disagree with the statement: "I get a great deal of satisfaction from reading."[6]

Of course, Bauerline's is just one book on the impact of technology on children and young adults. What I am suggesting, however, is that if students matter to us—and they do—doesn't it make some sense to read at least one book about what not only matters dearly to them (i.e., technology in all of its manifestations), but the ways in which technology may have shaped them prior to their arrival on campus. In turn, to what extent does technology, its use and its impact, become a point of entry for the development of co-curricular programming, for a review of institutional policies, for informal yet purposeful cafeteria conversation, for a joint faculty and student development personnel workshop, and the like.

Jean Twenge's book, *The Narcissism Epidemic*, suggests that we are living in an unprecedented era of self-admiration.

Said another way, an ethos of entitlement is widespread, and commonly resides in young adults, including those who have made their way to our institutions. According to Twenge, cultural forces as diverse as the family, the media, technology, easy credit, the commercialization of goods and services, and the church routinely bombard young adults with the same message: You are just so very special; in fact, you must be the center of the universe. The result is that narcissistic self-centeredness supplants self-effacing self-esteem and enthrones entitlement as the to-be-expected reality for young adults. Listen to just one example that Twenge utilizes, one with direct, obvious relevance for colleges and universities:

> Two-thirds of students believed their professor should give them special consideration if they explained they were trying hard (apparently missing the point that grades are given for performance, not just for trying!). One-third believed they deserved at least a B just for attending class. And—perhaps most incredible—one-third thought they should be able to reschedule their final exam if it interfered with their vacation plans.[7]

What I am suggesting is that if students matter to us—and they do—doesn't it make sense to consider the extent to which they have drunk deeply from the well of entitlement. And, doesn't it make sense that, especially Christian colleges and/or Christian educators, would be resolute to undertake learning projects that intentionally set out to eschew entitlement? If so, what co-curricular programming might we envision and implement, what informal yet purposeful cafeteria conversations might we have, and how might we work collaboratively with our formal curriculum partners to deliver an educational experience that is rooted in another version of reality that rejects narcissism and entitlement in favor of the notion that one must lose her life to save her life.

A third relevant book that I would like to mention is Christian Smith's *Souls in Transition*, which largely focuses on how

18-23-year-olds in the US understand and express religiosity and spirituality. In Chapter Two, Smith summarizes more than 30 general characteristics of this age group. Several of these characteristics seem to have significant import for our work as Christian educators. Please listen closely to this partial list:

1. Emerging adults expressed stress and overwhelm with trying to "figure things out."[8]
2. "Many [emerging adults] are stinging with the hurts of living problemed lives in what seems [to them] like a broken world[,] and are still working on recovering."[9]
3. Emerging adults say that they are "unable to know the real truth of anything beyond themselves."[10] Or, said another way, "The absolute authority for every person's beliefs or actions is his or her own sovereign self."[11]
4. Emerging adults consider college important for two reasons, and two reasons alone: its instrumental value (getting a job, making more money), and for the fun they can have there.
5. Emerging adults have no qualms whatsoever with being materialistic consumers.
6. Emerging adults frequently "do not really know where they stand or how they relate to a lot of the people they interact with,"[12] particularly in what might be called romantic relationships.

Once more, I am suggesting that if students matter to us—and they do—would it make some sense to examine Smith's research on emerging adults with an eye toward evaluating the extent to which his findings may coalesce with the emerging adults who happen to matriculate to our institutions? And, then, if the students at our institutions *do*, in fact, resemble the emerging adults that Smith studied, and precisely because students do matter to us, does it not seem reasonable to make haste to implement, strengthen and/or augment co-curricular programming that is intent on engaging students on these issues; does it not seem reasonable to make haste to craft our casual cafeteria conversations to engage students intentionally on these issues; and, does it not seem reasonable to make haste to concoct creative interchanges with our faculty colleagues about these issues such that our corporate and individual efforts may be more clear and more difference-making.

The final book example is Tim Clydesdale's *The First Year Out*. Clydesdale studied students from their senior year of high school through their first year of college. What he concluded was that many, if not most, mainstream first-year college students spend a vast majority of their time on two things: first, managing interpersonal relationships, particularly with their peers; and, second, maximizing personal gratifications including entertainment, technology, food, and clothing. What these students are virtually uninterested in pursuing in earnest is coming to terms with their civic, political, intellectual, religious, racial, and gender identities. They store away those identities—such as they are at the moment—in secure "lockboxes" until later…if later ever comes. In fact, according to Clydesdale, they postpone engaging these identities, at least in part, because they believe that doing so may interfere with their inexorable pursuit of personal happiness and personal fulfillment. Clydesdale concludes:

> [The vast majority of teen American that I studied] have narrowed their perspectives to the private worlds that they can capably and efficiently manage and left the wider world to its own devices… Lacking [any kind of] broader perspective that meaningfully links their private worlds to local communities, national issues, and global realities leaves these teens charting the course of their lives with dated and erroneous cultural maps. Some will therefore run aground, others will be lost at sea, still others will land in an undesirable place…we do possess the resources to begin the correction process and the capacity to alert teens to flaws in their maps. It is a question of how many adults have the will to start…[13]

Indeed. If students matter to us—and they do—and if students at our institutions seem to fit Clydesdale's description, and if we believe that Christian faith has implications far beyond effective life management skills and far different than pursuing and achieving personal happiness and comfort, then does it not seem worthwhile to consider co-curricular programming that will embrace and engage students on Clydesdale's findings? Does it not seem worthwhile to ensure that our serendipitous interchanges with students are somehow informed by Clydesdale's findings? And, does it not seem worthwhile to invite constructive dialog with our faculty counterparts regarding Clydesdale's findings to the end that we may collectively and collaboratively "have the will to start" to understand and to address the realities that our students may bring with them to our campuses?

Our Institution

Our institution must matter to us as student affairs professionals. For those of you in more senior level positions, I suspect that this comes as a simple truism of sorts. That is, if your role involves cabinet meetings and/or budget bickering, you know that institutions matter—or, at least that their survival as organizations matters. What leads me to make a big deal of the point that our institutions must matter to us as student affairs professionals, however, is my nagging sense that the default setting for many of us, particularly those younger than 35 or so is simply to steer clear of institutions of any kind, at least as much as is possible. Certainly notions of relying on institutions or investing in institutions or trusting in institutions or giving our lives to serving institutions—all because we somehow believe that we won't be able to understand what it means to be fully human or fully part of the way that God created the world unless we do—seem at best unrealistic, if not laughable altogether.

Allow me to suggest several reasons that may shed light on our institutional-avoidance dispositions. As you will notice, the subtext for each of the reasons that I offer is that it is simply easier *not* to be concerned about institutions in general. So, first, many of us have come to believe that all institutions are too complicated, too impersonal, too technical, or too bureaucratic. We consider them to be, in the words of sociologist Robert Bellah, simply "over our heads,"[14] way beyond our comprehension much less investment without significant amounts of time and energy. The institution of civil government is a good example here. Regardless of where you stood on the recent health care debate, it most likely wasn't because you had taken the time to read the report; it was way too technical; it was way too long; it was way too obtuse. It was easier just to have a personal opinion. Closer to home, I wonder if the comment, "My job is just to love the students in my residence hall," though certainly sincere, belies a culturally-reinforced inability or unwillingness to recognize that loving students in a residence takes shape best, in my view, to the extent that it occurs in concert with other institutional efforts to do the same.

A second reason for our allergy about institutions is that many of us have come to know that institutions may cause significant personal pain. All of you can see the faces of persons that you know for whom the institution of the family has perpetrated unthinkable distress and lasting damage. All of you can see the faces of persons that you know for whom the institution of education means anything except cultivating curiosity and wonder and an interest in becoming wise. And, all of you can see the faces of persons that you know for whom the institution of church has created deep cynicism or moribund religiosity. In each case, you know in your heart of hearts that the very institutions that are intended by the Lord to contribute richly and routinely to human flourishing can do just the opposite—they can destroy people. So, why bother with them at all?

A final reason that I would like to suggest for our reticence to invest in institutions is that many have come to believe that disparate subworlds are not only the best we can hope for given the complexity of institutions and the painfulness that they may cause, but a subworlds approach is simply also the regnant *modus operandi* of the contemporary academy, divisions are normative, parts of wholes are not really expected to work coherently, a balkanized academy is the way things are supposed to be, silos are standard procedure in institutions. In fact, is it really all that necessary for units even in the same department or division to collaborate on common goals? I mean, do residence life and campus ministries really have to take the time to partner when they each have so much of "their own" work to do?

Notwithstanding our concerns with institutions that arise from reasons that I have mentioned or for other reasons that you may have, I want to be clear that we must find ways to demonstrate that if our institutions matters to us—not just our own programs or projects, not just our own office or building, and not just our own unit or division—we must make the time, as part of our jobs, to understand and to appreciate our institution more thoroughly and more fully, including its people, its offices and departments, its programs and projects, its processes and policies, its history and ethos, its glories and glitches, and its hopes and future.

In their recent book *Beyond Homelessness: Christian Faith in a Culture of Displacement*,[15] co-authors Steven Bouma-Prediger and Brian Walsh consider the metaphors of home and homelessness as lenses through which to examine contemporary culture. I wonder if these metaphors may also be instructive for considering our institutions. As I have intimated already, institutions certainly can be characterized by the vacuity and dysfunction of homelessness as such. But I wonder if we might also do well to imagine institutions as homes of a sort, in which persons regularly experience, in the words of the authors, "identity, connectedness, order, and care"[16] and "the point of orientation around which all else makes sense."[17] Moreover, I think it was Peter Garland who suggested in a monograph years ago that student affairs practitioners contribute most effectively to institutional vitality to the extent that they serve as integrators of the college-wide experience, particularly for students. If Garland is right, how would our work as student affairs be different than it is now? That is, if our primary task—irrespective of particular role in a student affairs division—was to help students (and maybe even the entire institution) weave together all of the parts of the learning experience regularly, sensibly, and coherently, what programs would we dream up? What offices would we invent? What budget would we submit? What cafeteria conversations would we intentionally initiate? What resources would our divisional website include? Who would we get to know better on campus and how? What in the world would we do if institutional coherence and wholeness and integration mattered most?

The Profession

The student affairs profession must matter to us as student affairs professionals. I will say at the outset that I am somewhat nervous about making this claim because I do not want us to fall prey to a certain kind of professionalism. That is, I am in no way interested in pursuing or embracing a vocational neo-Gnosticism in which we become enamored with honing and flaunting "our own" vocabulary and "our own" theories and "our own" methodologies and "our own" journals and "our own" professional preparation trajectories and "our own" handshakes…all of which result in us being isolated within our institutions in "our own-ness." As I have already intimated, far too much of that kind of professionalism already resides in the academy in the form of autonomous academic departments and their respective "unique" or "special" faculty. I do not want to ignore the fact that student affairs has been, and continues to be, marginalized, ignored, taken for granted, demeaned, and/or treated as "extra" educational at plenty of institutions, including institutions represented by this gathering. I am simply suggesting that for student affairs professionals to adopt the problem as the solution to the problem reinforces and perpetuates the problem rather than eliminates it.

So, then, what am I advocating when I suggest that the student affairs profession must matter to us as student affairs professionals? Well, I am advocating that we view our profession as an office. I am not talking about the kind of office that has walls and tables and chairs and files where we hold meetings and respond to email. Instead, I am talking about office as inhabiting a place in which one has the honor of fulfilling important obligations with integrity for the good of others, in league with others, and to the end that the deepest hopes of the organization may be more fully manifest. Listen to scholar Hugh Heclo's explanation of office seen in this light:

> [The concept of office]…is about occupying, not a physical place, but a moral space in society…[It]…indicates the performance of a task, with heavy overtones of a duty to perform properly…There is therefore a fiduciary quality in office-holding that is missing from job-doing…This means acting out of an underlying loyalty to the purpose or purposes that lie behind there being such a job in the first place. It is the difference between acting a part and fulfilling the responsibilities of a position.… an office-oriented view…entails the obligation actually to *be* something.[18]

It strikes me that the implications of such a view make a difference. We are positioned by, we are set in place by (notice the passive voice here), our profession and our institution and ultimately by the Lord to *be* something and to *do* something that will really matter. And, so as not to miss it, it is demanded of us that we come to understand more fully and more deeply and more clearly what those somethings are that really matter! Further, we invest ourselves relentlessly to grow in our understanding of those things, because to do otherwise is to vacate our office and to hinder progress toward those somethings that really matter.

So, then, how do we proceed in these regards? Let me suggest just two ideas:

1. Read. I hope that I am wrong, but I fear that student affairs professionals don't read intentionally enough and/or simply enough; we much prefer action and doing. Now, I fully agree that action and doing are absolutely crucial. But, in the context of office that I have just highlighted, I wonder if our actions and our doings would be strengthened and enhanced and perhaps even made more effective, if they were shaped at least a little bit by ideas in addition to our innate energies and endearing personalities. So, bear with me; I am requesting that you don't just do something, but that you simply stand there for a moment. What should you read? I think that it seems reasonable to read in several areas. First, read things about students. Second, read things about your particular office. That is, if you are an RD, read about residence life; if you are an admissions counselor, read about college admissions; if you are a multicultural education coordinator, read about multicultural education; and so on. Third, read things about student affairs more broadly. For example, later this month a new book will hit the shelves written by a long-time friend, Marilyn Amey, and two of her colleagues, Linda Kuk and Jim Banning. It is called *Positioning Student Affairs for Sustainable Change*.[19] I am not suggesting that you read the whole book necessarily. I am simply suggesting that you know that the book exists and that perhaps you read one chapter in it. Fourth, read things about college student learning, including success stories, exemplary practices, innovative approaches, and the like. Fifth, read things about higher education more broadly. Sixth, read things about Christian higher education more broadly, particularly if you work in a Christian college or university, and with a particular eye toward understanding the ways that Christian faith sources and shapes knowing, learning and professional practice. Seventh, read some Christian theology, philosophy, biblical studies, or church history. I will say a bit more about this in a moment in a slightly different context. And eighth, read good novels, novels that have the power to grow your imagination. I think that, particularly in our day, we stand to benefit from cultivating more fertile imaginations. Now, I know what you're thinking: How am I possibly going to *do my job* if I have to read all of this? Well, here's all I'm suggesting that, over the next year, a) you scan *the Chronicle of Higher Education* for 30 minutes once a month; b) you read two essays in the *Christian Scholar's Review*; and c) you read a novel. If you do that, we're good.

2. Converse with one another about office. The good news is that I think we generally like each other, and we likewise enjoy talking with one another about all kinds of things. But I want to offer three suggestions for how to converse. First, schedule regular opportunities (i.e., once a semester, once a month) for those within the student affairs division to talk about the office. You may want to utilize the various categories that I provided above to organize areas within which to read to do so. Second, consider ways to meet and to interact with educators outside of the student affairs division about office. For example, identify a panel of faculty to converse with students in your residence hall about what they wish they had understood when they went to college. Or, invite admissions personnel to an event to discuss an overview of Tim Clydesdale's *The First Year Out.* Or, create and maintain a web page on your institution's website called something like "Investments in Learning," and invite division members and non-division members to submit things for it. And, third, consider ways to interact about office with student affairs counterparts at other institutions in your region. This could take various forms, of course, but I believe that we have much to gain from the cross-fertilization of ideas and strategies across institutions. My sense is that such an approach was/is behind establishing ACSD regions at one time, but I would suggest not necessarily limiting these efforts to other ACSD institutions alone.

Christian Faith

Christian faith must matter to us as student affairs professionals. To be clear, I have every confidence that we have come to believe that, as the Heidelberg Catechism puts it, "Our only comfort in life and in death is that we that we are not our own but belong—body and soul, in life and in death—to our faithful Savior Jesus Christ."[20] What I am less confident about—if only because I know my own shortcomings in this regard—is our success in understanding the implications of the lordship of Jesus Christ for all else. If it is true that "He's got the whole world in His hands"—and you and I believe that to be the case—then what must I be and do as a son, a spouse, and a parent? What must I be and do as a parishioner, a citizen, and a professor? If it is true that Christian faith is intended to be socially relevant in addition to being privately engaging, if Christian faith is intended to be a totalizing faith rather than a compartmentalized faith, if Christian faith is intended to be as much about Jesus as Lord of all as it is about Jesus as "my" savior, then what are the ramifications for student affairs professionals who have pledged their allegiance to Jesus?

Three recent books have challenged me to redouble my efforts in considering my faith-sourced and faith-shaped efforts in the academy. I hope that my brief comments about each may provide similar prodding for you. The first is Stanley Hauerwas' *The State of the University*.[21] Hauerwas wonders if Christian colleges may be graduating "students who are unable to recognize when they are serving powers foreign to the Gospel."[22] I am quite certain that Hauerwas' concern is clearly reflected in the sentiment of Jamie Smith when he wonders in his new book, *Desiring the Kingdom*,[23] the extent to which: "Christian colleges and universities generate an army of alumni who look pretty much like all the rest of their suburban neighbors, except that our graduates drive their SUVs, inhabit their executive homes, and pursue the frenetic life of the middle class and the corporate ladder 'from a Christian perspective.'"[24] Returning to Hauerwas for succinct summary: "The challenge is whether any of us live lives as Christians that are sufficient to force us to think differently about what is and is not done"[25] in the academy and beyond. Hauerwas challenged me and perhaps will challenge us to consider how we might become more faithful heralds—apprenticed well in "the knowledge of God" through our faith traditions, churches, and in the scriptures—as we muse about and as we implement plans, practices, and programs in our institutions.

The second book that provided a wake-up call for me is a book called *Divided by Faith*[26] by Michael Emerson and Christian Smith. The authors contend that many evangelical Christians overemphasize pragmatic or utilitarian action and personal relationships to the extent that they overlook careful, cultural analysis and engagement. The result, and the focus of their book, is that evangelical Christians, by their actions and inactions, have historically "done more to perpetuate the racial divide"[27] even though their rhetoric suggests a "[sincere] desire to end racial division and inequality."[28] Emerson's and Smith's argument is similar to Hauerwas' argument: Because they understand the gospel as assent to particular doctrine alone, or to personal piety alone, or to saving souls alone, kind, well-meaning, church-going, interested-in-faithfulness Christians can vacate a concern for understanding ways in which the gospel may have relevance and power for understanding and for shaping life within all parts of society's fabric.

The last book that I would like to mention is *Christianity and Moral Identity in Higher Education*, by Perry Glanzer and Todd Ream.[29] This book is not principally concerned with what is typically referred to as moral development theory. Rather, its thesis is that many colleges and universities have jettisoned any viable, orienting moral tradition from which "to educate students about the good, form their love for the good, and encourage them to do the good."[30] Instead, many institutions simply employ pragmatic versions of the good, ones that reduce the nature of persons to their professional, political, or personal dimensions alone. The authors go on to posit that Christian colleges and universities may have something profoundly better to offer precisely at this point to the extent that they tap the Christian moral tradition in general and particular faith traditions in particular in pursuing educational visions of the good that—by virtue of being animated by these robust, totalizing traditions—are more completely human.

Just so. This is what each of these books have reminded me of, namely, that the gospel is totalizing—by it and through it we are to see and to understand and to live all else. Abundant life should mean nothing less! And so, yes indeed, Christian faith must matter—must really matter—to us as student affairs professionals.

Conclusion

What matters to us as student affairs professionals? I have suggested four things: Students, Our Institutions, The Profession,
and Christian Faith. Irrespective of how long the Lord has had
you in this work, I sincerely hope that my comments have been
appropriately challenging, helpfully suggestive, and sufficiently
motivational. Our commitments, our investments, our efforts
matter; there is something significant to be lost if we are not "all
in" in the offices to which God has called us. In his recent book,[31]
Calvin College philosophy professor James K.A. Smith suggests
that colleges and "universities are for lovers," that what educators
ultimately love will be reflected in why and how they attempt
to form students' loves. I pray that our ultimate love for Jesus
and His kingdom will grow deeper and higher and longer and
wider to the end that our love for students, and for our institutions, and for the profession—and our efforts to shape students'
loves—might bring honor to the One who loved first.

Notes

[1]C. Smith, *Souls in Transition: The Religious and Spiritual Lives of Emerging Adults* (New York, NY: Oxford University Press, 2009).

[2]T. Clydesdale, *The First Year Out: Understanding American Teens After High School* (Chicago, IL: University of Chicago Press, 2007).

[3]J. Twenge and W. Campbell, *The Narcissism Epidemic: Living in the Age of Entitlement* (New York, NY: Atria Books, 2010).

[4]M. Bauerline, *The Dumbest Generation: How the Digital Age Stupefies Young Americans and Jeopardizes Our Future (Or, Don 't Trust Anyone Under 30)* (New York, NY: TarcherPerigee, 2009).

[5]Ibid., x.

[6]Ibid., 52-53.

[7]Twenge, 232.

[8]C. Smith, 35.

[9]Ibid., 38.

[10]Ibid., 45.

[11]Ibid., 49.

[12]Ibid., 58.

[13]Clydesdale, 200.

[14]R. Bellah, R. Madsen, W. Sullivan, A. Swidler, and S. Tipton, *The Good Society* (New York, NY: Vintage Books, 1992), 19.

[15]S. Bouma-Prediger and B. Walsh, *Beyond Homelessness: Christian Faith in a Culture of Displacement* (Grand Rapids, MI: Eerdmans, 2008).

[16]Ibid., 62.

[17]Ibid., 65.

[18]H. Heclo, *On Thinking Institutionally* (New York, NY: Oxford University Press, 2011), 136-137; 139; 141-142.

[19]L. Kuk, J. Banning, and M. Amey, *Positioning Student Affairs for Sustainable Change: Achieving Organizational Effectiveness Through Multiple Perspectives* (New York, NY: Stylus Publishing, 2010).

[20]G.W. Richards, *The Heidelberg Catechism: Historical and Doctrinal Studies* (Philadelphia: Publication and Sunday School Board of the Reformed Church in the United States, 1913).

[21]S. Hauerwas, *The State of the University: Academic Knowledges and the Knowledge of God* (Hoboken, NJ: Wiley Blackwell, 2007).

[22]Ibid., 124.

[23]J. Smith, *Desiring the Kingdom: Worship, Worldview, and Cultural Formation* (Grand Rapids, MI: Baker Academic, 2009).

[24]Ibid., 213.

[25]Hauerwas, 32.

[26]M. Emerson and C. Smith, *Divided by Faith: Evangelical Religion and the Problem of Race in America* (New York, NY: Oxford University Press, 2001).

[27]Ibid., ix.

[28]Ibid.

[29]P. Glanzer and T. Ream, *Christianity and Moral Identity in Higher Education* (New York, NY: Palgrave Macmillan, 2009).

[30]Ibid., 227.

[31]Smith, *Desiring the Kingdom.*

CHAPTER 10

Student Conduct: Balancing Expectation and Motivation

This essay was prepared for the annual meeting of the John Henry Newman Society in Washington DC in November 2002.

Introduction

Rules and regulations governing campus life have been present since the earliest beginnings of American higher education. And, though the rationales for and contents of these codes have changed since the 17th century—as well as the relative nature and seriousness of actual student misconduct—I think that most will agree that at least the idea of addressing student conduct continues to be important, perhaps even necessary. It is important and perhaps necessary because, at the very least, we still resonate with Laurence Veysey's comment, though originally made in reference to Noah Porter's Yale, that "although [students'] mental faculties were sharpened three hours each day, one could rest assured that countervailing forces were safely at work during the remainder."[1]

Countervailing forces indeed. Perhaps that is why over one hundred years prior to Porter's arrival as President, the "Yale Laws" included such statements as the following:

3. If any Scholar shall be Guilty of Profane Swearing, Cursing, Vowing, any Petty or Implicit Oath, Profane or Irreverent Use of the Names, Attributes, Ordinances or Word of God; Disobedient or Contumacious or Refractory Carriage toward his Superiours, Fighting, Striking, Quarrelling, Challenging, Turbulent Words or Behaviour, Drunkenness, Uncleaness, Lacivious Words or Actions, wearing woman's Aparrel, Defrauding, Injustice, Idleness, Lying, Defamation, Tale bareing or any other Such like Immoralities, He Shall be Punished…

6. If any Scholar Shall Play at Cards or Dice at all; or at any Lawfull Game upon a Wager: or Shall bring any Quantity of Rum, Wine, Brandy or other Strong Liquor into College or into his Chamber where he Resides without Liberty from the President or Tutors…he shall be Fined…

7. That if any Scholar…Shall jump out of College Windows…he Shall be Fined…

8. That Every Student Shall abstain from Singing, loud Talking and all other Noises in Studying Time…

9. That if any Scholar Shall associate himself with any Rude, Idle Disorderly Persons: or Shall Entertain Companions at his Chamber either in College or out after Nine o'Clock, or Shall Take any Person who is not a near Relation to Lodge with Him without Liberty from the President or a Tutor he Shall be Fined…[2]

Though paternalistic disciplinarianism is no longer the regnant motivation in American higher education, and the nature of many of the particular rules and violations has changed, student conduct codes persist. This paper is an attempt to offer a contemporary, alternative motivation for institutional expectations for college student conduct. More specifically, I will offer two observations regarding potential problems to regulating student conduct and, second, I will outline what I consider to be appropriate motivations for developing and implementing rules for college student conduct. Finally, I will suggest several ideas for pursuing moral community, based on David Hoekema's book, *Campus Rules: In Place of* In Loco Parentis.[3]

Potential Problems

A first potential problem comes in the form of an objection. The objection might go something like this: Focusing on the importance of student conduct places too much emphasis on what might be called "regulations," which are out of place in an otherwise permissive American culture; norms, rules, expectations, accountability, and constraint are simply anachronistic—perhaps even draconian—in what might be described as a "have it your way" postmodern society. Arguing further, historian Andrew Delbanco[4] suggests (lamentably so) that American society is currently organized around the idea of Self, having earlier been predominantly shaped by the ideas of God and Nation in succession. And, at an institutional level, Catholic theologian James Burtchaell[5] suggests that American colleges have moved from being animated by Christian pietism to an uneasy pietism, then to an indifference to pietism, and finally to postmodernism, whereby individual realities, preferences and aspirations supplant allegiance to any external, overarching purposes or goals. Isaiah Berlin's creative essay juxtaposes two animals—the hedgehog and the fox—to illustrate the same point.[6] The hedgehog "relate[s] everything to a single central vision" while the fox "pursue[s] many ends, often unrelated and even contradictory." The hedgehog touts law, order, unity, and certainty, while the fox embraces freedom, serendipity, multiplicity, and uncertainty. In short, some may object that codes, much less expected behaviors, are passé in contemporary postsecondary institutions. And, it also may be fair to say that the "some" is not solely comprised of students, but of student life professionals and faculty members as well.

A specific college-related example may also illustrate the source of the objection. The scene is a commencement ceremony within the last decade at one of the most prestigious institutions in the land, at which an honored graduating undergraduate stated: "Among my classmates...I believe that there is one idea, one sentiment, which we have all acquired at some point in our [college] careers; and that, ladies and gentlemen, is, in a word, confusion." That same year, an honored graduating graduate student made these remarks to the assembled crowd: "They tell us that it is heresy to suggest the superiority of some value, fantasy to believe in moral argument, slavery to submit to a judgment sounder than your own. The freedom of our day is the freedom to devote ourselves to any values we please, on the mere condition that we do not believe them to be true."[7] Notice the disregard for a sense of grand story or for meaning beyond self-referential understanding or personal choice. It is little wonder that within several years of these addresses that a story in *The Chronicle of Higher Education* coined the term "absolutophobia" to describe the American college scene. Perhaps sociologist David Lyon is on to something when he suggests that American culture has moved successively from Providence to Progress to Nihilism.[8]

Shifting the focus a bit from the relative attractiveness of championing behavioral expectations in a permissive environment (the "should we?" question) to the feasibility of pursuing proactive measures in the interest of the personal formation of college students (the "can we?" question), the news at least in certain quarters is rather bleak. For example, University of Virginia social philosopher James Hunter opens his most recent book, *The Death of Character*, with a chilling three-page "Postmortem" that begins with these words: "Character is dead. Attempts to revive it will yield little. Its time is passed...The social and cultural conditions that make character possible are no longer present and no amount of political rhetoric, legal maneuvering, educational policy making, or money can change that reality. Its time has passed."[9] In a more explicit higher education context, Peter Sacks contends that large numbers of today's traditional-aged students confidently belong to what he terms "the entitlement society." Sacks argues that many students are interested in being gratified—even quickly—in and out of the classroom. And, if they are not, they may express that they have been victimized unfairly—like one of Sacks' students who provided the following feedback on a teacher evaluation form early in his career:

> I hated this class and found it hard to get up in the morning to get here. I would have dropped it except that I am graduating in June. You must understand that we are beginning college writers and not graduate students. Your attendance grading is "BS" because we pay for our school and should be able to choose whether to attend or not...If I don't get a decent grade because of your critical attitude, I will be speaking to your superiors.[10]

Something tells me that this student—and others like him/her—might not buy the idea that campus rules exist to "strengthen community" or "to maximize his/her college experience" or as "a natural expression of institutional values." Is it possible that some, maybe many, students come to college convinced—even if subconsciously—by a self-referencing worldview that convinces them that what matters most is individual choices, unrestrained lived experiences with friends and by oneself, and personal satisfaction and hassle-free comfort now and into the future? Moreover, is it possible that some, maybe many, institutions of higher learning are complicit—even if subtlety—in purporting values and priorities that may unwittingly emphasize student autonomy and may cater to a certain spirit of anomie within the larger culture? Finally, do Catholic colleges and universities have anything to offer in addressing these issues, particularly when it may be the case, as Sandy Estanek contends, that there is a "disconnect between the values and assumptions of [their] [student affairs] profession and the values and assumptions of the Catholic institutions where they work."[11]

A second and final potential problem in emphasizing the importance of student conduct is what might be termed institutional muddle. The issue here is not so much whether student conduct may or may not be a worthwhile or good undertaking, but rather that institutional life is so confused, diffuse, and conflicted that attention to student conduct is relegated to, well...part of the muddle. Although I suspect that the institutional muddle can and does show up in various ways, permit me two examples, both of which are concerned with the muddle in communicating student expectations. Example One: David Hoekema explains that, based on the contents of many student handbooks, "The problems of sexual exploitation and drug abuse pale to insignificance in comparison to the threat posed by extension cords."[12] He cites the handbook of his former institution that included just one sentence regarding what was expected of students regarding cohabitation: "The University does not condone members of the opposite sex staying overnight in a residence hall." But, when it came to extension cord usage, the handbook included "three columns of detailed rules and specifications, with fourteen numbered subsections."[13] All of this is to say that muddle can result when the nature and amount of institutional words that we use to communicate student expectations may not square with our deepest interests for student behaviors.

Example Two: Muddle in communicating student expectations can occur because of the frequently muddled relationship between academic affairs and student affairs. Although the muddle may look differently at different institutions, the source of the muddle can be identified univocally—many institutions currently operate a bipartite system in which student and academic affairs divisions coexist but have relatively little to do with the other. Whether this bifurcated arrangement endures due to the efforts of those perceived to possess relative power (i.e., academics) or due to those perceived to wield relatively little power (i.e., student affairs staff), the net effect is unchanged—inside-of-class learning and outside-of-class learning are dichotomous tasks that, though both operate within the same institution, hold little in common. Clarity and coherence regarding student expectations may fall victim to the fragmentation of such "two-curriculum" institutions as faculty communicate little or no interest in "the rules" since "babysitting" is not part of their job; or, worse, communicate that institutional expectations should not stand in the way of "having some fun," or "letting boys be boys," or "doing what comes naturally"—even if tacitly or with a timely wink, wink, nod, nod. Conversely, clear communication regarding appropriate student conduct may suffer to the extent that student affairs professionals are ignorant of or insensitive to academic standards, procedures, or rigor; or, worse, convince students that they shouldn't let academics get in the way of their college education. In either case, a coherent stance regarding appropriate student expectations—in or out of the classroom—is jeopardized and muddle retains a privileged position.

Appropriate Motivations

Having very quickly mentioned a couple of the potential problems with regulating student conduct, allow me to focus now on what I consider appropriate motivations for developing and implementing rules for college students. I would like to argue that affirming the importance of student conduct and embracing specific student expectations for student conduct depends, in an inordinate way, on institutional motivations. Stated another way, the foundational values that animate and give texture to institutional life are also the appropriate context for understanding why and how student conduct may be affirmed as important, and why and how specific student expectations may be embraced as worthwhile.

So, what are the possible motivations for affirming the importance of student conduct and for embracing specific student expectations for student conduct? I submit just two propositions for you to consider.

Proposition 1: An institution affirms the importance of student conduct to the extent that it is motivated by student learning. From my perspective, when student learning is a primary motivation for the educational enterprise, the importance of and attention to student conduct is *fait accompli*. What does this all mean? Let me suggest several things. First, an institution that is motivated by learning will understand that a student conduct code is simply one part of the larger learning culture of an institution. When done well, it is far different and infinitely better than a perfunctory list of dos and don'ts. Rather, it becomes one symbol among a host of other symbols that reveals the particular purposefulness of an institution; the code makes one statement among all other kinds of statements regarding the kind of learning impact that an institution desires to effect.

Second, and related to the first, an institution that is motivated by student learning will understand that a student conduct code is just one dimension of a multidimensional educational experience. Needless to say, students will learn the theories, issues, and applications of various academic disciplines. However, they will also learn about career options, cultural differences, and decision-making. Students will learn what constitutes a thoughtful, well-reasoned term-paper as well as what counts as plagiarism, how to avoid late fees, and when to "just say no." The point is that student conduct codes ostensibly offer a window into and out from particular dimensions of learning that an institution hopes to impress upon its students.

Of course, a multidimensional understanding of learning shouldn't give way to a sum of fragmented parts view of learning. In my view, efforts must be made to integrate the various dimensions of the learning enterprise into a unified whole. This leads me to a third consideration, namely, that an institution that is motivated by student learning will understand that a student conduct code must resonate easily with other aspects of the learning experience.[14] If an integrated learning experience might be described as understanding the entire college experience as a singular course or class, student conduct codes can be viewed as a valuable, harmonious, contributing aspect of this one course.

Further, for the same reasons that a professor would not frame a classroom course by assembling 14 weeks of unrelated issues, student conduct codes must be coherently connected to and supportive of the overarching educational institutional vision. In short, it should seldom be the case that campus participants experience a "disconnect" between the institution's student conduct code and all else involved as part of its learning ethos.

Finally, an institution that is motivated by student learning will understand that a student conduct code codifies, at least in part, a vision of community that is characterized by mutual respect, willing collaboration and self-effacing partnership.[15] When an institution is motivated by a view of learning that includes a commitment to community, student conduct codes become an important touchstone, though not the entire word, for what might be called "life together." Stanford University's policies for conduct provide a helpful illustration:

> The disciplinary requirements that form the content of the Fundamental Standard are not meant to be a comprehensive account of good citizenship within the Stanford community. They are meant only to set a floor of minimum requirements of respect for the rights of others, requirements that can be reasonably and fairly enforced through the disciplinary process. The Stanford community should expect much more of itself by way of tolerance, diversity, free inquiry and the pursuit of equal educational opportunity than can possibly be guaranteed by any set of disciplinary rules.[16]

Proposition 2: An institution embraces specific student expectations for student conduct as a reasonable outworking of its ethos or mission. I say this because I believe that education is inexorably shaped by basic beliefs about life. An institution's learning project is not undertaken neutrally but reflects what Mark Schwehn refers to as "morally directive" principles.[17] These moral directives provide substance, form, and purpose to the educational enterprise. For example, the "living community" of St. John's College (Annapolis) rests on the conviction that "the best preparation for action is contemplation guided by the reading of the best books known to [its founders]."[18] Or, the colonial colleges took their direction from some variation of the belief that "Everyone shall consider the main End of his life and studies, to know God and Jesus Christ which is Eternal life."[19] All of this is to say that the ways in which postsecondary education is enacted—including the expectations for students that appear in conduct codes—are related to an institution's fundamental moorings, values, or convictions, many of which may be reflected in its mission statement. Jon Dalton summarizes this idea quite succinctly: "The central issue...is not whether [to] advocate certain essential values but which values should be advocated and how these values can be advocated in a clear and intentional manner."[20]

Is it possible for an institution not to be consciously aware of its convictions? Yes. Is it possible for an institution to be deceived about its values? Sure. Can institutional mission statements be irrelevant to "life on the ground?" Absolutely. And one more question: Can expectations for student conduct be out of step with other aspects of institutional life? Indeed. However, I suggest that institutions do well to understand and clarify their ultimate commitments and then strive to establish and cultivate affinity between these foundational values and all other aspects of institutional life. More specifically, given this view, it simply makes sense to me that the specific expectations for student conduct at Catholic institutions are appropriately motivated by a Catholic identity. While dialog regarding what constitutes a Catholic identity is crucial and must be ongoing,[21] and though honest differences have and will exist among discussants engaged in this task, it nevertheless remains sensible that a Catholic college enflesh its ideals within the entire fabric of institutional life, including how it conceives the relevance of student conduct for the larger educational enterprise, what and how it chooses to include as specific expectations for student conduct, and the end to which such expectations proceed. In this regard, I was pleased to be alerted to the recent book edited by Sandy

Estanek, because it so lucidly offers support for the argument that I am making. For example, in her essay within the book, Dolores Christie states: "Flowing from the articulated mission and identity of the institution for which they work, [student affairs practitioners] may be expected to bear some responsibility to represent the tradition of the Church and to encourage the development of other human-worthy values it espouses."[22]

Although not Catholic myself, and though I have not read Catholic higher education literature extensively, I am also intrigued by Monika Hellwig's summary of Catholic distinctives.[23] Further, I wonder if the five characteristics that she offers may be instructive for affirming the importance of student conduct and for identifying specific expectations for student conduct at Catholic institutions. Hellwig's identifies the following five distinctives: "An emphasis on the continuity of faith and reason, respect for the cumulative wisdom of past generations in the tradition, an effort to be inclusive in membership and values, acknowledgement of the communitarian aspect of the redemption, and the pervasive appreciation of the sacramental principle."[24]

Without much effort, I think that one can begin to see the relevance of these five characteristics to Catholic institutions in general and to student conduct in particular. For example, the Catholic tradition has long been committed, as Hellwig states, "To apply[ing] the faith to worldly challenges."[25] Assuming that establishing expectations for student conduct, communicating expectations clearly, and mediating disciplinary hearing with wisdom are sufficient "worldly challenges," the good news is that the Catholic tradition has long been in the business of not leaving faith out in responding to such challenges. Better news is the realization that the Catholic tradition, as a matter of course, pays homage to past wisdom, thus offering shoulders on which to stand as contemporary institutions tackle student conduct issues of various kinds. Still better—in reference to "an effort to be inclusive in membership and values"—is the ready affirmation that, in Hellwig's words, "conversion to Christ is a lifetime enterprise." Seen in this light, perhaps student conduct

codes at Catholic institutions could be construed as instructors in faithfulness, helping students make gradual progress in
understanding more deeply, more clearly, and more constantly
the nature of life lived in the shadow of the Cross. The fourth
distinctive—"acknowledge[ing] the communitarian aspect of
the redemption"—appears to have particular weight in framing
specific expectations for student conduct at Catholic institutions
because it emphasizes what Hellwig calls "practical concern for
peace and social justice."[26] Perhaps more importantly, according to Hellwig, this distinctive stresses *cura personalis*, or a concern for the whole person.[27] From my perspective, emphasizing
peace and social justice as well as whole-person concern can go a
long way toward laying the foundation for expectations regarding appropriate human relationships, speech, and behaviors. The
final characteristic—a "pervasive appreciation of the sacramental principle"—may come most readily to mind when examining
Catholic identity. The sacramental principle underscores the notion that all of life can point the way to greater understanding of
the presence and power of God. Hellwig writes:

> To be fully Catholic the institutions ought to be differ-
> ent in a sensible, tangible way that strikes all who step
> onto the campus. The identity of the institution should
> be evident in the calendar of events, the central loca-
> tion of campus ministry and privileged placement of
> chapels, the privileged place given to library holdings in
> theology,...the unashamed use of religious motifs and
> images in the adornment of buildings, and most of all
> in the easy inclusion of religious topics and themes in
> conversations of faculty and administrators on campus,
> allowing students to realize that this is the integrating
> factor of scholarship on campus.[28]

To this list of things that give testimony to Catholic identity and
more, to the spiritual reality of life in the Lord, might we add
student conduct? That is, could the underlying motivations for
and specific expectations for student conduct be so designed,

communicated, and employed such that students could surmise that they must be attending a Catholic institution and that they are involved in a spiritual pilgrimage? I hope that from my remarks you can ascertain that my answer to this question is a resounding "yes!"

In my own tradition, we might talk about the idea that a Christian college education can be a small part of the sanctification process. That is, students are introduced to ideas, people, experiences, events, and the like, such that they will cultivate ways of thinking, acting, questioning, and living that are—in the truest sense of the term—godly. The purpose of such an education is to help students think Christianly and to relate faithfully what one learns to what one does. In this regard, it strikes me that student conduct codes, when done thoughtfully and with an eye toward coherence, is an essential ingredient for this purpose.

Concluding Comments

In closing, allow me to be a bit more practical than I have been thus far. What are some specific suggestions for "balancing motivation and expectation" at Catholic institutions? I have several suggestions.

First, begin by exploring the relevance, importance, and nature of Catholic perspectives for college student conduct. If it is true that a disconnect between belief and behavior is the order of the day, then it strikes me that we have much work to do to argue that beliefs and behaviors simply belong together. By all means, involve students, faculty, and staff in these discussions; articulate clearly the ways in which Catholic values are threatened when certain standards are not pursued; and, perhaps even present real-life offenses that undermining or obfuscate these values at your institution. Conversely, offer examples of behaviors or conduct that positively affirm institutional values consonant with Catholic identity.

Second, revisit your institution's student conduct code with an eye toward developing a compelling and winsome rationale for creating and cultivating a community of mutual and moral responsibility. What is not acceptable on campus should be tempered by what is acceptable and encouraged on campus; and both should have preamble and body regarding why and to what end. Stated another way, moral community has its reasons and we must be adept at explaining them.

Third, revisit your institution's student conduct code with an eye toward ensuring that it adequately addresses what Hoekema considers the two most important, specific ingredients of students' conduct,[29] namely, that behaviors that exploit or harm other members of the academic community will be prevented and punished, and that behaviors that undermine academic values will be prevented and punished. As important, I would quickly add that the particular behaviors that a Catholic institution places within both of these categories should be there or not be there, as the case may be, as a reflection of Catholic identity.

Fourth, revisit your institution's student conduct code with an eye toward considering how to prevent or deter unacceptable behavior, on the one hand, and how to encourage and support admirable behavior on the other. This is to say that student affairs professionals not only must consider what goes into the code regarding good and not so good behavior, but also must develop strategies for how to promote the good and curb the not so good.

Finally, revisit your institution's strategies for enforcing the student conduct code and adjudicating breaches of it. These institutional efforts not only should be undertaken with a Catholic accent in mind, but also may go a long way toward enhancing the academic, moral community that is desired. In contrast, an overzealous safety and security officer or a capricious judicial hearing not only bespeaks a breakdown in Catholic sensibilities, but also does significant—and quick—damage to the type of community that the code hopes to engender.[30]

Perhaps the epilogue of Edward Long's exceptionally good book, *Higher Education as a Moral Enterprise*, offers the most fitting way to conclude. He is worth quoting at length:

While the academy offers the possibility of creating a richer habitat for humanity, if the skills it bestows are placed in the service of the wrong ends life will become worse, not better…if the scholarly life pursues only the safe security of routinized inquiry about the factual and the materially productive, it will provide only the tools of submission to the growing horrors of a violent world and not the promise of an alternative; if colleges and universities are the seat of training only to indulge in the narcissistic and not the fount of an impulse to engage in the philanthropic, they will harden the lump in the pit of our stomachs rather than inspire our spirits… [Learning] is at its best when it enlarges horizons, magnifies the capacity for empathy, commends the importance of dialogue, and recommits us to the search for life in working viability with others and with an awareness of that which individuals and groups experience as the ground for their most essential being. The importance of practicing the life of learning in that way in the company of a committed guild will never be outdated.[31]

Indeed!

Notes

[1]L. Veysey, *The Emergence of the American University* (Chicago, IL: University of Chicago Press, 1970), 30.

[2]R. Hofstadter and W. Smith, *American Higher Education: A Documentary History, Volumes I and II* (Chicago, IL: University of Chicago Press, 1961), 56-57.

[3]D. Hoekema, *Campus Rules: In Place of* In Loco Parentis (New York, NY: Rowman and Littlefield Publishers, 1994).

[4]A. Delbanco, *The Real American Dream: A Meditation on Hope* (Cambridge, MA: Harvard University Press, 1999).

[5]J. Burtchaell, *The Dying of the Light: The Disengagement of Colleges & Universities from their Christian Churches* (Grand Rapids, MI: Eerdmans, 1998). See Chapter 8 for a helpful summary.

[6]I. Berlin, *The Hedgehog and the Fox* (New York, NY: Simon & Schuster, 1953), 1-2.

[7]As cited in R. Bellah, et al., *The Good Society* (New York, NY: Vintage Books, 1991), 43-44.

[8]D. Lyon, *Postmodernity* (Minneapolis, MN: University of Minnesota Press, 1999).

[9]J. Hunter, *The Death of Character: Moral Education in an Age Without Good or Evil* (New York, NY: Basic Books, 2000), xiii.

[10]P. Sacks, *Generation X Goes to College: An Eye-Opening Account of Teaching in Postmodern America* (Chicago, IL: Open Court, 1996), 154.

[11]Sandra M. Estanek, "Student Development and the Catholic University: Philosophical Reflections," In S. Estanek (ed.), *Understanding Student Affairs at Catholic Colleges and Universities: A Comprehensive Resource* (Franklin, WI: Sheed and Ward), 22. I believe that Estanek correctly identifies this disconnect as an epistemological issue since the student affairs profession and the Catholic intellectual tradition "hold different understandings of the nature of the human person and the nature of society and, therefore, while each tradition may on the sur-

face hold dear the same values, such as community and freedom, each means something completely different," 23.

[12]Hoekema, 66.

[13]Ibid.

[14]Hoekema seems to draw together these first three ideas when he compellingly writes: "The moral vacuum that now obtains on many campuses, the absence of any clear motivation or direction for student conduct or for the institution as a whole, has corrosive effects on faculty and students alike. Faculty are encouraged to see their responsibility as limited to research and lecturing; students are given help with the intellectual aspects of self-definition but not with the equally essential moral and personal aspects," 165.

[15]Hoekema strongly affirms this idea: "Students and faculty do indeed have communal interests—that is to say, literally, that they have interests not merely as individuals but as a community. To form a genuine community, by fostering and encouraging the numerous smaller communities in which students and faculty find their place and form their identify [sic], is the ultimate goal of the entire system of student conduct regulation and discipline," 166.

[16]As quoted in Hoekema, 111.

[17]M. Schwehn, *Exiles from Eden: Religion and the Academic Vocation in America* (New York, NY: Oxford University Press, 1992), 94.

[18]E. Brann, "St. John's Educational Policy for 'Living Community,'" *Change,* September/October, 1992), 36-43; 43.

[19]Hofstadter and Smith, 8.

[20]J. Dalton, "Organizational Imperatives for Implementing the Essential Values," In R. Young (ed.), *Identifying and Implementing the Essential Values of the Profession (New Directions for Student Services, No. 61)* (San Francisco, CA: Jossey-Bass, 1993), 87-96; 88.

[21]This may be substantially more true than I know (as a non-Catholic) given the sentiment conveyed in Philip Gleason's article, "What Made Catholic Identity a Problem?" In J. Heft (ed.), *Faith and the Intellectual Life* (South Bend, IN: Notre Dame University Press, 1996), 87-100.

[22]Dolores L. Christie, "Student Affairs and Conscience Formation," in S. Estanek (ed.), *Understanding Student Affairs at Catholic Colleges and Universities: A Comprehensive Resource* (Franklin, WI: Sheed and Ward), 75.

[23]M. Hellwig, "What Can the Roman Catholic Tradition Contribute to Christian Higher Education?" in R. Hughes and W. Adrian (eds.) *Models for Christian Higher Education: Strategies for Success in the Twenty-First Century* (Grand Rapids, MI: Wm. B. Eerdmans Publishing, 1997), 13-23.

[24]Ibid., 14.

[25]Ibid.

[26]Ibid., 16.

[27]Ibid,. 21.

[28]Ibid,. 22.

[29]Hoekema, 134ff.

[30]Again, I am indebted to D. Hoekema with respect to these last two points. He expands on each of them on 146ff.

[31]E. Long, Jr., *Higher Education as a Moral Enterprise* (Washington, D.C.: Georgetown University Press, 1992), 221.

CHAPTER 11

Magnanimity, Higher Education, and Me:
Notes to Myself About What I Still Want to Believe and Be

This essay was presented at the Symposium on Faith and Culture at Baylor University in October 2016.

Historian Patricia Limerick suggests that "lecturing is an unnatural act, an act for which providence did not design humans."[1] At the outset, then, I apologize for violating providential norms. I do find solace, however, in Dom Scibilia's idea that teaching—or perhaps a conference presentation—may have a "eucharistic accompaniment."[2] That is, in the same way that parishioners gather at the Lord's table to break bread, we gather in a classroom to, what Scibilia suggests, "break wisdom together."[3] I pray that that will be so.

As the title of my presentation suggests, I intend my remarks as a self-reflection, to remind myself (and perhaps others) of why it may be that I do what I do as an educator in the midst of what can feel regularly like tumultuous times socially and institutionally, and a flagging or, at times, cynical spirit personally. Redoubling my efforts to embrace certain virtues while eschewing others can be tough sledding. Still, for many years now, I would like to think that I have attempted to teach undergraduate and graduate students to understand and to face challenges while maintaining commitment and energy in addressing them well. So, I wrote these "notes" as reminders for myself in the pursuit of the enduring task and the enduring joy of higher education.

I do not think that I would be a teacher unless there was something about higher education—its purposes, its prospects, its opportunities, its people—that fascinated me, that confounded me, that thrilled me, that bid me come. Just last week, for example, I had grad students report on some things that they were reading on insidehighered.com, a great online news feed—free speech on campus and first amendment rights; 60% of instruction at Dutch universities is now in English; unionization of adjunct faculty at a private institution; limiting students' transfer options; improving campus police training; and the list goes on. At the end of those presentations I said something like: Is this a great field or what? And, on many days, I believe it! In fact, on many days, I would say that I love higher education.

At the same time, I would like to think that my love for colleges and universities is not blind, nor must it be so. Higher education jingoism will not sustain us. Rather, as G.K. Chesterton writes: "Love is not blind; that is the last thing that it is. Love is bound; and the more it is bound the less it is blind."[4] Indeed. Dangers, toils, and snares are part of the package that we recognize and confront as we bind ourselves to the good work that there is to do in colleges and universities. And, based on a recent, short presentation that I was privileged to attend, I have been wondering about the ancient virtue of magnanimity as a resource worthy of our attention and even embrace as we consider sustenance for our journeys.

The presentation occurred at a conference that I attended in St. Louis in late March 2015. The conference was sponsored by the Council of Independent Colleges as a bi-yearly feature of one of its initiatives called NetVUE, or the Network for Vocation in Undergraduate Education. The presenter was Dr. Paul Wadell, a professor of theology and religious studies at St. Norbert College in Wisconsin. Paul's remarks that day can now be found in an essay called "An itinerary of hope: Called to a magnanimous way of life."[5] Allow me to share some of what I learned from Paul, and what I have explored just a bit further since.

Not all words are like this but isn't it true that you can tell that some words just sound like they must mean something positive, while other words convey negative impressions. For example, words like nefarious or vile or obsequious just sound bad. And they are! But words like...well...words like 'magnanimous' sound so good!

And, indeed, this is so. The list of synonyms for magnanimity are amazingly positive. Listen to some of them: generous, unselfish, charitable, great in courage, large-hearted. For Aristotle, magnanimity was a virtue that could be summarized as "great-souledness." A person who possessed the virtue of magnanimity was, according to Aristotle, a person that pursued a life worthy of and expressing great honor; a person willing to offer "generous disregard" or "forgiveness" for any manner of pettiness or insult perpetrated by others.

Likewise, for Thomas Aquinas, typically regarded as the father of modern Catholicism, magnanimity was the central virtue among the virtues, as it bolstered one's resolve to embrace and to live into the entirety of the virtuous life. Philosopher Rebecca DeYoung, writing about Aquinas' sense of magnanimity said it this way: "Magnanimity is a wholehearted readiness to attempt the great acts of virtue to which we are called, however impossible or daunting the task may seem and however much the attempt may 'stretch' us."[6] DeYoung suggests that we think of the annunciation of Mary as a fitting example.[7]

Perhaps another way to understand the meaning and power of magnanimity is to explore what magnanimity is not. In the classical tradition, the virtues stood in sharp contrast to the vices. And, the two vices that were opposites of magnanimity were pusillanimity and acedia. The pusillanimous person lacks courage, is faint-hearted, and regularly petty. He is small-souled; she shies away from pursuing her potential. Again, DeYoung is helpful here. She writes: "[The pusillanimous person] is one who, when considering some action, looks around, sees others doing a much better job, is certain that she will look inferior in comparison or fare poorly by their standards or expectations, and therefore decides not to make the attempt."[8] According to DeYoung, Aquinas used the example of Moses at the burning bush—before he "got it"—as an appropriate example.[9]

Acedia is related to pusillanimity, but it has some particularities as well. Acedia is often translated as sloth, but poet and writer Kathleen Norris suggests that, to the extent that we may interpret sloth simply as laziness, it simply doesn't reach to the depths of the real meaning of acedia, and to why acedia is such the opposite of magnanimity. That is, Norris suggests that acedia has to do with "being so not able to care that you don't care that you don't care."[10] For Norris, acedia is indifference with capital letters; it is what she calls "commitment phobia"[11]—it is a life that is cauterized to what really matters and to a resolve to live honorably, to be great-souled, no matter what.

Magnanimity. Pusillanimity. Acedia. Me. Higher Education.

- Am I charitable in explaining perspectives and practices other than the ones that I privilege?

- Am I faint-hearted in preparing for class?

- To that extent has any commitment that I ever had to a visionary and courageous educational project waned? To what extent would I care if it had?

- Am I generous in my professional and personal dealings with student, staff, and faculty colleagues?

- Am I a petty or disengaged committee member?

- Would a teaching evaluation point to me as a great-souled or as a small-souled educator?

- After all these years in the academy, am I willing to be stretched with respect to perspectives and practices and strategies? Can I still imagine? Be wrong? Hope?

One of the books that I have come back to in preparing for my remarks is John Bennett's *Academic Life*.[12] It is a book that, at least in part, commends virtues for teachers/scholars. In fact, Bennett says this: "hospitality is a cardinal value in our work as academics."[13] There are simply too many good things from the book in general and for the specific chapter on hospitality, but let me mention just two from the chapter. First, for Bennett, hospitality is a corrective to what he calls an "insistent individualism" that can all too often characterize the academic life, lamenting that "academics are known more for arrogance than humility"[14] and suggesting that hospitality requires a kind of humility that necessarily "attend[s] to the other rather than dwelling on the self."[15] A second nugget that captures my attention is his belief that courage is an important aspect of practicing hospitality. He poignantly remarks: "Courage in the pursuit of learning requires the strength to risk the disapproval of less imaginative colleagues."[16]

Perhaps my favorite theologian over the last ten years or so is Walter Brueggemann, who was a keynote at this conference a few years back. One of Brueggemann's enduring themes is the notion of "relinquishing and receiving."[17] His sense is that people of faith do well to always be in the process of letting go of certain beliefs and practices that run counter to Yahweh's designs for life, and of embracing anew beliefs and practices that reflect and signpost the Lord and the kingdom. Brueggemann's relinquishing and receiving idea captures my "notes to myself"—I do well to relinquish the ways that pusillanimity and acedia and "insistent individualism" show up in my professorial work and personal life and, by grace, receive anew the gifts of magnanimity and hospitality.

I am quite sure that some of you are *Lord of the Rings* fans. One of my favorite scenes is the last 45 minutes of *The Two Towers*. The siege at Helm's Deep is looking grim, but, just as he had promised to Aragorn, at first light on the fifth day from the east, Gandalf shows up...and he's not alone. Elsewhere, Pippin and Merry have done their part to cajole the Ents to take action and take action they do. They, shall we say, lumber over to, shall we say, liquidate Isengard and to foil Saruman's evil operations. And, of course, Frodo and Sam are setting out from Gondor for Mordor, to face Sauron and to destroy the One Ring. You may remember that as they're walking and talking at the end of the film, Sam earnestly asks Frodo something like this: "Mr. Frodo, do you think that someday others will recite tales and sing ballads about us?"

Citizens all of Middle-Earth, do you think that someday others will recite tales and sing ballads about you and your labors as educators? Maybe this weekend, we should take some time to write ballads about one another, eh? My sincere hope is that such tales and ballads will provide ample testimony that, in my labors and in your labors in the fields of higher education, you will be known throughout the land not for pusillanimity nor acedia nor insistent individualism, but for magnanimity in abundance.

In the Epilogue of the wonderful book entitled *Higher Education as a Moral Enterprise*, Edward Long writes these words:

> While the academy offers the possibility of creating a richer habitat for humanity, if the skills it bestows are placed in the service of the wrong ends, life will become worse, not better. If the academic odyssey provides only an operational intelligence but no valuational purposes, it will be more likely to exacerbate than to counteract the social antagonisms that plague us; if the scholarly life pursues only the safe security of routinized inquiry about the factual and the materially productive, it will provide only the tools of submissions to the growing horrors of a violent world and not the promise of an alternative; if colleges and universities are the seat of training only to indulge in the narcissistic and not the fount of an impulse to engage in the philanthropic, they will harden the lump in the pit of our stomachs rather than inspire our spirits.[18]

In my view, avoiding the kinds of insidious perils—the kinds of professional and institutional vices—that Long describes requires willing folks to seek with intention and resolve the virtues of magnanimity and hospitality. DeYoung identifies these dear folks as those who "attempt[s] and achieve[s] great things [simply] because they are appropriate expressions of the excellence"[19] that motivates them from within, even at great cost. May we be those folks as we take our places serving the academy day by day, even amidst its structural, professional, and personal challenges.

Notes

[1] As quoted in P. Smith, *Killing the Spirit* (New York: Penguin Books, 1990), 210.

[2] D. Scibilia, "Pedagogy as Eucharistic Accompaniment," in S. Haynes (ed.), *Professing in the Postmodern Academy* (Waco, TX: Baylor University Press, 2002), 195-214.

[3] Ibid., 209.

[4] G. Chesterton, *Orthodoxy* (San Francisco, CA: Ignatius Press, 1995), 76.

[5] P. Wadell, "An Itinerary of Hope: Called to a Magnanimous Way of Life," in D. Cunningham (ed.), *At this Time and in this Place: Vocation and Higher Education* (New York, NY: Oxford University Press, 2015), 193-215.

[6] R. DeYoung, "Aquinas's Virtues of Acknowledged Dependence: A New Measure of Greatness," *Faith and Philosophy*, Vol. 21, No. 2 (April 2004), 214-227, 219.

[7] R. DeYoung, "Pedagogical Rhythms: Practices and Reflections on Practice," In D. Smith and J. Smith (eds.), *Teaching and Christian Practices: Reshaping Faith & Learning* (Grand Rapids, MI: Wm. B. Eerdmans, 2011), 24-42.

[8] DeYoung, "Aquinas's Virtues," 216.

[9] DeYoung, "Pedagogical Rhythms," 26.

[10] L. George, "Kathleen Norris Battles 'The Demon of Acedia,'" Los Angeles Times, September 21, 2008, latimes.com/entertainment/la-ca-kathleen-norris21-2008sep21-story.html.

[11] Ibid.

[12] J. Bennett, *Academic Life: Hospitality, Ethics, and Spirituality* (Eugene, OR: Wipf and Stock Publishers, 2003).

[13] Ibid., 46.

[14] Ibid., 65.

[15] Ibid., 66.

[16] Ibid., 61.

[17]W. Brueggemann, *Tenacious Solidarity: Biblical Provocations on Race, Religion, Climate, and the Economy* (Minneapolis, MN: Fortress Press, 2018). See Chapter 8 in particular.

[18]E. Long, Jr., *Higher Education as a Moral Enterprise* (Washington, D.C.: Georgetown University Press, 1992), 221.

[19]DeYoung, "Aquinas's Virtues," 217.

CHAPTER 12

Autobiographical Reflections on My Life and Calling(s)

I prepared a version of this essay for a position for which I had applied earlier in my career.

Introduction

I originally penned a version of the comments that follow in 2012 as part of an application process for an administrative position at a Christian college. They represent a bit of a different feel than much of the rest of this volume. I nevertheless thought this chapter important to include because its words reflect certain personal commitments that have and do provide scaffolding for plenty of other issues and ideas and undertakings that are represented elsewhere in the book, and for my professional career in the academy.

As in the former version of these remarks, I have arranged these according to specific questions that to which I was asked to respond. Perhaps one could say that what follows reads as a kind of interview of myself. In addition, compared to the previous version of this document, I have edited out questions that did not quite fit my design for this chapter, and I also updated several items as well, to account for current circumstances.

Q1: What significant events, compelling writings, and personal interactions have contributed to your growth as a Christian and particularly as a Christian educator?

Although I had the privilege of being raised in a Christian home and in a church that was committed to nurturing its youth in Christian discipleship, a church-camp experience when I was a teenager made most clear and compelling the gospel of Jesus Christ. In college, my faith was expanded and strengthened extensively by faculty mentors (particularly in the Religion department), by close friends that remain to this day, and through serving in the ministry of Young Life. My work after college in campus ministry further convinced me of the totalizing nature of the gospel, as well as the scope of Jesus' redeeming work. This campus ministry experience also confirmed to me that the Lord was calling me to pursue a career in the academy. I continue to be fully captivated by this high calling. And, colleagues in graduate school, at Calvin, at Geneva, at Penn State, and at other institutions; colleagues in face-to-face conversations, in emails, in presentations, and via published writings; and, colleagues living and deceased continue to help me understand it more fully, more clearly, and more faithfully day by day, year by year.

I will quickly add that my wife, Cindy, has been a constant conduit of God's love and grace to me for 38 years. Her honest faith and deep devotion to Christ and His kingdom are inspiring to me; she lives the gospel contagiously. Likewise, our three children—from their births to the present—as well as our two daughters-in-law regularly tutor me on love, forgiveness, grace, joy, and hope. In his wonderful book, *Jesus, My Father, the CIA, and Me*, Ian Cron writes that the gospel reveals that "love always stoops."[1] My wife and kids help me to know this to be profoundly true.

Regarding compelling writings, where does one even begin? Here is a very partial list of books that have shaped me personally in powerful ways during the last almost 40 years: Van Auken's *A Severe Mercy*,[2] Wolters' *Creation Regained*,[3] Augustine's *Confessions*,[4] Hardy's *The Fabric of this World*,[5] Sloan's

Faith and Knowledge,[6] Marsh's *The Last Days*,[7] Marsden's *The Soul of the American University*,[8] Plantinga's *Engaging God's World*,[9] Robinson's *Gilead*,[10] Lahiri's *The Namesake*,[11] and, Brueggemann's *Testimony to Otherwise*.[12]

Q2: What is your philosophy of a Christian liberal arts education? How do you see it differing from any other liberal arts education? What books, articles, or people have helped you to formulate your philosophy of education?

Liberal arts education in the context of historic Christian faith generates rich meaning. The liberal tradition most broadly emphasizes truth, beauty, and virtue; exploration, creativity, and discovery; learning how to think, communicate, and live; and, responsible, courageous leadership within society. Liberal arts education in the context of Christian faith involves similar foci. Moreover, far from being a contaminating constraint to the educational process, Christian faith offers a freeing framework for scholarship, study, and personal development. With God's covenantal faithfulness and redeeming work as backdrop, each member of a Christian liberal arts college is commissioned and admonished to uncover and cultivate, with both wonder and license, God's good intentions for all dimensions of life. In these very efforts is the joy—and the challenge—of liberal arts education in the context of historic Christian faith.

To accomplish this vision requires three fundamental activities according to Christian educator Nicholas Wolterstorff.[13] First, faculty and students alike must engage and wrestle with historic and contemporary, secular and Christian, individuals, theories, and ideas. Clearly, the acquisition, analysis, and synthesis of knowledge are the frontispieces of any education. In a Christian context, however, such activity is undertaken with a principled and honest discernment that is rooted within a biblical view of all things. Second, students must be nurtured in the development of various skills. Such skills may be related directly to vocational aspirations (e.g., learning how to conduct an audit), but also may include personal skills (e.g., understanding more fully what characterizes friendship), or social skills (e.g., discovering more clearly the contours of responsible citizenship). Once again, in a Christian context, the strategies for cultivating these skills as well as the ends for which they are developed are given particular substance and texture rooted in biblical principles. Finally, liberal arts education in the context of historic Christian faith aims to nurture appropriate "tendencies" within its participants. Less tangible perhaps than the previous two elements, but equally important, tendencies refer to those habits, styles, characteristics, and manners of life that demonstrate a profound and enduring commitment to live life in all of its fullness in response to and in honor of the God who created and sustains it.

At a time in which American culture in general is reevaluating the nature and importance of postsecondary education, liberal arts institutions that are animated by historic Christian faith have the opportunity—and perhaps even the responsibility—to offer a liberating beacon of light.

In addition to some of the books that I mentioned in the previous question, I would add the following as some of the sources that have contributed to my philosophy of education: Long's *Higher Education as Moral Enterprise*,[14] Wolterstorff's *Educating for Shalom*,[15] Clark's *The Distinctive College*,[16] Budde and Wright's *Conflicting Allegiances*,[17] Newman's *The Idea of a University*,[18] Pelikan's *The Idea of the University*,[19] Kerr's *The Uses of the University*,[20] Hauerwas' *The State of the University*,[21] Hutchins' *Higher Learning in America*,[22] Walsh and Middleton's *Transforming Vision*,[23] Holmes' *The Idea of a Christian College*,[24] Bowen's *Investment in Learning*,[25] Keller's *Academic Strategy*,[26] Rudolph's *The American College and University*,[27] Geertz's *Interpretation of Cultures*,[28] Berger's *The Sacred Canopy*,[29] and Garber's *The Fabric of Faithfulness*.[30]

Q3: In a Christian liberal arts curriculum, many of the disciplines face particular challenges as they interface with both the wider evangelical sub-cultures as well as members of the broader academy. Using specific examples, explain how you maintain the balance between academic freedom/disciplinary integrity and biblical orthodoxy.

Stated succinctly, educators at Christian liberal arts colleges steward their academic vocations most effectively to the extent that they utilize resources from both the Christian community and from the broader academic community. But several additional things are important to note, as follows, and in no particular order of importance:

- Christian resources do not automatically "get it right" nor do resources from the broader academic community automatically "get it wrong." On the contrary, Christian perspectives can "get it wrong" and the broader academic community can "get it right." Thus, from my perspective, two practices are critical. First, educators at Christian liberal arts colleges must know about, search for, and utilize well resources from both Christian and non-Christian quarters. And, second, educators at Christian liberal arts colleges must embrace and cultivate biblical discernment/wisdom as a critical practice of their professional service.

- "Christian resources" is not a monolith. That is, not all Christians agree on all things, including with regard to their perspectives on economics, human origins, politics, the arts, and the like. In addition, though many may not easily include them in the term "evangelical sub-culture," Catholic brothers and sisters in Christ— historically and currently—produce thoughtful and compelling perspectival resources in every academic field that must not be overlooked.

- To the extent that the faculty culture at your institution has affinity with the faculty culture at Geneva where

I currently work, many if not most faculty seem most prepared in their respective disciplinary homes, but far less comfortable in knowing about much less having digested extant Christian resources for their respective fields. For example, it would not be uncommon for a prospective faculty member at Geneva to offer a statement like this: "I know my field very well, but I have never really thought about the relationship of Christian faith to my field." All of this is to say that achieving "a balance between disciplinary integrity and biblical orthodoxy" may require redoubling and/or recalibrating faculty development efforts.

- During the last 35 years or so, the bibliography of integration of faith and learning in all fields has grown dramatically. As I said earlier, although not all of these resources are helpful (for various reasons), opportunities for strengthening a "through the eyes of faith" perspective in all fields is more reasonable now than perhaps ever before.

- Pursuing a "balance between disciplinary integrity and biblical orthodoxy" is a communal task; it may even be the peculiar task of a Christian collegium. It may require eschewing the disciplinary balkanization and rigid departmentalism of the larger academy, but exploring and executing the nature and texture and nuance of "the balance" is done best not in isolation, but in the company and fellowship of others, as is customary in the body of Christ whether gathered to worship or to teach for Jesus' sake.

Q4: Describe your leadership style. Give several examples to illustrate that you have strong communication skills, both one-on-one and in groups (small and large), including the ability to adjudicate among differing viewpoints while making sure all parties feels as if their perspectives have been heard.

I offer two observations about my leadership style and, at least implicitly, my communication skills. I will respond to the last portion of this question (i.e., ability to adjudicate) in the next question below.

First, during graduate school, I read one of the classic organizational culture books called *Reframing Organizations* by Lee Bolman and Terrence Deal.[31] Toward the end of the book, Bolman and Deal offer four leadership approaches, each of which they connect to one of the organizational "frames" that they discuss earlier in the text. The four leadership approaches are: architect, catalyst, advocate, and poet/prophet. I think that effective leadership necessarily must involve all four of these approaches because, as the authors state, specific circumstances may be more appropriately addressed with a particular leadership style. I suspect that this is precisely why Bolman and Deal, in the final analysis, consider leadership as artistry. I would like to believe that my leadership experiences have helped me to become more aware of and more adept at exercising leadership styles that comport well with the situations and/or the person or group of persons in view.

And, second, I completed Bass' and Avolio's Multifactor Leadership Questionnaire (MLQ, Form 6S)[32] right along with the students that enrolled in a Work, Vocation, and Leadership course that I taught last spring. This instrument purports to measure transformational leadership with seven factors. Prior to revealing my own scores to the students, I asked them to suggest the particular factors on which they believed I would score more highly. As a group, they were dead on. My three highest scores were: intellectual stimulation, idealized influence, and, inspirational motivation. A brief interpretation of each is below:

> Intellectual stimulation shows the degree to which you encourage others to be creative in looking at old problems in new ways, create an environment that is tolerant of seemingly extreme positions, and nurture people to question their own values and beliefs and those of the organization.

Idealized influence indicates whether you hold subordi-
nates' trust, maintain their faith and respect, show ded-
ication to them, appeal to their hopes and dreams, and
act as their role model.

Inspirational motivation measures the degree to which
you provide a vision, use appropriate symbols and images to help others focus on their work, and try to make
others feel their work is significant.

I sincerely hope that my self-perceived leadership style and the
judgments of the students in this class have some basis in reality!
At the very least, I aspire to the particular leadership traits that
are identified by these three factors.

*Q5: Liberal arts colleges of all types face many challenges. What
do you perceive as significant challenges that our institution will
be facing in the next ten years?*

A short list of significant challenges that your institution may
face in the next decade includes college costs/graduate indebtedness, fundraising, diversity, capacity for change, and institutional distinctiveness. Allow me to make a few brief comments
on each. First, college costs and graduate indebtedness is a ubiquitous concern in public policy debates, higher education literature, and in families' homes. Private institutions have had to
contend with this issue for years, but with insufficient funds to
maintain current education funding levels in many states, many,
if not most, public institutions will begin to feel this tension
more acutely. Understanding the complexities and realities of
college affordability will be critical in the years ahead.

Second, and related to the first challenge above, there is no
substitute for effective fundraising in private higher education,
including among Christian institutions. It may well be that success in these endeavors may make the difference for a Christian
institution's survival.

Third, diversity is a continuing challenge for many, if
not most, Christian institutions whether it takes the form of

increasing the numbers of various campus subpopulations, greater exposure to and understanding of other cultures in comparative perspective (e.g., off-campus study), or what might be called a "diversity across the curriculum" effort. In my view, Christian colleges must redouble their efforts to embrace this challenge in the next decade, acknowledging that the kingdom of God has been, is, and will be comprised of every "nation, tribe, people, and language" (Rev. 7:9).

Fourth, I believe that an institution's capacity for change will be critical in the next decade. It is unclear to me if a capacity for change is a more difficult proposition for private, Christian institutions compared to other types of institutions; historically it is fair to say that postsecondary education as a whole tends to be conservative when it comes to change. Whatever the case, it may be that, in the next decade, institutions that are willing to innovate, "think outside the box," be responsive to social forces, be educationally unorthodox, and the like may distinguish themselves well—and perhaps find that hoped-for student learning is enhanced in the process. Gap year programs, interdisciplinary or multidisciplinary studies, three years to degree, alternative semester formats (e.g., 15 week semesters split into 12-week and three-week components), technology-based self-directed study, centralized back-office functions, institutional collaborations, and more may become more prevalent in the years ahead...for good and for bad I suspect.

Finally, I conclude with the challenge of institutional distinctiveness. I sense that pressure to soft-pedal the central premise such as the one often linked to Christian institutions (e.g., higher education within a framework of vibrant, evangelical Christian faith) may become even more acute in the next decade. This is not to suggest that change and "tradition" are mutually exclusive. It is, however, to note that understanding and navigating their relationship is a continuing challenge that must be met wisely and effectively.

Q6: Our faculty members come from a variety of denominations and theological positions, but all agree to our statement of faith. Describe a way in which you have had to engage in respectful dialog with people with whom you disagreed. How comfortable are you with differing opinions and how would you approach this aspect of your task?

In large measure, to work in the academy—Christian or otherwise—is to work in a context of differing opinions about many things. Faculty everywhere disagree about ideas, theories, curricula, policies, and strategies. And, Christian faculty also disagree about theology and ecclesiology. For many years at Geneva—including when I was the academic dean and dean of faculty development—I led a faculty development workshop for recently hired faculty (and some others) on the reformed tradition and the integration of faith and learning. Knowing that Geneva's faculty are theologically and ecclesiastically diverse, I structured this workshop to acknowledge that Christianity is represented by several faith traditions, that each has distinguishing features, and that each has implications for Christian higher education. I revealed to them that I am one who finds himself in the neo-Calvinist tradition, but I also encouraged them to dig more deeply into their respective faith traditions, including ways in which it may shape their efforts at Geneva. Inevitably, cordial, respectful disagreements emerged during these conversations. But, more importantly, many of these same faculty sought me out as someone who was "for" them in developing a more sophisticated sense of the integration of faith and learning, though they recognized that we may still differ on various theological particulars. Almost in every case, they also wanted to hear more about the reformed tradition, particularly as they tried to navigate the distinctions between the reformed tradition and the Reformed Presbyterian Church of North America, which owns and operates Geneva.

Speaking more generally rather than regarding theological differences explicitly, I think that it is important to create a culture that welcomes differing opinions. This is not to suggest that some opinions—including my own—may not be as valuable as others', that my own opinion will not be important to make clear, and, that particular decisions often must be made although differing opinions persist. I simply am suggesting that I believe myself to be an approachable and amiable colleague that is unthreatened by differing opinions.

Q7: Give an example of how you have handled professional failure. What did you learn from that experience?

Shortly after I became the academic dean, I was responsible for writing a letter that evaluated a colleague as he came up for tenure. I wrote in support of this colleague, including an endorsement of his integration [of faith and learning] paper. Based on the drastic unevenness in the quality of these papers in previous years, I had come to the conclusion that simply submitting one was sufficient. Although I thought that his paper was not the approach to integration in his particular field that I would have outlined personally, I wrote tersely but positively about it in my letter on his behalf. The composition of the faculty committee that reviewed tenure portfolios had recently changed dramatically and had come to include several faculty members who had significantly more sophisticated understandings of the integration and faith and learning. What I did not know was that the committee also had been asked by the provost with the encouragement of the Board to set the bar higher for integration papers.

My colleague was not granted tenure. If I had provided specific advice to him regarding his integration paper (including how it needed to be revised before he submitted his materials), perhaps this may not have been the outcome. I apologized to him for believing that I had failed him, and was deeply grateful that he did not blame me. In fact, he asked me to be a professional reference in subsequent job searches.

This experience taught me never to underestimate the critical importance of taking time to evaluate preexisting assumptions; establishing thorough and clear expectations; the left hand knowing what the right hand is doing; and, asking for forgiveness.

It was a hard lesson to learn, but I do believe that it was a useful baseline experience from which I drew as I continued in my role.

Q8: What will be the most important factors for you in determining your consideration of this post?

In the late 1980s, when I was in graduate school at Penn State, I came across a book called *The Distinctive College*, written by Burton Clark almost 20 years earlier in 1970.[33] In this book, Clark develops the idea of "organizational saga" based on his research at three prominent, historically liberal arts institutions. He contends that these colleges were distinctive precisely because of their respective strong sagas. To be distinctive was to have a compelling saga. Clark goes on to suggest that institutional distinctiveness consists of a clear and vibrant identity; forged intentionally over time *de novo* or in response to crisis, need, or opportunity; around which institutional participants have consensus and express loyalty; and, of which all institutional structures and practices routinely testify. In such an institution, "Deep emotional investment binds participants as comrades in a cause…; participants "behave as if they knew a beautiful secret that no one outside the lucky few could ever share."[34]

So, what will be the most important factor for me in considering this role? Simply this: I want to be part of, contribute to, and be nurtured by an institutional saga. And, although I am quite sure that your institution is not perfect, I believe that it has embraced and is poised to strengthen its embrace of the characteristics that attend Clark's notion of saga. I would sincerely like the privilege of joining such an ambitious effort.

Notes

[1]I. Cron, *Jesus, My Father, the CIA, and Me: A Memoir of Sorts* (Nashville, TN: Thomas Nelson, 2011), 175.

[2]S. Van Auken, *A Severe Mercy: A Story of Faith, Tragedy, and Triumph* (New York, NY: HarperOne, 2009).

[3]A. Wolters, *Creation Regained: Biblical Basics for a Reformational Worldview, 2nd Edition* (Grand Rapids, MI: Eerdmans, 2005).

[4]M. Boulding (trans), *The Confessions: The Works of St. Augustine: A Translation for the 21st Century, Volume 1* (Hyde Park, NY: New City Press, 2002).

[5]L. Hardy, *The Fabric of this World: Inquiries into Calling, Career Choice, and the Design of Human Work* (Grand Rapids, MI: Eerdmans, 1990).

[6]D. Sloan, *Faith and Knowledge: Mainline Protestantism and American Higher Education* (Louisville, KY: Westminster John Knox Press, 1994).

[7]C. Marsh, *The Last Days: A Son's Story of Sin and Segregation at the Dawn of a New South* (New York, NY: Basic Books, 2002).

[8]G. Marsden, *The Soul of the American University: From Protestant Establishment to Established Nonbelief* (New York, NY: Oxford University Press, 1996).

[9]C. Plantinga, *Engaging God's World: A Christian Vision of Faith, Learning, and Living* (Grand Rapids, MI: Wm. B. Eerdmans Publishing Company, 2002).

[10]M. Robinson, *Gilead: A Novel* (New York, NY: Picador, 2006).

[11]J. Lahiri, *The Namesake: A Novel* (Boston, MA: Mariner, 2004).

[12]W. Brueggemann, *Testimony to Otherwise: The Witness of Elijah and Elisha* (St. Louis, MO: Chalice, 2001).

[13]N. Wolterstorff, *Educating for Responsible Action* (Grand Rapids, MI: Christian Schools International and Wm. B. Eerdmans Publishing Company, 1980). See Chapter 1 in particular.

[14]E. Long, *Higher Education as a Moral Enterprise* (Washington, D.C.: Georgetown University Press, 1992).

[15]N. Wolterstorff, *Educating for Shalom: Essays on Christian Higher Education* (Grand Rapids, MI: Eerdmans, 2004).

[16]B. Clark, *The Distinctive College* (Piscataway, NJ: Transaction Publishers, 1992).

[17]M. Budde and J. Wright, *Conflicting Allegiances: The Church-Based University in a Liberal Democratic Society* (Grand Rapids, MI: Brazos Press, 2004).

[18]J. Newman, *The Idea of a University* (South Bend, IN: University of Notre Dame Press, 1981).

[19]J. Pelikan, *The Idea of the University: A Reexamination* (New Haven, CT: Yale University Press, 1992).

[20]C. Kerr, *The Uses of the University, 5th Edition* (Cambridge, MA: Harvard University Press, 2001).

[21]S. Hauerwas, *The State of the University: Academic Knowledges and the Knowledge of God* (Hoboken, NJ: Wiley-Blackwell, 2007).

[22]R. Hutchins, *The Higher Learning in America* (New York, NY: Routledge, 1995).

[23]B. Walsh and R. Middleton, *The Transforming Vision: Shaping a Christian Worldview* (Downers Grove, IL: IVP Academic, 1984).

[24]A. Holmes, *The Idea of a Christian College* (Grand Rapids, MI: Eerdmans, 1987).

[25]W. Bowen, *Investment in Learning: The Individual and Social Value of American Higher Education* (Baltimore, MD: Johns Hopkins University Press, 1997).

[26]G. Keller, *Academic Strategy: The Management Revolution in American Higher Education* (Baltimore, MD: Hopkins Fulfillment Service, 1984).

[27]F. Rudolph, *The American College and University: A History, 2nd Edition* (Athens, GA: University of Georgia Press, 1991).

[28]C. Geertz, *The Interpretation of Cultures* (New York, NY: Basic Books, 1977).

[29]P. Berger, *The Sacred Canopy: Elements of a Sociological Theory of Religion* (Norwell, MA: Anchor, 1990).

[30]S. Garber, *The Fabric of Faithfulness: Weaving Together Belief and Behavior* (Downers Grove, IL: IVP Books, 1997).

[31]L. Bolman and T. Deal, *Reframing Organizations: Artistry, Choice, and Leadership, 6th Edition* (San Francisco, CA: Jossey Bass, 2017).

[32]See: https://www.statisticssolutions.com/wp-content/uploads/wp-post-to-pdf-enhanced-cache/1/multifactor-leadership-questionnaire-mlq.pdf.

[33]Clark, "The Distinctive College."

[34]Ibid., 235.

CHAPTER 13

Vibrant Christian Faith in the 21st Century

This essay was prepared for the Lilly Endowment's Christian Faith and Life Consultation in May 2016.

As noted in the introductory chapter, I include this chapter to provide readers a partial sense of my personal commitments. It is organized by a list of questions to which I was asked to respond for the Lilly Endowment's Christian Faith and Life Consultation, in May 2016. I did so in the form of what musicians may call "fragments" that, in some way, represent a coherent melody.

What are the Marks of Vibrant Christian Faith in the 21st Century?

Fragment 1: As I think about this question, I am conscious that I do so as a middle-aged, middle-class, White, American, well-educated (comparatively) Christian.[1]

Fragment 2: As I think about this question, I am conscious that I do so as one shaped right up to this present moment by persons and experiences and "the times."

I don't mean to suggest that I do not likewise construct reality. It is simply to draw attention to the notion that "society" shapes me.

Fragment 3: As I think about this question, I am conscious that I do so as one shaped and informed by particular Christian traditions, most central of which is neo-Calvinism.[2]

Fragment 4: As I think about this question, I am conscious that I do not see clearly or live faithfully because, though a follower of Jesus, I continue to be taken by the continuing effects of the fall.[3]

Fragment 5: My sense is that the mark[4] of vibrant Christian faith has something to do with seeking to honor the Lord in all things. I recognize that making such a claim may sound cliché or vapid. But, I am trying to draw attention to the notion that vibrant Christian faith has something to do with Christian faith that is "totalizing"—that vibrant Christian faith has as much to do with one's sacrificial love and care of a family as it does daily prayer; that vibrant Christian faith has as much to do with how and why one spends as it does regularly reading the Bible; that vibrant Christian faith has as much to do with advocating for economic and racial justice as it does worship; that vibrant Christian faith has as much to do with affirming epistemic non-neutrality as it does tithing; that vibrant Christian faith has as much to do with why and how one votes as it does with being a deacon. This is not to suggest that prayer, Bible study, church, tithing, and serving as a deacon are unimportant to Christian faith. To be sure, prayer, Bible study, and worship are indispensable foundations/wellsprings for what Walter Wangerin calls "faithing"[5] the faith beyond Sunday services and "quiet times." But I simply want to call attention to the idea that vibrant Christian faith has something to do with "faithing." Perhaps this is why the noun version of faith (*pistis*) is not found in the Gospel of John; only the verb for faith is used by the apostle (*pisteuo*).[6] Or, to put it another way, theologian Gordon Spykman says, "Nothing matters but the kingdom; but because of the kingdom, everything matters."[7] Such it is with vibrant Christian faith in my view; one with vibrant Christian faith recognizes that all things matter to the Lord, and humbly and gratefully and intentionally and passionately strive to live by the spirit, with the support and challenge of fellow believers living and departed, to signpost the kingdom—albeit through a glass darkly—in thought, word, and deed, in all parts of living, each day.

Fragment 6: Notwithstanding my comments in the preceding fragment, I must say that I am immensely inspired by the faith of those who champion the faith in more traditional missional ways: William Borden,[8] Mother Teresa, and Carolyn McKinstry,[9] to name just three. All seemed/seem to have a vibrancy to their Christian faith that eludes me much of the time. There is a vibrancy that they and others like them had/have that I wish was more "second nature" in me.

What is The Ecology of Institutions that Shape and Support Faith Formation and Discipleship?

Fragment 1: All institutions—families, schools, governments, markets, and the like—shape and support the formation of some type of faith system.[10]

Fragment 2: Some/many may feel disillusioned, betrayed, or violated by social institutions and doubt that they are in any way contexts for human flourishing. If true, what is the impact of this for faith formation *vis-à-vis* institutions?[11]

Fragment 3: All persons construct or form a faith of some kind, based on the interactions they have with their environments.[12]

Fragment 4: Might it be possible to truncate vibrant Christian faith to the extent that Christians think of "faith formation" and "life formation" as considerably mutually exclusive (except perhaps when it comes to certain behaviors). That is, to what extent might it be possible to form faith as if it had very little to do with life, other than one's personal, private "spiritual" life as such?[13] In this scenario, faith formation concerns regular Bible study, prayer, small groups, church school/worship, and participation in episodic "spiritual events" such as conferences, short-term missions, or church leadership roles.[14] In contrast, "life formation" simply happens via…well, via the things that are part of life—media, friends, technology, family, school, personality, neighborhoods, consuming, and the like. To go further, in this scenario, faith and life may be related only insofar as "appropriate" behaviors are involved (e.g., Christians should be kind and not get high). But, to what extent are persons and institutions facile in forming faiths that are instructive to and for living?[15] Said another way, what is the relevance of Christian faith for: Forming a view of Bernie Sanders' democratic socialism? One's work/job? Responding to those who believe we live in a post-racial society? The environmentalism conversation? Buying one's 10-year-old child a cell phone? Voting in favor of a church-expansion project? What one purchases and why? Responding to grief? Watching a movie or listening to Coldplay? Discerning one's stance on war or nuclear weapons? Having a "good" date? In short: To what extent should the forming of Christian faith have something to do with lived life, in all of its dimensions? What would such faith formation look like?

Fragment 5: Though not all that follow are institutions as such, Christian families, Christian churches, Christian schools/colleges/seminaries, Christian camps, Christian organizations (parachurch organizations; mission organizations; gap-year programs; etc.), Christian "experiences" (e.g., short-term mission; internships; youth groups; summer programs; etc.), and Christian comrades/friends, all have been and are currently part of the forming and ongoing nurture of Christian faith. This is not to say that any Christian institution or person undertakes formation efforts on others' behalf perfectly. Clearly, neither Christian institutions nor Christian persons nor the formation efforts of either are automatically holy. But it is to say that these institutions and persons are entrusted with such formation and are, in most cases, intentionally and conscientiously committed to such formation as well. Perhaps three important results of the consultation will be to: 1) Identify what faith formation most often currently means and includes, 2) explore a version of faith formation that includes explicit attention to forming a faith that has lived life in mind, and 3) consider ways that faith formation efforts of any kind—existing or new—may be done more effectively.

Fragment 6: In reflecting on Fragments 4 and 5 above, perhaps it is also important to consider that faith forming efforts take shape based on a particular vision/version of Christianity.[16] Particular Christian faith traditions beget particular ways to think about and to enact faith formation. For example, a Christian faith tradition that emphasizes a robust theology of culture may construe faith formation differently than a Christian faith tradition that emphasizes ascetic piety.

Fragment 7: Faith formation efforts in Christian churches will be better or worse depending on the extent to which the particular approach to faith formation aligns with desired outcomes, on the skill of those who lead the efforts, and on those who participate in such efforts. Relatedly, this raises the question: What vision/version of faith formation is currently being espoused in today's seminaries? The response to this question offers insight into the vision/version of faith formation that currently exists and will continue to exist in Christian churches in the immediate future.

Fragment 8: As one associated with Christian higher education for a long time (though not currently), I would remiss to add that insofar as faith formation occurs in Christian colleges, such efforts will be better or worse depending on the extent to which the particular approach to faith formation aligns with desired outcomes, on the skill of those who lead the efforts, and on those who participate in such efforts. Again, the question emerges: What vision/version of faith formation is currently being espoused in today's Christian colleges and universities? I must also add that, in the same way that I wondered in Fragment 3 about the separating of faith and life, I wonder about the extent to which those in academic institutions (including Christian ones) separate learning and life, faith and learning, or both? Perhaps the challenge before us has something to do with seeing things more coherently connected. The good news is that Christians may understand such integrality more than many; integrality simply "fits" our worldview.[17]

Fragment 9: Related to Fragment 8, I am reminded that some have recently argued that formation is the vocation of Christian colleges and universities.[18] To the focus of our conversation, is this vocation a faith formation project? A life vocation project? Are they one and the same thing? Are they related? Could the faith formation project and the life vocation project at a Christian college be in conflict?

Fragment 10: In terms of what might be called "next steps" (i.e., What is missing? What could strengthen, be created) I wonder if Clayton Christensen's notion of "disruptive innovation" may be useful.[19] That is, perhaps para-institutions, para-organizations, "institutes" within/among colleges or churches are promising strategies for re-envisioning and strengthening faith formation efforts. To give one example, gap year programs are, in a sense, disruptive innovations that seem to be having some success, including with respect to formation.

What Resources Have Been Helpful to You as You Consider the Marks of Vibrant Christian Faith in the 21st Century?

For me personally, my family, my personal study and reading, and close friends have been indispensable to me for pursuing vibrant Christian faith. In addition, my work and the opportunities that it has afforded me over the years has contributed richly to my formation. To highlight just one thing in regard to personal study and reading, the resource of Hearts and Minds Bookstore (www.heartsandmindsbooks.com) cannot be understated. It represents a treasure trove for me that I continue to cherish, even though I am able to take in just a small fraction of what it offers. Its website offers the following greeting: "Welcome to a bookstore which attempts to create a new space for serious, reflective readers. Unabashedly Christian, we are often told that we are different than most religious bookstores. Our name, we trust, gives a good first clue to what we are about."

One last, brief comment, since I am already far past the page length: I wish that I could say that the church/worship has been a critical, rich resource for my faith formation, but it largely has not. This is not to say that I have been distant from the church and its opportunities; on the contrary, I continue to invest in the life of a local church. It is to say that, in my experience over the last many years, the message that church conveys is that church and life have little relationship.

Notes

[1]How might brothers and sisters in Christ in China or Honduras or Nigeria respond to this same question?

[2]Al Wolters' book *Creation Regained: Biblical Basics for a Reformational Worldview, 2nd Edition* (Grand Rapids, MI: Eerdmans, 2005) may be representative of my sense of things generally.

[3]Writing in the *Confessions* (Chapter VIII, XI [26]), Augustine discussed how his "old loves...tugged at the garment of [his] flesh...trying to persuade [him] to look back." (See H. Chadwick, translator, *Confessions* (New York, NY: Oxford University Press, 2009), 151.

[4]I used the singular here in an attempt to consider the idea that "marks" may flow from "a mark," perhaps in the same way that perhaps one could say that "ethics" flow from "an ethic."

[5]W. Wangerin, *The Orphean Passages: The Drama of Faith* (New York, NY: HarperCollins, 1986). See the Prologue in particular, 1-15.

[6]The apostle uses it 98 times, more than three times more than the other Gospels combined!

[7]G. Spykman, *Reformational Theology: A New Paradigm for Doing Dogmatics* (Grand Rapids, MI: Eerdmans, 1992), 266.

[8]See H. Taylor, *Borden of Yale (Men of Faith)* (Minneapolis, MN: Bethany House Pub, 1988).

[9]See C. McKinstry, *While the World Watched: A Birmingham Bomb Survivor Comes of Age During the Civil Rights Movement* (Carol Stream, IL: Tyndale House Publishers, Inc., 2013).

[10]To this end, in *An Other Kingdom: Departing the Consumer Culture* (Hoboken, NJ: Wiley, 2016), Peter Block, Walter Brueggemann, and John McKnight suggest that American society shapes and supports the formation of a consumerist faith.

[11]In his little book, *On Thinking Institutionally* (New York, NY: Oxford University Press, 2011), H. Heclo writes: "...a fundamental distrust of institutions is the one mark we have in common as inhabitants of these times...Ordinary citizens on the receiving end of the persuasion industry [of institutions] have

every reason to believe that public life is a spin cycle where nobody ever comes clean," 11; 29-30.

[12]I am persuaded that Peter Berger, in his book *The Sacred Canopy: Elements of a Sociological Theory of Religion* (Norwell, MA: Anchor, 1990), is on to something when he suggests that to be human is to be about the business of what he calls "world construction" and "world maintenance." That is, all humans construct lives that, for them, is life!

[13]Some identify what I am describing here as "dualism" or the separating of those things that God really cares about from the things that "just are." To be clear, I admit to being a functioning dualist myself; I act as if plenty of things don't really matter to the Lord. But, in my best moments, I want to believe that "all things" *do* matter in the kingdom (cf., Colossians 1:15-20) and, as importantly, live and act accordingly. To give just one compelling example for me personally: Both M. Emerson and C. Smith's *Divided by Faith: Evangelical Faith and the Problem of Race in America* (New York, NY: Oxford University Press, 2001) and C. Marsh's *The Last Days: A Son's Story of Sin and Segregation at the Dawn of a New South* (New York, NY: Basic Books, 2002) poignantly reveal a gaping incongruence regarding the invidious racism of Bible-be-livin', well-meaning Christian persons. In what ways might a biblically and theologically trained, go-to-church-every-Sunday, longtime Christian educator, Presbyterian elder, trying-to-be-thoughtfully Christian person like me currently be getting it all wrong?

[14]To be clear, I am not against any of these things. On the contrary, I fully support efforts to address what seems to be rampant biblical and theological illiteracy among Christians. And, I would like to think that such undertakings can occur in such a way as to both increase literacy and the relevance of the biblical/theological narrative for lived life.

[15]To what extent are Christian churches as interested in forming discipleship groups around those in similar work roles (e.g., business; allied health; law; education) compared to having Lenten services? To what extent are Christian churches as interested in hosting a Sunday school series on "The Election 2016 from a Christian Perspective" compared to a Sunday school series on prayer? To what extent are Christian churches as interested in planning ordination services for all vocations (parent; child; student; spouse; teacher; friend; etc.) compared to ordination services for church officers?

[16]I have recently come across, for example, Gabe Lyons' depiction of Christians based on what they tend to emphasize and, in turn, its relative impact

on their lived lives (See *The Next Christians: The Good News About the End of Christian America* (New York, NY: Doubleday Religion, 2010). He referred to three main groups identified as "separatists," "cultural," and "restorers."

[17]*The Idea of a University* (South Bend, IN: University of Notre Dame Press, 1981) comes to mind here when John Henry Newman, in explaining his "circle of objects" approach to faith and learning (and life), says: "I lay it down that all knowledge forms one whole, because its subject-matter is one; for the universe in its length and breadth is so intimately knit together, that we cannot separate off portion from portion, and operation from operation, except by a mental abstraction; and then again, as to its Creator...He has so implicated Himself with it, and taken it into His very bosom, by His presence in it, His providence over it, His impressions upon it, and His influences through it, that we cannot truly or fully contemplate it without in some main aspects contemplating Him," 45.

[18]I am thinking here of the book *At This Time and in This Place: Vocation and Higher Education* (New York, NY: Oxford University Press, 2015), edited by David Cunningham. In one chapter, "Finding the center as things fly apart: Vocation and the common good," Cynthia Wells writes that "by developing a capacity for providing students with the time and space they need to explore and discern their vocations, higher education may be fulfilling one of its *own* essential vocations" (71). And, later in the book, David Cunningham references a keynote address that he delivered several years ago entitled "Colleges Have Callings, Too: Planning, Programming, and the Politics of Institutional Vocation," 152.

[19]See: https://www.christenseninstitute.org/disruptive-innovations/.

EPILOGUE

Life Has Killed the
Dream I Dreamed?

In December 2019, I attended a luncheon at Messiah University in which a small group of its faculty gather on occasion to discuss a selected reading. I was invited because the discussion was enjoined around an essay that I wrote about Christian higher education and the common good.[1] Though I thoroughly enjoyed reconnecting with longtime friends and colleagues and meeting new friends as well, and though the dialog was warm and robust, I think that we also experienced a certain soberness. On one hand, we resonated with and were buoyed by the dreams conveyed by the essay such as thinking of "the mission of Christian colleges and educators as common good discipleship for Jesus' sake,"[2] or of "imagin[ing] the task of Christian colleges and universities as designing curricular and co-curricular programs to prepare students to 'increase the net amount of shalom in the world.'"[3] On the other hand, our enthusiasm was disrupted when noting other parts of the essay such as the stark "environmental realities" that many Christian institutions may currently face: "stay-afloat-no-matter-what marketing strategies, budget cuts (including to faculty and professional development), layoffs, program discontinuations, early-retirement packages, and the resulting impacts on human morale may challenge even the heartiest of personal and institutional hopes and practices."[4]

Herein is the rub. Dreams confront realities; faith meets lived life. It was not lost on me or others that the luncheon occurred during the season of Advent. Christian colleges wait and hope and follow the star and behold the One and Only and dream kingdom dreams.[5] But Christian institutions also experience the weariness of longings, and the darkness of the nights, and the absence of words like Zachariah, and the painfulness of birthing, and the Herods within and without, personal and structural, that seek to squash dreams.

This side of Jesus' coming again to make all things new, life will not be any other way. Advent is more than seasonal for Christians and for Christian institutions; it is a way to see and to live every season. Living in God's world, for now, is frustrating and disappointing, compromises are regular, and failures are certain. But, like the faithful throughout the ages, Christians and Christian institutions must dream, they must plant fields, they must testify to new possibilities, and they must pursue, with hope and joy, the calling of the king.

What, then, do I conclude? Has "life" killed my dreams for Christian higher education? No. May it never be so. Responding no, however, does not preclude plenty of laments over the years. For example:

- I lament that many faculty members at Christian colleges have little or no functional theology of culture.

- I lament that a seemingly growing number of Christian colleges flail about for chimerical curricular and co-curricular silver bullets to stay afloat.

- I lament that "standard" disciplinary and departmental structures persist at most, if not all, Christian colleges and universities.

- I lament that many Christian institutions mostly serve as "decompression chambers that make the passage from home to the larger world less traumatic for the shy or the provincial."[6]

- I lament the Christian faculty member who opposed moving from 55-minute class periods to 50-minute class periods because PowerPoint slides were already prepared.

- I lament that diversity and its principled embrace continues to be a difficult proposition at Christian colleges.

- I lament the budget crises and their implications at many Christian colleges and universities, including the ways in which personal cutbacks are often communicated.

A partial list to be sure, and one that readers that work in Christian higher education may easily increase. So, sure, I lament. But, hand in hand with lament, I continue to dream dreams for Christian higher education. In doing so, I am reminded of a book that was instrumental in my earlier years of faith, *A Long Obedience in the Same Direction*, by Eugene Peterson.[7] The opening chapter begins with words from Jeremiah 12. Jeremiah is entreating Yahweh with heartfelt pain, "Why do the wicked seem to prosper?" and "How long will the land be parched and the grass in every field be withered?" And Yahweh responds to Jeremiah with these challenging words: "If you have raced with men on foot and they have worn you out, how can you compete with horses? If you stumble in safe country, how will you manage in the thickets by the Jordan?"

Christian discipleship is neither easy nor immediate nor painless; dreaming dreams for Christian higher education, to use Peterson's words, is not for "the tourist who only wants the high points,"[8] and quickly. Rather, dreamers are enjoined to explore further, to seek further understanding—come hell or high water. I do not mean to suggest that the most faithful option for a Christian college may be to shutter its doors; perishing in the fight has long been a possibility for Christians. I hope that by God's grace, I will be able to affirm—to paraphrase the last line of a popular contemporary Christian hymn—'Til He returns, or calls me home, here in the power of Christ, I will dream (about Christian higher education).

Two such dreams I would like to offer in conclusion. Both are dreams that I dream in solidarity with the authors that envisioned and penned them. Neither derive from some of the more recent commendable dreaming about Christian higher education.[9] Instead, my imagination was taken with both of these dreams as I was preparing this last word.

The first dream comes from Dallas Willard, from an article that he wrote called "Observations on Current Leadership Issues in Higher Education."[10] Willard's dream might be construed as a more general vision of Christian higher education. It is driven by deep concerns that he sees at the time that he wrote this essay almost 20 years ago. For example, Willard lamented that "faculty minds are under *de facto* control of their professional field" rather than on a "curriculum [that] would produce…a Christianly educated person."[11] He also was distraught about the lack of coherence in the curriculum, commenting that "the idea that the whole course of studies is a curriculum is laughable."[12]

Willard's vision for addressing these concerns is for Christian colleges and universities to reduce "the number of different things we do and do[ing] a few things well."[13] He adds that "think[ing] outside of established categories"[14] is critical as well. Willard's admonitions are generic, but they may also provide the kinds of simple starting points for conversation. For example, reductions in what Christian institutions do has occurred of late in response to budget cuts. But, to what extent would a Christian college be willing to partner with several other Christian colleges to "divvy up" academic programs among them? Or, as regards Willard's comment on "established categories," it strikes me that, at the very least, this may be a rich conversation with imaginative minds going forward.

The second dream comes from Nicholas Wolterstorff, in an article titled "The Mission of the Christian College at the End of the 20th Century."[15] The dream is of a "Stage III" for evangelical Christian colleges. According to Wolterstorff, Stage I was prominent in the early 20th century and lasted until well after World War II. It was characterized by an approach in which Christian colleges "sought to quarantine and inoculate their students against the cultural developments of the day."[16] In short, "education in the evangelical Christian colleges became culturally and socially disembodied."[17]

Stage II of evangelical higher education developed in the 1950s and Wolterstorff believed it be in "full flower"[18] in the 1980s. In contrast to Stage I, the suspicion with which Christian colleges treated culture was significantly diminished, and "quarantines [had] been lifted."[19] Instead, a majority of Christian institutions "resolutely insisted on introducing their students to the full breadth of...high culture."[20] Moreover, the language of the integration of faith and learning became the shibboleth of Christian colleges during Stage II in which "the calling of the Christian scholar is to practice scholarship in Christian perspective and to penetrate to the roots of that scholarship with which she finds herself in disagreement—along the way appropriating whatever she finds of use."[21] Many readers will readily recognize Stage II of the history of evangelical American higher education, having been nurtured in it personally, having read one or more of the extraordinary number of books animated by it over more than the last generation, and/or believing it still to be the regnant stage today.

But, almost 40 years ago, Wolterstorff dreamed of a Stage III. He is worth quoting at length:

> Is [Stage II] the final stage? Is it now the mission of the Christian college simply to do more of the same and to do it better—with more penetration, more imagination, more creativity, more courage, more self-confidence, more fidelity to the gospel of Jesus Christ? Or could it be that we are called to enter a third stage? Could it be that our mission at this point in our history and at this point in the history of the world requires us to take a large step and enter the uncertain future of a Stage III? I think that it does.[22]

Wolterstorff admits that he is unsure what may characterize Stage III. But in this short article, he dreams that it may importantly include three things. First, and perhaps foremost, Stage III Christian higher education must help students "build[ing] bridges from theory to practice."[23] That is, "The goal is not just to impart to the student a Christian world-and-life-view—it is to equip and motivate students for a Christian way of being and acting in the world."[24] Wolterstorff implicates the importance of preparing students for the various vocations/callings that they will occupy upon graduation in this discussion as well by emphasizing the social roles, social practices, and social institutions that they will experience and within which they are called to be faithful to the gospel.

Second, Wolterstorff suggests that Stage III Christian institutions will be "much more international in [their] concerns and consciousness."[25] His interests in these regards seem to be rooted in the critical importance of helping students understand the impact of other parts of the world on the United States and on themselves. And, third, Wolterstorff envisioned that Christian colleges that enter Stage III in their development must "explore new ways of packaging the learning it presents to students."[26] He elaborates, "When our concern is simply to appropriate the stream of culture, then the relevant packages are available and familiar: physics, literary criticism, music theory, economics, etc."[27] But, Wolterstorff contends that if the focus of Christian colleges is to "know the structure and dynamics of [that] society" and to nurture "the Christian in society,"[28] then "perhaps we shall need programs in peace and war, nationalism, poverty, urban ugliness, ecology, crime and punishment."[29] Wolterstorff concludes his dream with these powerful words:

> The church of Jesus Christ is called to be agent of shalom in the world and [that] we in the Christian colleges must no longer be content with evasive answers when we are asked why we act so hesitantly in promoting the social dimension of that mission…it has a liberating word to speak to that society and a healing hand to extend to it.

> It may not withhold that word and that hand. We are
> ready for Stage III.[30]

Perhaps I am self-deceived, but I would not characterize myself
as a cynical person. I have been called a "troubler of Israel" in the
past, but that is a different badge, and one that I would continue
to be honored to wear. My point is simply this: Over the almost
30 years since Wolterstorff's dream, I wonder if Christian higher
education has embraced either "more of the same but better"
while staying in Stage II, or if it has embraced a Stage III. Are
faculty members at Christian colleges and universities more facile at the integration of faith and learning today than ever before? Are administrators at Christian institutions more imaginative, creative, and courageous in providing leadership? Perhaps
Christian colleges and universities have entered a Stage III, but
not one resembling what Wolterstorff dreamed. Of course, that
may be fine for a variety of reasons. I will add, however, that if
Christian higher education has, in fact, entered a Stage III, but
one that is characterized by significant commodification, or by
flippantly promoting education as job training, or by ambiva-
lence regarding [Christian] faith-based teaching and learning,
or by required chapel and OT and NT survey courses but "neu-
tral" student learning otherwise, to name a few possibilities,
then I would be disappointed. From my perspective, all of these
options are backwards, the wrong direction, or both.

In retrospect, I wonder if my efforts over the last 20 years,
at least in part, represent an attempt at what Wolterstorff called
Stage III Christian higher education. I wonder if I was dreaming
about ways to build further and differently on the gains of Stage
II and in light of the relative successes, strengths, and resources
of the Christian higher education movement at the time (i.e.,
15-20 years ago). Perhaps some of the dreams included in this
book still have some merit and are worth revisiting. Perhaps
some of the dreams included in this book have merit but do well
to be recast given our current moment in time. Or, as I intimated
above, perhaps Christian higher education is currently in Stage
III, but simply not the Stage III that Wolterstorff preliminarily

imagined—or that I dreamed. Perhaps Christian colleges and universities have already moved on to a Stage IV!

Whatever the case, I am hopeful that scholars and practitioners—seasoned and younger alike—will explore these things further. Likewise, I hope that organizations such as the Council for Christian Colleges and Universities may renew their interests in doing the same, perhaps even sponsoring national conversations and empirical research around the idea of "Stage III (or IV) Christian higher education." In short, understanding more about the present realities, shortcomings, and opportunities of Christian higher education may be the *sine qua non* for new, imaginative, faithful dreams to emerge. May the Lord be well pleased to inspire and to superintend these developments.

Notes

[1]D. Guthrie, "Revisiting a Christian View of the Common Good for Christian Higher Education" (*Christian Higher Education*, Vol. 17, Nos. 1-2, 2018), 20-32.

[2]Ibid., 20, quoting C. Plantinga, *Engaging God's World: A Christian Vision of Faith, Learning, and Living* (Grand Rapids, MI: 2002), 129.

[3]Ibid., 28.

[4]Ibid., 29.

[5]It may sound odd to ascribe to institutions what is most often ascribed to persons. But that is my point.

[6]D. Riesman, "The Evangelical Colleges: Untouched by the Academic Revolution," *Change*, January/February 1981, 13-20), 19.

[7]E. Peterson, *A Long Obedience in the Same Direction: Discipleship in an Instant Society* (Downers Grove, IL: Intervarsity Press, 1980).

[8]Ibid., 13.

[9]A few that come readily to mind are: P. Glanzer, N. Alleman, and T. Ream, *Restoring the Soul of the University: Unifying Christian Higher Education in a Fragmented Age* (Downers Grove, IL: IVP Academic, 2017); L. Schreiner (ed.), *Re-Imagining Christian Higher Education* (New York, NY: Routledge, 2018); K. Longman (ed.), *Diversity Matters: Race, Ethnicity, and the Future of Christian Higher Education* (Abilene, TX: Abilene Christian University Press, 2017); E. Meadors (ed.), *Where Wisdom May Be Found: The Eternal Purpose of Christian Higher Education* (Eugene, OR: Pickwick Publications, 2019).

[10]D. Willard, "Observations on Current Leadership Issues in Higher Education," Retrieved from http://www.dwillard.org/articles/individual/observations-on-current-leadership-issues-in-higher-education.

[11]Ibid.

[12]Ibid.

[13]Ibid.

[14]Ibid.

[15]N. Wolterstorff, "The Mission of the Christian College at the end of the 20th Century" (*The Reformed Journal*, Vol. 33, No. 6, June 1983), 14-18.

[16]Ibid., 15.

[17]Ibid.

[18]Ibid.

[19]Ibid.

[20]Ibid.

[21]Ibid.

[22]Ibid., 16.

[23]Ibid., 17.

[24]Ibid.

[25]Ibid.

[26]Ibid.

[27]Ibid.

[28]Ibid.

[29]Ibid.

[30]Ibid., 18.

Afterword

A letter from Eric Miller, professor of history at Geneva College and Dave's colleague and friend.

Dear Dave,

I've just finished your book. It has unsettled me. I sit here typing, and my stomach feels like it missed the Dramamine I always take while traveling—my head is spinning, my eyes are teary, my heart rate is up. Last week I watched an episode of "Better Call Saul" (my quarantine survival tactic, or one of them) that featured the best portrayal of motion sickness I've ever witnessed—the poor guy was forced to travel in the back of a van with a bag on his head. When the ride finally ends there is nothing to do but sit still, drink water, breathe deeply, and wait for the nausea to pass. That is where your book has left me: motion-sick from time travel.

Vertigo of the soul.

It's so personal, at all levels. I found myself wondering what I looked like, a 33-year-old assistant professor just beginning his second year of teaching, sitting there at that faculty lunch listening to you pound question after question on the true nature of Geneva's Reformed identity. It was courage, it was audacity, it was truth.

Your ending is what I remember most vividly—"While it is the case that I drink beer and wine on occasion; swear here and there; have mowed my grass, grocery shopped, and played tennis and golf on Sunday...let me assure you that I am honestly and diligently striving to be a faithful servant of Immanuel who, in the words of Abraham Kuyper, is our 'skin-draped point of fellowship with the Father.'" That was institutional beauty, Dave. You, ten years ahead of me, were making it count—making your life count. And you were showing me and so many others the way.

I wasn't at the Wooden Angel that January night, more than five years later, when you imagined Geneva's story in terms of a "saga." I can't remember why. I know I was by then in the midst of the worst burnout of my life and was jettisoning every obligation I could. But reading your speech and the one that (in the book) precedes it, on Geneva's "educational future," I feel again that sense of swelling hope, that thrill of true achievement in the offing. Then I fall back, look around, and see that, yes, it's 2020 somehow, and we are fighting for dear life. The nausea, the vertigo return.

I well remember you talking about the address you gave at Grove City, though I'd never read it. Looking back now, I have to laugh, wryly, at the ways the generational story has shifted, and the ways it hasn't. It's easy to forget now that Gen X was once the object of so much concern and disdain—we Gen Xers are barely noticed today, I think, thanks to the glories of the Millennials and the universal (and justified) preoccupation with Gen Z. But your observations were penetrating, your vision (in this essay and others) utterly piercing. You take the Delbanco thesis and its prophetic examination of American individualism and show exactly what it looks like in the context of the academy. How I wish you were still part of our conversation, as we strive to lead our students toward health, wholeness, hope.

The opening essay stirs as much emotion as any. I was going nuts that summer when we five were meeting to reckon with those themes, to discover and hammer out our common stance. I wrote the second half of my dissertation over those weeks; my mind was a fever. And I can see now that part of what fueled that fever—that remarkable stimulation—was those conversations. What I am most struck by is how disturbed we seemed at the "transforming society" slogan that Geneva, in the company of so many others, was touting. I see why Brian Walsh, after hearing you read the paper, dubbed us the "angry Genevans"! But it was productive anger, I think. We were coming off of the 1990s, when so much seemed possible, with Christian higher education and evangelical intellectual life in general hitting what we can today recognize as a peak. We were trying to seize the day, give the dream flesh. The Geneva College of President White still empowered that kind of action, blessed it even, perhaps. We were in motion, heading forward...and not quite seeing well enough which parts of the college were heading elsewhere, following other visions, heeding other voices, singing other songs.

Thanks for recapturing that weekend in New England and the night in Providence. It was a magical few days, mystical and earthly at once—the best kind of "visionary" episode, perhaps. The vision unfolding seemed so full of promise as to be a portent. In faith, I will choose to continue to see it as that—one day, my friend, one day.

But your book isn't just personal because of moments and hopes I recall. It's personal because you are so fully revealed in it, heart and soul and mind and strength. Day after day, year after year, you put yourself out there. It is beautiful to see and remember this, page by page. Your pastoral compassion for the students, in all of the essays, is a bracing reminder of why we are here, and how we need to go about this calling. Your book is scholarly—so many citations, so much evidence of your sustained, intense engagement with all kinds of reading; so many authors. Yet it is the farthest thing I can imagine from stuffy, preening, pretentious scholarship. No—it's driven by the personal, by the intimate, by the deepest parts of you appealing to the deepest parts of us. You show us how it's done and why it's done.

Your book is a gift, Dave. Its great beauty lies in the fact that it as much a collection of documents as essays. You've given us remarkable documentary evidence of what this thing we in Christian education are striving to achieve actually looks like in real time. Where else can you get that? This is not the usual collection of essays. The various pieces are not theoretical and philosophical in, say, a Wolterstorffian kind of way. They were written, rather, by someone who absorbs Wolterstorff, Brueggemann, Boyer, and friends and tries to put it all in motion, impelled by a keen sense of vocation. And so, as readers we walk not simply through your ideas—we walk through your life.

It is entirely fitting that at the book's close you include laments. What dreamer doesn't need to go there, at some point? But along the way you teach us what dreamers of your kind know well: that redemption is in the offing—that it's already happened, in fact; that it's never not happening.

I'll keep walking alongside you, my brother and friend— dreaming for dear life.

Yours,

Eric
Beaver Falls, PA
19 May 2020

About the Author

David S. Guthrie is Teaching Professor of Higher Education at Penn State University, where he has specific responsibility for coordinating the M.Ed. program for University Park students. He has over 20 years of full-time teaching experience at undergraduate, master's, and doctoral levels, has served as a dean in both student affairs and academic affairs, and also worked for eight years in campus ministry.

Dave is the author of two monographs, many journal articles/book chapters, numerous conference presentations, and has directed a multi-million dollar grant focused on the theological exploration of vocation. His intellectual interests include the vocation of higher education in general and of church-related colleges and universities in particular; the integration of faith, learning, and living; and, connections among religion, society, and higher education.

Other Titles from Falls City Press

The Enneagram of Discernment:
The Way of Vocation, Wisdom, and Practice
Dr. Drew Moser

Reforming the Liberal Arts
Dr. Ryan McIlhenny

Storied Leadership:
Living and Leading from the Christian Narrative
Brian Jensen
Dr. Keith R. Martel

Unleashing Opportunity:
Why Escaping Poverty Requires a Shared Vision of Justice
Michael Gerson
Stephanie Summers
Katie Thompson

On Mission Together:
Integrating Missions into the Local Church
Dr. Richard Noble

For news and a complimentary copy of *Storied Leadership*,
sign up for the Falls City Press mailing list:

www.fallscitypress.com/list